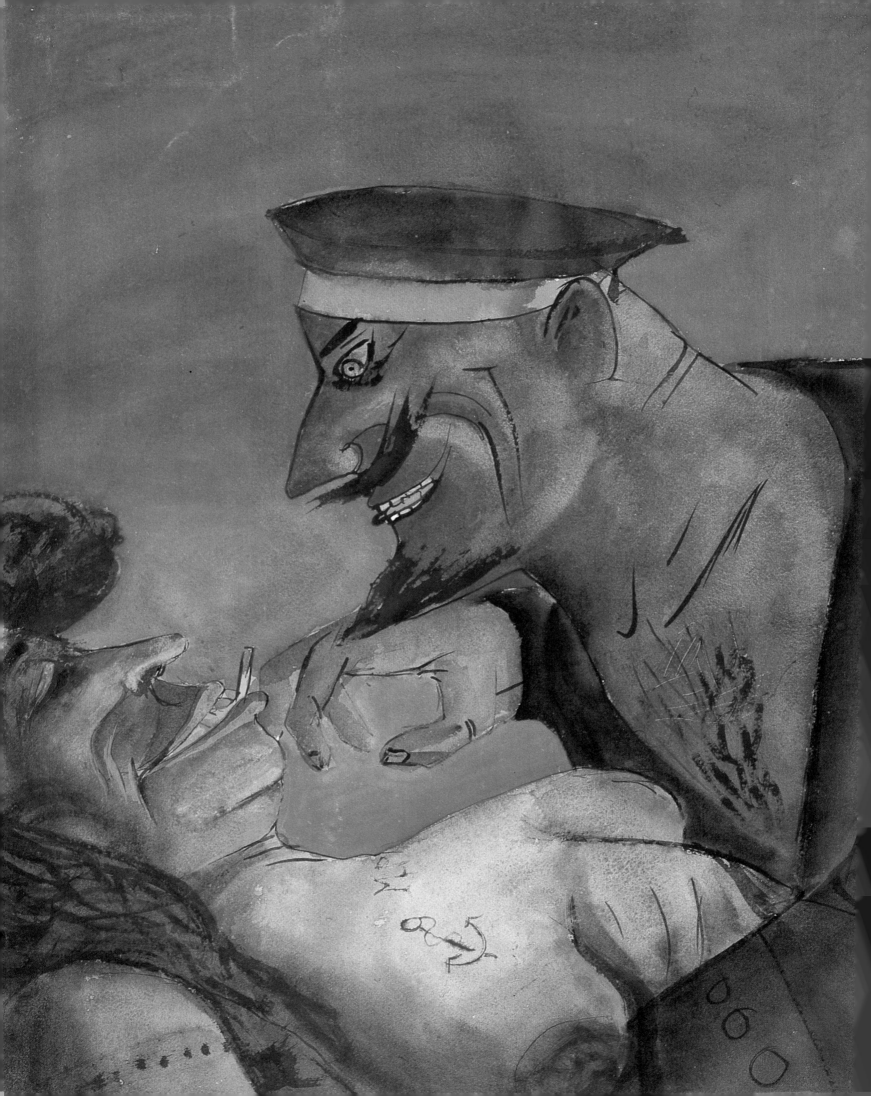

Eva Karcher

Otto Dix

1891–1969

"I'll either be famous – or infamous."

Benedikt Taschen

For Rainer Pfefferkorn

PAGE 1:
Three Nudes, 1923
Drei Akte
Pen and ink, 61.8 x 48.6 cm
Vaduz, Otto Dix Foundation

PAGE 2:
Sailor and Girl, c. 1925
Matrose und Mädchen
Watercolour, 61 x 48.5 cm
Vaduz, Otto Dix Foundation

This book was printed on 100 % chlorine-free bleached paper in accordance with the TCF standard.

© 1992 Benedikt Taschen Verlag GmbH,
Hohenzollernring 53, D-50672 Köln
© 1988 Otto Dix Foundation, Vaduz, for the illustrations
Edited and produced by Ingo F. Walther, Alling
English translation: Doris Linda Jones and Jeremy Gaines
Cover design: Angelika Muthesius, Cologne;
Mark Thomson, London

Printed in Italy
ISBN 3-8228-0272-7
GB

Contents

"Sachlichkeit" – Objectivity and the Age

"Objective (*sachlich*)…who's objective, after all? I mean, is there any artist who is truly objective? Of course, in contrast to Expressionism and the later abstract style, the world of objects seems close to factual reality! The strong emphasis on the subject matter, on the material, in my work at the time might have been called objective, for example. Tangible matter." (From an interview with Otto Dix by Maria Wetzel, 1965).

Otto Dix was the artist of *Neue Sachlichkeit*, the New Objectivity, *par excellence* – precisely because he did not give in to the precepts of that style. The concept pervaded an entire period, the way it felt about life, and its world view. It became the undisputed normative standard, and applied not only to art criticism and art theory, but also to politics and the humanities. The term was used by those of every political persuasion – Marxist, conservative, liberal, and so forth – to identify the enemy, and in due course was even raised to the status of the underlying value of a new introversion: "*Sachlichkeit* is the emotional and intellectual tendency to act, not for personal gain, but in the service of a higher cause" (Helmut Lethen).

An entire generation practised *Sachlichkeit*, glorified functionality as well as rationality, and celebrated objectivity – yet it meant something different to everyone. Ambiguity was the most conspicuous feature of the *Neue Sachlichkeit*, a term that changed its colours like a chameleon. During the post-war period of economic stabilization – from 1923 to 1929 – *Sachlichkeit* referred to an overall trend in social development that could not at that time be fully described. The term signified a claim to value neutrality. The "objective" value of money – which as a consequence of economic development had become the focus of attention – was viewed as a neutral standard of individual and social communication.

The aim was above all to create a perfect outer shell that was as impenetrable as possible in order to conceal the "vulnerable" ego at all costs (in terms of the power of money). At the same time, bodies were transformed into metaphors of *Sachlichkeit*, the new principle of life. *Sachlichkeit* was in itself regarded as a cognitive value, and thus deemed to have an "exposing", "uncovering", indeed a general "analytic" capacity. The widest variety of blatantly contradictory value concepts were projected onto it – "self-control", "generosity", "freedom from arbitrari-

Small Self-portrait, 1913
Kleines Selbstbildnis
Oil on canvas, 36.5 x 28.5 cm
Löffler 1913/1
Stuttgart, Staatsgalerie Stuttgart

ness, and imagination". *Sachlichkeit* seemed on principle to lend the invariably subjective experience of reality an objective quality. A generation which had been shaken in its very foundations, morally as well as physically and emotionally, by the inferno of the First World War, sought in this way to regain its stability and find an enduring social identity. Owing to his sceptical nature, Dix, who was inquisitive, voyeuristic, totally averse to ideologies, and loved to experiment, was immune to the cult of *Sachlichkeit*. His motto – "For me at any rate, the object remains primary" – was diametrically opposed to the position held by *Sachlichkeit*, which was based on a claim to "objectivity" – in other words, objects are perceived with a vision already distorted by its own idea of what constitutes the objectivity of things and bodies. In art, this approach may well do justice to its idea, but not to the object it wishes to depict. Dix, on the other hand, is adamant in retaining his subjective perception as the point of departure for creation. He does not behave in an objective manner, "like an object", but "in relation to the object". He takes the

Foundry, 1910
Gießerei
Oil on paper, 48 x 57.3 cm
Löffler 1910/3
Vaduz, Otto Dix Foundation

Waxing and Waning, 1911
Blühen und Vergehen
Oil on canvas, 60.5 x 47.5 cm
Löffler 1911/1
Bautzen, Stadtmuseum

"objects", i.e. the subjects of his pictures, seriously in the forms in which they appear; he studies their material qualities and substance meticulously, down to the last detail. This gives rise to multi-layered analyses, not painted pamphlets documenting class hatred, such as those of George Grosz. Grosz thought of his art as "an effective weapon...against the stupidity of the people of our time", and repeatedly stressed the "drastic and unmitigated harshness and lovelessness" of his objects. He said in unequivocal terms that his "observations were dictated by absolute misanthropy at that time": "I drew and painted out of protest and tried with my works to show the world in all its ugliness, sickness, and hypocrisy." Grosz used his painting as a medium of political struggle against "the fatted rabble" and philistinism. In 1925 he still considered it his "new great mission (to create) tendentious art in the service of the revolutionary cause".

Rigid political convictions of this kind were foreign to Dix. Obstinate as he was, he stressed his fundamentally conservative attitude, and on numerous occasions cited his roots in the tradition of painting, especially that of 16th century Germany: "One slogan has been vital for the generation of creative artists in recent years: 'Create new forms of expression!' was the catchword. It seems highly doubtful to me whether that is even possible... If people contemplate the pictures of old masters or become engrossed in studying these creations, some of them will surely say I am right. At all events, what I see as the new element in painting lies in the expansion of subject matter, in the intensification of those expressive forms which, after all, were already present in the works of the old masters."

Understanding the unique quality of Dix's perception, which at the same time conditioned his approach to human life in general, takes us to the heart of his art. Dix was fascinated by all the different forms in which human life appeared, especially those that were extreme in nature. He registered them without prejudice or bias, with the most finely tuned senses, and rendered them with pictorial directness in all of the facets of their exposure to Eros and Thanatos. As a matter of fact, nearly all of the themes that preoccupy Dix – prostitution, war, the city, religion – touch on that all-embracing existential drama of the indissoluble bond between Eros and Thanatos. Whenever Dix began to explore the phenomena he observed with curiosity and pleasure, he always started, strangely enough, with the body: "The outside of things is important to me, for in the process of rendering external form one also captures the internal...The first impression is the right one and has to be preserved in all its freshness. If I can only see the outside, the inside then follows of its own accord." In other words, Dix attributed substantive expressive qualities to the specific appearance of an object. The consistency and application with which Dix remained committed to his position of openness and impartiality throughout all the phases in his career makes him an outsider within the group of *Neue Sachlichkeit* artists. Together with Max Beckmann, his polar opposite, Dix is the greatest lone wolf in the art of the 1920s.

As in every period, critics of the 1920s sought both identifiable criteria by which to classify works and patterns by which to interpret them, and necessarily overlooked nuances and fine points as a result. Even Dix's work was not exempt from being dealt with in such a manner, and was often interpreted in terms of simplified blueprints.

In general, the concept of *Sachlichkeit* had evolved in art criticism and art theory of the 1920s in counterpoint to the "inflation of subjectivist 'isms' of the late Expressionist period" (H. Lethen), and was likewise opposed to the stylistic orientation of Expressionism. Gustav Friedrich Hartlaub, director of the Mannheim Gallery at the time, was the first to apply the term *Neue Sachlichkeit* to works of art. He coined the term in 1925 on the occasion of an art exhibition he had organized for "those artists who have recognizably remained true or have again become true to positive, tangible reality and are prepared to attest to this..." Hartlaub

Self-portrait with Carnation, 1912
Selbstbildnis mit Nelke
Oil on paper, 73 x 50 cm
Löffler 1912/3
Detroit, Detroit Institute of Arts

himself was aware that the wide-ranging terms failed to cover the socially related contents with respect to some representational works. He attempted to render the concept flexible by making a distinction between a "right wing (Neo-Classicist, as it were)…and a left, Verist wing, which can be said to include Beckmann, Grosz, Dix, Drexel, Scholz, etc."

Superficially, certain of the *Sachlichkeit* clichés seemed applicable to Dix's style of painting. For this reason, early critics found evidence of such "objectivity" in his works on account of their quality of "detachment" and "unrelenting cognition"; "Otto Dix represents the attempt to achieve a new kind of objectivity for painting" (*Frankfurter Zeitung*, 1923), "…he looks at things objectively and seems to portray them with

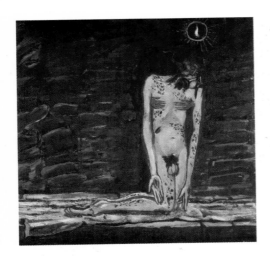

Pietà, 1912
Oil on paper on chipboard
50.5 x 49.5 cm
Löffler 1912/1
Private collection

the calm of the detached observer" (Paul Ferdinand Schmidt, 1923). "And a new kind of objectivity prevailed – the principle of unrelenting cognition" (*Magdeburger Zeitung*, 1922). Dix was regarded as a "relentless fanatic for the truth" (*Neue Zürcher Zeitung*, 1929), who "analysed, dissected, deformed, exposed, unmasked". His art was described as "disillusioning the visible", as "exposing the futility of life". Furthermore, Schmidt found in Dix's works a "relentless truth in the media of presentation" and an "unusual honesty vis-à-vis all impressions of the world around him".

Any number of further examples could be cited here. Aside from apt statements such as those made by Carl Einstein, there were others, such as Erich Knauf's, that were eccentric and quite beside the point. Passages are quoted here by way of illustration. In 1923 Einstein maintained that "...others such as Grosz, Dix and Schlichter destroy the real with trenchant *Sachlichkeit*, uncover this period and force it to be ironic about itself. Painting as a medium of bold assassination, observation as an instrument of harsh attack. The painting of critical observation. A banner against times that are ridiculous in themselves: iconoclasm. It is a war that is being waged, through formal invention and annihilating portrayal." Einstein puts it quite bluntly: War is being waged... In 1928 Knauf writes with bombastic pathos: "In the sultry perfume of the military hospitals the 'lovers' bliss' of the survivors blossomed in screaming beauty on a barrel-thin stalk", and at another point: "Dix developed the style of ice-cold objectivity...with the same brutality Dix digs his pencil into the festering wounds of society."

These statements presuppose that Dix's paintings debunk reality. In general, reality in the 1920s was experienced rather as being negative and ugly – the events speak for themselves. Dix's paintings supplied his contemporaries with a welcome confirmation of their projections of reality's "ugliness". Unfortunately, because of this presumptuous way of looking at Dix's works, people failed to inquire as to how Dix himself viewed reality. Nor, unfortunately, did anyone ask how Dix portrayed this reality, with what kind of subjectivity. Do the pictures really convey an appraisal of reality as something ugly and negative, or are they intended to portray something else? What subjective perception are they based on?

We shall approach Dix's life and works as coolly and clearly as possible by taking up these questions, but first a number of quotes by contemporaries of the period will serve to convey an impression of the Weimar Republic in which Dix created his major works.

Ernest Bornemann was surely the most acrid critic of this republic of contradictions. In his memoirs he says: "When I, doting babbler that I am, hear the yarns on television about the 'Golden' Twenties, it still turns my stomach. They were 'Golden' for the wheelers and dealers, the warmongers, the speculators, who were profiting from inflation. That was a minority, so small you would hardly have noticed them...It is one of the best-kept secrets of bourgeois nostalgia production that all of these 'Golden Twenties' creatures who were dancing the Charleston, drinking champagne, and gobbling up caviar, got their gold by exploiting the poor

Night in the City, 1913
Nacht in der Stadt
Oil on paper on cardboard,
70.8 cm x 52.5 cm
Löffler 1913/11
Rome, private collection

to the point of atrocity. That made their arrogance, their shamelessness, their boastfulness, all the more revolting."

Alfred Döblin aptly describes the ambivalence of this period: "Any age is invariably a cross-over of various epochs, is unfermented for larger periods of time, half-baked, carries residues of other forces, seeds, in itself." Fritz Raddatz (to whom the present author is indebted), analysing the "unloved republic", says of the chameleon-like properties of this republic that it is like unravelling threads out of a tangled, colourful fabric. "No matter whose personal destiny one investigates, no matter which work or political theory and practice one addresses, one keeps coming back to the republic's bad start and its gruesome end. Sherds at best." And he finds this common denominator for Weimar culture: "It was constantly in the process of helping to formulate its own end. Hans Sahl provided a wonderful description of this dance towards death, as if he had the choreography in his head." What Sahl so aptly wrote was this: "This epoch had its own dialect, an esperanto of communication whose

Streetlamps, 1913
Straßenlaternen
Oil on paper on chipboard,
52.5 x 64.3 cm
Löffler 1913/16
Vaduz, Otto Dix Foundation

Sunrise, 1913
Sonnenaufgang
Oil on paper, 51 x 66 cm
Löffler 1913/25
Stuttgart, private collection

precondition was that one had to have seen the latest play by Brecht, the latest production by Piscator, Jessner, Reinhardt, to have read the latest review by Kerr or Ihering, that one had to be up-to-date on the concerts of Furtwängler, Toscanini, Klemperer, Kleiber, Bruno Walter, on Tairow's *Unbound theatre*, Habima's *Dybbuk* and Meyerhold's latest guest performance in Germany, on the black dancer Josephine Baker and the whispering baritone Jack Smith, on Eisenstein's *Potemkin* and Chaplin's *Gold Rush*, on Gershwin's *Rhapsody in Blue* and Thomas Mann's *Magic Mountain* and Hermann Hesse's *Steppenwolf*, on the six-day race and Fritz Kortner as Richard III, on Bergner as Rosalinde and Albert Bassermann in Sternheim's *1913*, on Stravinsky's *Oedipus Rex* and Mies van der Rohe's skyscrapers made of glass and steel, on Freud and Einstein and atonal music. Between the two world wars Kurt Tucholsky turned this Berlin eloquence into a language fit for literature. (...) The Berliner's curiosity for 'the latest', the Berliner who had become a cosmopolitan in an amazingly short time, and for whom only one thing mattered: being part of it all. And when the absolute 'latest rage' arrived on the scene, namely, Hitler, he had to be part of it all in the cruellest way, either as the one who was sacrificed or the one who did the sacrificing."

Dix's Childhood and Early Works

Dix came from a working-class background. Wilhelm Heinrich Otto Dix was born on 2 December, 1891 at Mohrenplatz 4 in Untermhaus near Gera in what is now the GDR. He was the eldest son of Franz Dix (1862-1942), an iron-foundry worker, and his wife Louise, née Amann (1863-1953). Dix's social background repeatedly led biographers and interpreters of his work to jump to the hasty conclusion that he was to be classified as a political artist, that he necessarily felt it was his calling to avenge the ills of capitalist society. The myth of Dix the "proletarian" was soon established and became entrenched, particularly as Dix's straightforward idiom could easily be misinterpreted as "proletarian jargon". The fact of the matter, however, is that everything Dix ever said ran counter to his being labelled a proletarian in the political sense. Dix was and remained indifferent to all political viewpoints – something which cannot be stressed enough – unless, as in the period of National Socialism, it directly threatened his existence and that of his family. He also had, and maintained, an instinctive aversion to all ideologies, all forms of preconceived thinking in terms of fixed categories, all forms of intellectualism and bloodless theories. When his friend, the painter Conrad Felixmüller, a pacifist and member of the German Communist Party, called on Dix in 1919, shortly before the convention that led to the Dresden secession, to join the party as well, Dix reacted sarcastically: "…stop bothering me with your pathetic politics – I'd rather go to the whorehouse." In an interview with Maria Wetzel many years later (1965) he said something in much the same vein: "No, I did not become a supporter of any political programme – probably couldn't stand all those platitudes. Whenever they came around and tried to start telling us something, they couldn't get anywhere with me. I didn't want to let myself be roped into it."

Much to the contrary of all the bourgeois clichés about exploitation, Otto, the "working-class child", grew up under conditions that were not typical of his class. Not only was his mother a "creative, poetic" type, who wrote poetry as a young woman; a cousin of his, Fritz Amann from Naumburg, was a painter. As a result, Dix was exposed to the artist's craft at an early age. The memories of his childhood in Gera, which he set down on paper some seventy years later (in 1966), are marked by sensory

Self-portrait as Smoker, 1913
Selbstbildnis als Raucher
Oil on paper, 70.5 x 56 cm
Löffler 1913/6
Denzlingen, private collection

Squatting Woman, 1913
Kauernde
Pencil, red and blue ink,
25.3 x 18.3 cm
Albstadt, Walther Groz Foundation,
Städtische Galerie Albstadt

Self-portrait as a Soldier, 1914
(on the reverse: Self-portrait with
artillery helmet, 1914; cf. page 26)
Selbstbildnis als Soldat
Oil on paper, 68 x 53.5 cm
Löffler 1914/4
Stuttgart, Galerie der Stadt Stuttgart

impressions: "The first impression I can remember was that I was lying in a dark room. It was very cold. I saw a large, full expanse of light and heard the sombre, droning sounds of an organ." The acoustic sensations are followed by tactile and olfactory impressions: "Later we lived in my Uncle Rudolf Amann's house. I had a babysitter (probably because my mother worked in the porcelain factory). The girl had reddish-blond hair, and for the first time I was bowled over by what fat behinds girls have. My uncle had a store that smelled of paraffin, coffee, sour pickles and all kinds of things. Smells were in fact the most important of my memories ... At my cousin Fritz Amann's, who was a painter, I sometimes posed for him. The wonderful smell of the oil paints and varnishes, mixed with the smell of the tobacco smoke from my cousin's pipe, plus the beautiful colours on the palette, aroused the wish in me, even while still a little boy, to become a painter. It may be that the sense of smell is more fundamental than the sense of sight, the primordial sense, so to speak."

Dix's childhood was apparently carefree, close to nature, and marked by a love of discovery. His delicate constitution made him susceptible to illness (he had repeated bouts of pneumonia) and to minor injuries. However, his physical instability was balanced out by remarkable endurance and energy; bubbling vitality was the main source of Dix's work as an artist throughout his life. According to Dix himself, he was actually "always able to paint without following in someone's footsteps, but naturally I had my old teacher Schunke (his primary school teacher in Gera) to thank for a lot that led me to find my creative freedom". Far from having an idealized image of himself, Dix, an old man when he wrote his memoirs in 1966 – three years prior to his death – continued: "It was not until later, at commercial art school, that I shouldered the main burden of the drill entirely of my own free will, after having escaped the bitter constrictions of Herr Senff's rules of painting. 'You will never be a painter, you will always be a dauber' was his inspired assessment of my work."

As the academy was for many other young artists, so the Dresden school for commercial arts, which Dix attended between 1909 and 1914, was for him a necessary evil, "burdensome drill", rather than an enriching educational experience or source of inspiration. Schunke, his former teacher, had arranged for him to receive a scholarship to attend the commercial art school, and Dix made use as best he could of the classes in decorative, three-dimensional and ornamental design, taught by Richard Mebert, Paul Naumann, Richard Guhr and Paul Rade. In addition, he continued above all to learn more on his own. He often visited the art gallery and the exhibitions of avant-garde German and French painting on show during this period of bustling cultural activity in Dresden. Thus Dix was exposed to Symbolist, Impressionist and Cubist tendencies early on, and was also familiar with the painting of Vincent van Gogh and the *Brücke* artists. It was at this time that he produced his first paintings, drawings and gouaches; from 1908 onwards he completed his first landscapes showing Dresden, Thuringia, and the Elbe, followed by the first group of self-portraits in 1912/15. The studies of himself that Dix drew, painted, lithographed or etched with remarkable frequency throughout

Prostitute, 1913
Dirne
Pencil and red ink, 28 x 18 cm
Albstadt, Walther Groz Foundation,
Städtische Galerie Albstadt

his career provide an important measure of the uniqueness of his perception, and that uniqueness, of course, shaped his attitude towards all aspects of human life. The early paintings, such as the 1912 *Self-portrait with Carnation* (p.11), *Self-portrait against Landscape with Cliffs, Mountain Meadow and Lake* and *Self-portrait with Red Gladiolas*, both completed in 1913, betray stylistic elements inspired by 16th century German painting as well as Art Nouveau.

As we shall see, Dix's use of quotation was one of the primary elements of his style in many of his later, much more representative portraits and self-portraits, as well as in numerous paintings. He drew them from the resources of art history or culled them from films and documentary photographs. However, this "stylistic pluralism" which is so noticeable throughout Dix's work has nothing to do with merely emulating the style of others. On the contrary, from the very beginning Dix made an effort to find his own formal pictorial medium. At the same time, he gave credit to the "accomplishments" of art and in a certain sense made them an integral part of his own art. One reason why he did so was presumably to free himself of them, even if by no other means than quotation.

In his early landscapes such as *Lennéstrasse in Dresden* or *Streetlamps* (p. 14) Dix rhythmically structured the painting's surface with the emphatic use of brushstrokes. In subsequent years, up until roughly 1919, the painted line in all of its dynamic variety became his principal formal and expressive medium. His striking ability to reproduce highly detailed forms, his sensitivity to the plasticity and substantive quality of the line, are particularly noticeable. Sense perceptions are converted into finely differentiated brush movements, making ample use of the action of painting. The brushstroke of colour, more or less heavily applied, becomes an independent vehicle of expression. Lines in both parallel and interwoven patterns, in juxtaposition with others, are the predominant feature, for example, of the 1913 painting *Sunrise* (p. 15). As in *Streetlamps*, light is treated as substance, streams of light are rendered as materialized bundles of energy and circles. As one can already see from *Self-portrait as a Smoker* (p. 16) and above all *Self-portrait as Mars* (p. 28), Dix was growing ever bolder in his approach, dissecting and fragmenting space into animated structures of form and colour. Without having to forego conveying a precisely-defined message, Dix nevertheless transforms the painting's surface into the scene of simultaneous, interwoven events that build up dramatic, compressed momentum with a sense of breathtaking speed. This aspect was influenced only in part by the formal "linearism" which prevailed in those years in artistic currents such as Futurism and Cubism (cf. for example p. 21); the painter's experiences in the First World War played a far greater role in this respect.

For Dix, art was an act of banishment, of holding things at bay. "I did not paint pictures of war in order to prevent war; that would have been presumptuous. I painted them in order to banish the war. All art is banishment. I paint dreams and faces, too – the dreams and faces of my time, the dreams and faces of all people!" The statement "All art is

The Cannon, 1914
Das Geschütz
Oil on cardboard, 98.5 x 69.5 cm
Löffler 1914/1
Düsseldorf, Kunstmuseum Düsseldorf

Portrait of the Painter Carl Lohse I, 1914
Bildnis des Malers Carl Lohse I
Oil on paper on cardboard, 64 x 46.5 cm
Löffler 1914/7
Vaduz, Otto Dix Foundation

banishment" could stand alongside the motto "Trust your eyes!" which Dix himself chose as the overall guiding principle of his work. Dix banished what moved him, captivated him, terrified him. To a certain extent his perception was a creative pause in which he could understand what he was perceiving, gain clarity and come to terms with it. Banishment might be described as "active" observation that does not repress the tensions and anxieties which arise, but instead seeks to overcome and eliminate them by means of meticulous visualization.

One of Dix's earliest paintings, produced in 1911, is entitled *Waxing and Waning* (p. 9). A twig of blossoms in a vase is arranged in a virtually programmatic composition together with a skull. Both motifs, derived from the tradition of still-life painting, are classic symbols used to denote the bi-polar regularity of life and then death. Admittedly the confrontation between the two poles in this early work is treated in an academic, illustrative style. For example, the two objects, the vase and the skull, are positioned on the same level in the foreground, in front of a section of window. Nevertheless, Dix was already clearly formulating his theme of the indissoluble link between Eros and Thanatos. In early drawings and gouaches, such as *Crouching Woman* (1913) (p. 18) or *Walpurgis Night* (1914), the explosive intensity of the stroke of the pencil, pen or ink brush reveals a capacity for experience, which, with energy and directness, always seeks to convey the most extreme poles of human existence – those of procreation, birth, suffering and death. As already indicated, the body always serves as the point of departure when Dix tackles these experiences. In Dix's early works physicality is portrayed as formal or muscular vitality in a wider context that is anchored in the realm of myth. These early works, which were produced between 1912 and 1913, primarily visualize the cycle, mythical in origin, of procreation, birth and aging. Femininity and sexuality are seen as mysteries of untamed, tempting and at the same time threatening savagery and profusion.

The work *Pregnant Woman* (p. 40), painted in 1919, was the first in a series of paintings well into the 1930s that Dix devoted to the portrayal of pregnant women. It is completely spellbound by the vision of cosmic fertility. As homage to the body that bears and brings forth new life, the composition repeats the spherical form of the belly in variations: Dix fashions the body out of circles and spiralling forms, immerses it in the colours of space (blue) and the earth (red), thereby rendering in striking visual form the *urgestalt* of Eros and life: the spherical form of the earth and the sphere of the pregnant body merge into one.

In his early paintings Dix was impetuously inclined to affirmation, and shared the enthusiasm of German intellectuals of the 1920s for the hero of philosophical affirmation, Friedrich Nietzsche. Like Gottfried Benn, Thomas Mann, Ernst Jünger, Rudolf Schlichter or Arnold Zweig, Dix considered Nietzsche's "the only correct philosophy". As early as 1911 he began to study Nietzsche's thought. In 1912 this reverence for the philosopher led to the creation of a tinted plaster bust of Nietzsche, which, however, was confiscated in 1937; its whereabouts are not known today. Like Nietzsche, Dix conceived of the world as a "monster of

Billiard Player, 1914
Billardspieler
Oil on cardboard, 51 x 56.5 cm
Löffler 1914/21
Private collection

strength", a force beyond the categories of good and evil, which gives birth and devours in an eternal cycle of being and cessation. This cycle, however, is not some blindly arbitrary fate to which one must submit fatalistically. Rather, it is precisely what makes eternal rejuvenation possible at every moment and thus the ability to say "yes", even to death and destruction.

Nietzsche's conception of nihilism coincides in crucial respects with the structure of the nihilism that characterized *Neue Sachlichkeit*. Nietzsche's description of nihilism exposes its value system. "What does nihilism mean? – that the highest values are devalued. There is no goal, there is no answer to the 'why'." The "insight of nihilism, namely, that we do not have the slightest right to construe a Beyond or an In-Itself of things, that is the 'divine', or corporeal morality" leads to the conviction that existence is devoid of value. This constitutes a switch back into the

Gunner Löwe, 1914
Kanonier Löwe
Oil on canvas, 69 x 64 cm
Löffler 1914/12
Private collection

Self-portraits, ca. 1914
Selbstbildnisse
Oil on wood, 75.5 x 54.5 cm
Löffler 1913/3
Lawrence (KS), Spencer Museum
of Art

opposite extreme, yet at the same time the conceptual structure of absolute values is retained as before. Whereas God was hitherto believed to be the highest of all values, now nothingness is rendered absolute, where nothingness is belief in the valuelessness of existence.

However, precisely this adherence to old idealist value systems, which are merely inverted by giving them a negative twist, had certain fatal consequences for the "subject", i.e. the individual, in the era of *Neue Sachlichkeit*: because "subjects" could only take "nothingness" as an absolute value, they necessarily had to negate the historical-subjective existence of their own bodies. They had to posit themselves as "purposes" and attempt to objectivate themselves to a certain degree. At the same time, however, they completely blurred the relationships between ego, subject and object. The "valuelessness of Being" implied that the individual had become valueless, and signified, according to Nietzsche, the onset of "the end of the individual".

Dying Warrior, 1915
Sterbender Krieger
Oil on paper, 68.5 x 54.5 cm
Löffler 1915/3
Schaffhausen, Museum Allerheiligen

This process can be traced back to an erroneous understanding of the "subject" which fails to include its corporeal existence. Nietzsche believed the roots of this misunderstanding lay in the claim to unity and unequivocality intrinsic to the concept of "subject". Such qualities, however, are fictitious variables in his eyes: "Subject: that is the terminology used by our belief in a unity among all of the most disparate elements contained in the highest sense of reality; we understand this belief to be the effect of a cause – we believe so much in our belief that we imagine 'truth', 'reality', 'substantiality', if only for the sake of that belief. – The subject is the fiction, that many similar situations were to affect us as if a substratum: but we are the ones who first created the 'equality' of these situations, the act of equating them and making them fit the scheme is the fact of the matter, not the equality (– this, if anything, is to be denied)." Nietzsche counters this approach with the following hypothesis: "The subject as multiplicity." It can only be grasped as such in its corporeal

form, or as Nietzsche puts it: "Everything which becomes conscious as unity is already terribly complicated; we invariably have only the semblance of unity. The phenomenon of the body is the richer, clearer, more palpable phenomenon: preferable in terms of method, without this in any way predicating its ultimate meaning." This is why Nietzsche repeatedly demands that thought take as its starting point the body and its physiology. Only then, he maintains, would a new theory of values and evaluation be able to evolve, one that begins with the body.

The reader may wonder why this somewhat complicated digression into Nietzschean philosophy is necessary at this point. The fact is that the nucleus of this philosophy leads to the heart of the dilemma of the *Neue Sachlichkeit* generation. The war could not have given them a more brutal and crass display of the "valuelessness of being" and, by extension, of the valuelessness of their own existence. While it was not the only cause of the "end of the individual", it had irrevocably sealed the indi-

Self-portrait with Artillery Helmet, 1914
Selbstbildnis mit Artilleriehelm
(reverse side: Self-portrait as a Soldier,
1914; cf. page 19)
Oil on paper, 68 x 53.5 cm
Löffler 1914/5
Stuttgart, Galerie der Stadt Stuttgart

Self-portrait as Target, 1915
Selbstbildnis als Schießscheibe
Oil on paper on chipboard, 69.5 x 49.4 cm
Löffler 1915/2
Vaduz, Otto Dix Foundation

vidual's fate. Dix and his contemporaries could read Nietzsche to find out what had happened to them, so to speak; being "children of the times", however, they had no means of distancing themselves from it. They had to react in one way or another, either by deadening their senses with consumerism and drugs or by becoming *sachlich*. It is understandable that most of them adopted an illusionary or ideological approach to reality, and only few of them, such as Dix, were still able to analyze it. In Dix's work, as has already been pointed out, the body is the focus of all his studies, and this is precisely what Nietzsche had described as being the only fruitful point of departure in order to regain the subject "in its multiplicity" after the end of the individual.

The First World War 1914 – 1918

In 1914 Dix, like most of his contemporaries, enlisted voluntarily. Nearly all of the younger generation in Europe had initially welcomed the war as a symbol marking the advent of a new era. It was seen as the sign of a long-overdue departure from an era that had been imprisoned in bourgeois narrow-mindedness and prudery. Not only the early Expressionist writers such as Jakob van Hoddis or Johannes R. Becher and Klabund, but also a large percentage of university professors shared the young people's general euphoria about the war. University teachers compiled pamphlets calling on people to enter the "battle", referring to the war as "a miracle", as something "great", welcoming it as "salvation sent by divine providence". "For the just war is not only destructive, but also constructive. The most violent of all destroyers of civilization is at the same time the mightiest of all bearers of civilization", was the view held, for example, by Otto von Gierke, one of the leading law professors of his time and a staunch proponent of "German law" in Berlin. Germany was not the only place where such jingoistic patriotism was at its heyday; the war was glorified by French and Italian artists and intellectuals as well. Guillaume Apollinaire's "Adieu à toute une époque" in 1914 may be considered representative of all such statements. The Italian Futurists around Umberto Boccioni and Filippo Tommaso Marinetti saw the war as a new beginning and had hopes (as Marinetti put it in 1909) that it would have a self-purifying effect, "the only hygiene of any importance in the world".

All of these deluded projections of the war as the grand liberator of mankind are only understandable in light of the enormous changes that had been set in motion by the dawning of technology. In view of the ossified biedermeier-bourgeois social structure, and disgust at the double standards of Wilhelminian morality, the war could be equated with dynamics, strength, and progress. Not for long, however; the experience of war, which wrought destruction of unanticipated proportions, disillusioned the young men who were to die in the years to come, usually from one minute to the next, at the front, either in the massive battles of weaponry or through the merciless brutalities of positional warfare. In 1914, following the retreat from Grodek, Georg Trakl wrote the following poem as an existential resumé: "In the evening the autumn woods

Self-portrait as Mars, 1915
Selbstbildnis als Mars
Oil on canvas, 81 x 66 cm
Löffler 1915/1
Freital, Haus der Heimat

29

Concrete Trenches, ca. 1915-1917
Betonierter Schützengraben
Gouache, 29 x 28.5 cm
Italy, private collection

resound/with fatal weapons, the golden plains/and blue lakes, the sun above/rolling more gloomily by; the night embraces/dying warriors, the savage lament/of their broken mouths…" Trakl's lines sound like the verbalization of Dix's painting *Dying Warrior* (p. 25), in which he depicted the anguish of violent death in form and colour. Trakl died during the first year of the war, presumably by his own hand, in a military hospital in Cracow.

Dix experienced the war on the frontmost lines. Unlike Ernst Ludwig Kirchner, for example, who had a breakdown while in basic training, or Beckmann, who was sent on leave after suffering from traumatic shock, Dix, despite his sensitivity, took up the challenge of events. If one reads his observations on those years and compares the statements recorded "on site" in his "war journal" with those written from memory forty years later, one is struck by the uniform tenor. Dix neither "glorified" the war nor opposed it as a pacifist; rather, he looked at it sobrely: "I was afraid, as a young man. Naturally, when you then moved forward, slowly advanced to the front, in other words, at the front, the heavy barrage was like hell, oh well – it's easy to laugh about it now – there was some shit in people's pants, I tell you. But the further up you moved, the less afraid you were. At the real front, once you were up front, you weren't afraid at all. In other words, those are all phenomena that I absolutely had to experience. I also had to see how someone next to me suddenly fell, and was gone, the bullet hitting him right in the middle. I had to experience all of that very precisely. I wanted to. In other words, I'm not a pacifist at all. Or maybe I was a curious person. I had to see it all for myself. I am such a realist, you know, that I have to see everything with my own eyes in order to confirm that that's the way it is." Even as a young man, Dix was candid about himself as well as toward others, as one can see from the entries in his diary in 1915 and 1916: "Lice, rats, barbed wire entanglements, fleas, grenades, bombs, caves, corpses, blood, schnaps, mice, cats, gases, cannons, filth, bullets, machine-guns, fire, steel, that's what war is! Nothing but the devil's work!"

This "paperback scarred by the hailstorms of the war", as Dix scholar Otto Conzelmann described it, was Dix's "book of notes and observations on the continuously repetitive agenda of everyday life in wartime". Entire pages of the book are covered with the names of soldiers whom Dix, in his rank as sergeant, had to tell the place, time and nature of their duty. From November, 1915 until December, 1916 the theatres of war were Champagne, Artois in French Flanders (the site of trench warfare) and the banks of the Somme, where two major battles took place. Between 1915 and 1918 Dix drew brief, concise, but vivid sketches depicting the chronology of events on a total of 46 postcards from the front. As it was, the "business of war" often obliged the soldier to hole-up for nerve-racking, tedious periods of waiting things out in some shelter or underground tunnel. "It was fun being able to draw in the midst of this hard, boring grind", Dix said of these times many years later. "The rigidity and inhumanity of it has to be seen to be believed."

The postcards from the front as well as the entries in his war journal

are not only first-rate documents of the period, but are also revealing in terms of autobiographical content. They shed light on the personality of an artist for whom the war was in fact the "father of all things", as Heraclitus defined it, that is to say, the decisive experience in his development as an artist.

Dix's unique way of dealing with war, death and destruction is comparable to that of Ernst Jünger, the writer, who was born in 1895. The latter's early works are equally marked by a way of thinking that centres on the basic human drives and is rooted in myth. In his writings Jünger thematized the antagonism between human "instinctual nature" and the

Trenches, ca. 1917
Schützengraben
Gouache and opaque white, 29 x 29 cm
Private collection

progress of civilization, with its ineffectual attempts to tame the "animal" in humans. Like Dix, Jünger was a visually oriented person for whom "observation represented one of the highest and wildest processes of movement" and who summarized his observations in graphical, visual language. Like Dix, Jünger also possessed, in addition to his critical involvement and astute analysis of current trends, the kind of sensuality and vitality that led him to search for the "wild and primaeval" beyond the scope of historical events. The observations recorded in his diary contain a precise perception – comparable to Dix's – of the dynamics of the battles as well as of the atmosphere of the wartime scenarios and the whole gamut of the soldiers' states of mind. Jünger, too, reports on the events in a form free of pathos. With his passion for action and movement, he is somewhat like a surgeon who dissects what is happening. At the same time, he incorporates detailed descriptions of wounds, mutilation, gutted towns and landscapes, which Dix first thematized in a similarly complex way with his cycle of etchings on *War* in 1924 (pp. 118ff). Unlike Dix, however, Jünger emphasized the heroic dimension to adventure and battle: "In the same way that life is thoroughly warlike, and because it is, the essence of life is turmoil." Only in battle did it seem possible to satisfy the wild and primaeval elements of the "instinctual human nature". This attitude was linked to a code of proving oneself in battle, especially in the face of defeat; this, as Jünger saw it, was precisely

Tracer Flares, 1917
Leuchtkugel
Gouache, 40,8 x 39.4 cm
Albstadt, Walther Groz Foundation,
Städtische Galerie Albstadt

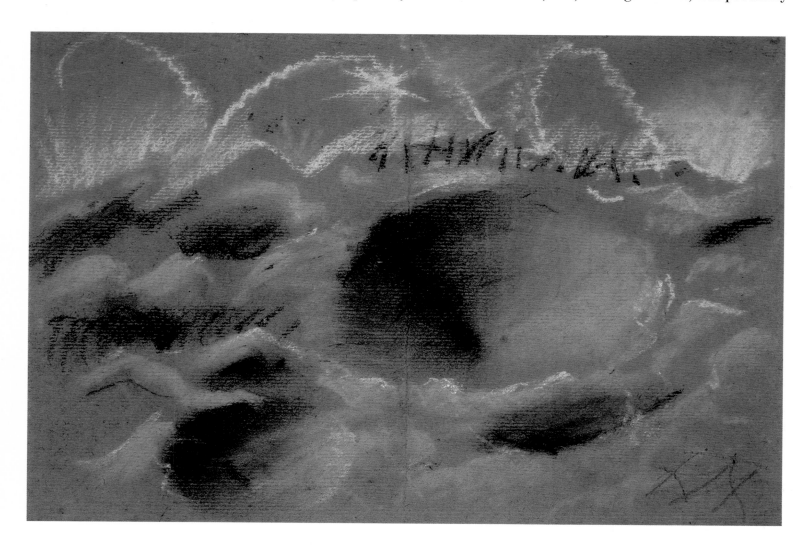

Shell Craters, ca. 1917
Granattrichter
Gouache, 29 x 28.3 cm
Leipzig, Museum der Bildenden Künste

what made war the great "teacher". Dix, on the other hand, thought and acted without any moral or value-oriented preconceptions. He was bent on probing into that tension-filled primordiality of human nature which had been transformed many times over in the course of socio-cultural evolution.

Dix, the sensitive man with the adventurous heart. Dix, the sceptic with the cool mind. Dix's person combined both devotion and distance. It is probably only because of this that he was able to "be a part of it" and paint at the same time. Notes in his diary such as "corpses are impersonal" or "war, too, must be regarded as a natural phenomenon" point to both a

The Position (Battlefield with Tree), 1917
Die Stellung (Schlachtfeld mit Baum)
Gouache, 41 x 38.7 cm
Freiburg, Augustinermuseum

vision unobscured by illusions and an audacity in his make-up, and at the same time to a slight complacency.

Even in 1963, while discussing art, religion and war with his friends, Dix insisted on his life-long "addiction" to reality: "Well, I simply happen to be a person who likes reality. I have to see everything. I have to plumb all life's depths myself. That is why I go to war. And that is why I volunteered in the first place." At another point, in 1961, he had this to say in an interview: "War is simply something so very animalistic: hunger, lice, mud, these insane sounds. Everything is just different. You see, before doing the early pictures I had the feeling that one side of reality hadn't been portrayed yet at all: ugliness. The war was horrible, but nevertheless gigantic. I couldn't afford to miss that. You have to see the human being in this uncontrolled state in order to know something about humankind."

Such statements reveal insights Dix had as a young man. War as a natural force, unleashed by the force of human aggression. Dix had already understood battle, suffering and death as fateful natural events in the works he produced before the war, and this view took on a more concentrated form in the paintings, drawings and sketches he made in 1915 and 1916, portraying the unconditional violence of destructive forces. The highly tense perception in these works focussed on observing

and rendering the battle campaigns in their totality, and less on the details or the extent and cause of the horrors. A large number of drawings from these years confirm Dix's fascination with the way in which the apparatus of war transformed the earth, in all of its organic-plastic variety, into thousands of burst and shredded entrails.

Sheets such as *Trenches with Flowers, Destroyed Farms* or *Bombarded Village*, all produced in 1915, but also the gouaches *Tracer Flares* (p. 32) or *Evening Sun* (p. 36) were composed of lines and cubic rectangles of colour: dismemberment rendered by means of discontinued lines converted into drawing and colour. The contours are never sharply delineated. Instead, they are layered over by hatching and this does not so much create a three-dimensional effect as achieve clear chiaroscuro qualities.

The brutality of all onslaughts – grenades and bombs exploding, attacks by night, surprise attacks – is conveyed directly by means of the technique of drawing marks, lines, zigzags and sharp edges which themselves seem to have been torn apart by explosions. The figures of the people involved in the battles are equally integrated into geometrically-based webs of lines, making them a part of nature that is detonating, being torn asunder. The wartime shelters, the dugouts, the tunnels as well as the trench systems created as fortification remain, for the most part, in subterranean, nocturnal darkness. The surfaces in nuances of

Evening Sun (Ypres), 1918
Abendsonne (Ypern)
Gouache, 39.2 x 41.3 cm
Albstadt, Walther Groz Foundation,
Städtische Galerie Albstadt

chalk, ink or charcoal, smeared or hatched in various dark tones, lend the structures of the objects their respective characters, created by the lesser light values. Rubble, ruins, exploding flares and grenades as well as the primarily nocturnal, subterranean existence allow one to see nothing but dismemberments, fissures and processes characterized by extremely chaotic speed. Dix translated them into an analogous technique of dismembered and dynamic lines.

The drawings and gouaches have a certain abstract quality about them, attributable to the idiosyncratic nature of a viewpoint which documents the war as the experience of the constant dissolution of organic and physical unity. Dix provided an anatomy of the war as a chain of destructive acts.

The cycle of etchings entitled *War*, produced in 1924, adds an additional dimension to the drawings. When asked why he had created this cycle, or the painting *Trenches* and the famous triptych *War* (pp. 172f), Dix replied: "I wanted to be rid of it!" Another statement reveals the distress and emotional burden of the war years in more unequivocal terms: "Well, it's like this – you don't notice it, as a young person you don't even notice that it has been weighing on you inside. Because for years, at least 10 years, I kept having these dreams where I would have to crawl through the ruins of houses, through corridors hardly wide enough for me to get through. The ruins were always in my dreams. Not that painting was a release for me!" It may not have been a release, but it was banishment, a means of holding something at bay.

Trenches, ca. 1918
Schützengraben
Gouache, 39 x 41 cm
Private collection

Awakening, 1918
Erwachen
Gouache over black chalk,
39.3 x 39.7 cm
Albstadt, Walther Groz Foundation,
Städtische Galerie Albstadt

Nevertheless, Dix documented the stages of the war and his experiences with extreme concentration – in the density of three-dimensional, corporeal portrayal. It was only at this point that a certain distance had been established from the remembered reality, which could thus be "held at bay" in all detail and revived again. We are shaken and unsettled in particular by the sharpness and precision with which the details of destruction are rendered. Some aspects of the scene Dix visually recreates and takes to the extreme are almost more than the eye can bear. Because we are hard-put to comprehend the reality of the meticu-

lously rendered atrocities, they almost seem to cross the threshold into the realm of the unreal. Dix's precision of detail allowed him to achieve an intensity that clearly showed how the forms of destruction are always essentially the same, above and beyond their immediate "historicity". Because of the contents, the individual etchings become general statements about destruction, suffering and death.

In its claim to general validity, Dix's cycle was comparable to the *Desastres de la Guerra* cycle of 82 etchings which Francisco de Goya began around 1810 and expanded around 1820. It was not until after

Warrior with Pipe, 1918
Krieger mit Pfeife
Gouache, 39.5 x 39 cm
Private collection

Red Head (Self-portrait), 1919
Roter Kopf (Selbstbildnis)
Oil on paper, 72 x 66 cm
Löffler 1919/8
Private collection

Pregnant Woman, 1919
Schwangeres Weib
Oil on canvas, 133 x 72 cm
Löffler 1919/6
Stuttgart, Dr. Freerk Valentien collection

Goya's death, in 1863, that the Madrid Academy published them as a series. Goya, whose cycle originated during the Napoleonic Wars, a national war of liberation fought by the Spanish people against the French invaders, attempted – like Dix – to depict misery and suffering in a way that transcended the respective historical context. The futility and hopelessness of this, as of any, war become painfully clear in Goya's work. A humanist, Goya saw war as a product of human instincts, and focussed on the fates of individuals.

Dix, who shared Goya's perspective on the individuality of the fates of humans affected by war, went one step further in his own etchings. He portrayed the successive stages in which individuality was suspended or brutally destroyed, a process which, not only according to Nietzsche, is closely linked to the concept of human dignity. In the etchings, Dix concentrates on portraying those events of war which were manifested in states of devastated physical existence as well as ravaged nature and civilization. This is what distinguishes the war cycle from the works produced on the subject during the war itself.

Dix had been using the technique of etching since 1920. It enabled him to present deformations of the body in minute nuances of substance and

plasticity. He considered it essential to find the technical medium best suited to the respective pictorial purpose. "After I had tried all possible techniques with Herberholz, I was suddenly taken with the technique of etching. I had a great deal to tell, I had a theme. Wash off the acid, put aquatint on it, in short, a wonderful technique that can be used to work step by step just as you like. The structure suddenly becomes colossally interesting; when you etch, you become the purest alchemist." With the possibilities afforded by the process, such as, for example, the repeated corrosion after coating the plate with asphalt varnish, Dix was able in a certain sense to reproduce the various stages of destruction, perceived as states of mutilated corporeality, by means of this technique. In this way he was also able to demonstrate the genesis of destruction as an invariably violent intrusion into organic material.

Portrayals of injured bodies and dead, gruesomely deformed, already putrefying bodies constitute the largest portion of the cycle. As in numerous other studies of bodies and nudes of the period, Dix emphasizes the face and hands, which once expressed human sensitivity and are now all that remains when tragic chance has taken its toll. The face of a *Dying Soldier* is disfigured, as is the hand, by black acid holes as big as fists, etched along the edges. The putrefaction of the *Corpse in the Barbed-Wire Entanglement* and of the *Dead Body in Mud* is depicted through the various steps of the acid-etching process, conveying the stages of decomposition in the skull and bones of the arm. The technique, central to many of the etchings, is also based on Dix's use of the line, which may range from the finest crosshatches and evenly distributed marks all the way to the terse contouring of flayed bodies. *Dance of Death Anno 17 (Height of Dead Man)*, taking up drawing experiments from 1915/16, is one of the best examples of Dix's deft deployment of chiaroscuro tonalities. A dead pile of soldiers' bodies luminates from the nocturnal darkness, exposed by the flickering light. The limbs are so twisted that macabre associations, such as those of the dance, rise to the surface and linger. This is why Dix did not hesitate to make an explicit reference (in his title) to this brutal "switch", whereby the abominable becomes the grotesque, indeed the ridiculous. The act of destruction occurs without reflexion. When consciousness later reasserts itself, it is no longer able to link the results of the destruction back to the moment of its genesis. It is undoubtedly this gap that makes violence and destruction possible in the first place.

In portraying the war, Dix, who was fundamentally fascinated by manifestations of vitality, did not see his role as that of an accuser or admonisher. He wished to shed his own feelings of consternation. And he was a meticulous chronicler of the phenomena of war. Much as he "trusted his own eyes" (his motto), Dix still tirelessly sought to support, filter, verify his own perceptions with additional documentation, such as photographs. For his cycle of *War* etchings Dix probably drew, among other things, on war photographs taken by Hugo Erfurth (cf. his portrait, p. 128); he was also familiar with Ernst Friedrich's book of photographs entitled *Make War on War*, published in 1924, and incorporated elements of it in his own work. In his book *The Other Dix*, Conzelmann describes

The Moon Woman, 1919
Mondweib
(Painted frame)
Oil on canvas, 120 x 100.5 cm
Löffler 1919/5
Berlin, Nationalgalerie,
Staatliche Museen zu Berlin

The Electric Tram Car, 1919
Die Elektrische
Oil on wood and collage, 46 x 37 cm
Löffler 1919/6
Whereabouts unknown

how Dix arranged to have entrails, intestines and corpses brought to him from the Department of Pathology at the hospital in Friedrichstadt, which he then "sketched, rendered in water-colours, or painted" – a love of truth that bordered on the cynical.

Far from merely copying, Dix quoted certain significant elements of destruction. His large four-part altarpiece *War* (pp. 172 f), which he worked on from 1929 to 1932, is a kind of pictorial synthesis of material drawn from knowledge, memory, observation, analysis and quotation. The same is true of *Trenches*, which was painted between 1920 and 1923, the whereabouts of which has been uncertain since 1938. This explains the tremendous impact both key works had on his contemporaries. *Trenches*, painted in oil on hessian, was purchased in 1923 for 10,000 reichsmarks by Hans F. Secker, the director of the Wallraf-Richartz Museum in Cologne. It provoked a scandal at the exhibition organized by Max Liebermann at the Berlin Academy in 1924. Julius Meier-Graefe, an influential art scholar and outstanding connoisseur of French 19th century and Impressionist painting, vented his anger in the *Deutsche Allgemeine Zeitung* of 5 July, 1924: "This trench is not only badly, but infamously painted with an overbearing…delight in detail…Brains, blood, guts can be painted in such a way that they make one drool…Rembrandt's second *Anatomy* with the gaping belly is enough to make you want to kiss it. This Dix is – if you'll excuse the expression – enough to make you want to throw up. Brains, blood, intestines are dressed up – not painted, mind you – in such a way that all of one's animal reactions are charged with high voltage." Anyone who speaks in terms such as these fails to acknowledge that war is a special subject which demands an unusual form of presentation that may even violate taboos. And perhaps humankind cannot bear too much cruel reality.

Although Dix was defended by Liebermann and the socially committed art critic Paul Westheim, among others, Secker had to rescind the purchase of the work in 1925. Carl Nierendorf, who had become Dix's art dealer in 1925, entered the picture in a touring exhibition organized that year by the "No more war" committee. Dix became popular – as a "pacifist". It was the beginning of a misunderstanding: since then (and up to the present) views of Dix have differed dramatically. One side considers him a revolutionary who accused society, and a pacifist; the other takes him for a militarist in disguise, a cynical advocate of wartime atrocities. The fate of his trench-painting in a sense documents the helplessness one frequently encounters in dealing with this artist, and which took an especially fateful turn under National Socialism. In 1933 the Nazis confiscated the painting and sent it to their ghoulish defamatory exhibition, "Entartete Kunst" (degenerate art). Together with his *War Cripples* (pp. 65/66), it was shown in Munich under the heading "Painted Sabotage of Defence by the Painter Otto Dix". It is assumed that the painting, which was seen for the last time in 1938, was burned in the courtyard of the main fire station in Berlin in 1939.

When asked to comment on the war triptych, which he completed between 1929 and 1932 in Dresden, Dix remarked in 1964: "The painting

was made ten years after the First World War. During these years I had conducted many studies in order to deal with the experience of war in artistic terms. In 1928 I felt mature enough to tackle this major theme, and its presentation occupied me for several years or more. At that time, by the way, many books in the Weimar Republic once more blatantly propagated a form of heroism and a concept of the hero that had long been taken to the point of absurdity in the trenches of the First World War. The people were already beginning to forget what unspeakable suffering the war had brought with it. It was this situation that led to the triptych."

On 30 January, 1933, one year after the painting was completed, Adolf Hitler was appointed chancellor by the Reich's president, Paul von Hindenburg. Dix, who had held a chair at the Dresden Academy since 1927, was dismissed without notice and forbidden to exhibit his works. The signs of the Weimar Republic's foreseeable downfall had been visible since as early as 1928. The unemployment figures had risen considerably, and the Nazi party had recorded a rapid growth in membership since 1929. Dix's tremendous efforts to master the theme of war again – in such monumental form – make the impression of a presentiment of

Male Head (Self-portrait), 1919
Männerkopf (Selbstbildnis)
Oil on canvas, 66 x 50 cm
Löffler 1919/9
Stuttgart, Galerie der Stadt Stuttgart

PAGE 46:
Portrait of the Poet Alfred Günther, 1919
Bildnis des Dichters Alfred Günther
Oil on paper, 76 x 54 cm
Löffler 1919/13
Stuttgart, Galerie der Stadt Stuttgart

PAGE 47:
My Friend Elis (with Self-portrait), 1919
Meine Freundin Elis (mit Selbstbildnis)
Oil on canvas, 57.5 x 50 cm
Löffler 1919/14
Denzlingen, private collection

The Printer and Collector Max John with Book, 1920
Der Drucker und Sammler Max John mit Buch
Oil on canvas, 69.5 x 59 cm
Löffler 1920/15
Freital, Haus der Heimat

The Skat Players, 1920
Die Skatspieler
Oil and collage on canvas, 110 x 87 cm
Löffler 1920/10
Stuttgart, Galerie der Stadt Stuttgart

things to come, including his own banishment. Only once was the war triptych displayed, in 1932 at the Prussian Academy's autumn exhibition in Berlin. Afterwards it was stored in boxes, to conceal it from the National Socialists.

Dix's choice of the mediaeval altarpiece as the form for his *War* triptych was well-considered. It was to be a contemporary version of human martyrs analogous to the holy pictures of the crucifixion. Indirectly, the Isenheim altar by Mathias Gothart Nithart called Grünewald served as a model for the composition. Its content, however, is completely the product of Dix's power of perception and imagination. The sequence of events includes morning, afternoon, night. It presents a season in Hell, conceived in cyclical terms. The left panel shows a column of soldiers marching to battle in the morning fog. This "develops" into gruesome proportions on the wooden centre panel. The only survivor is a soldier wearing a gas-mask crouching under the arched ruins of what used to be a bridge, on which a corpse is impaled. An apocalyptic landscape of trenches and craters spans the background, comparable in terms of arrangement to the middle panel of the Isenheim altar. The final version of the right panel (it was preceded by several drafts) shows Dix himself, who has escaped the inferno and has also been able to save a wounded comrade. On the predella, the "plinth", the drama ends in silence, in the soldiers' sleep of death.

It is impossible in a few lines to do justice to this work, which became a vision of "the last days of mankind". Numerous interpretations of the painting have been attempted, but none fully captures the timeless relevance of this 20th century masterpiece. However, it may suffice to say that it has an immediate impact. The magnificence of Dix's technique contributed decisively to its overwhelming effect. He made several drafts in pencil and red chalk, as well as a water-colour version of the composition; and the cardboard drafts and preliminary drawings to scale were essential for the final product. The use of a highly elaborate varnishing technique with the successive application of layers of transparent varnish is in keeping with the analytical nature of the work. We will return to Dix's adaptation of this technique, which was employed by the old masters, when we focus on the big-city triptych of 1927/28.

To complete our examination of this subject, however, we shall now turn to the "last" picture Dix devoted to the First World War, the painting entitled *Flanders* (p. 188), created between 1934 and 1936. In 1934 Dix, outlawed artist that he was, had nothing more to lose. Dix expert Fritz Löffler has rightly called the project Dix had begun in the middle of the "thousand years Reich" and which, as he knew only too well, had to be kept secret, "supremely self-confident": "Dix kept to his mission." He had to take this theme to the point of exhaustion, until the very last bit of it was "digested", as it were. Clearly the horrors of positional warfare in Flanders – which Dix had experienced for the last time in the spring of 1918 – had been particularly unforgettable. The French writer Henri Barbusse created the most intensive description of them in his novel *Le Feu*. It was no coincidence that Dix dedicated his Flanders painting to the author of

the book whose last chapter had inspired him to work on the theme: "We are awaiting daybreak at the same place where we threw ourselves to the ground at nightfall. – Hesitantly it approaches. Icily, gloomily and eerily stretching out over the fallow earth…Half dozing, half sleeping, staring with wide open eyes again and again, only for them to immediately fall shut again, paralyzed, shattered and freezing we stare at the unbelievable return of the light…With great effort and as unsteadily as if I were severely ill I half get up and look around. The weight of my wet army greatcoat is a clammy burden on me. Next to me three figures are lying distorted to the point of shapelessness. One of them with a shell of crusted mud on his back also gets up. The others do not stir in their sleep…"

Unlike all Dix's previous works on this theme, this painting is weighed down by the heaviness and fatigue of resignation. With it, Dix, who was then living in "internal exile" in Randegg Castle near Hemmenhofen, took leave, so to speak, from the self-assured, ebullient vitality of his earlier years.

Back to the year 1918. November 11. Armistice. Dadaism was the first artistic reaction to conditions immediately after the war: jarring, defiant of all authority, anarchistic, a nihilistic, playfully calculated affront to

Butcher's Shop, 1920
Fleischerladen
Oil on canvas, 80.5 x 70 cm
Löffler 1920/6
Italy, private collection

The Match Vendor I, 1920
Der Streichholzhändler I
Oil on canvas and collage,
144 x 166 cm
Löffler 1920/9
Stuttgart, Staatsgalerie Stuttgart

everything and everyone – and to the art movement which, prior to 1914, had seen itself as revolutionary, that is, Expressionism. "Did the Expressionists fulfil the expectations of an art that branded flesh with the essence of life? NO, NO, NO!", reads the Dadaist manifesto of 1918. "Dada: that is perfectly generous malice; in addition to exact photography, it is the only justified pictorial, communicative form and balance in shared experience – everyone who fulfils those leanings that are most intrinsically his is a Dadaist", wrote Raoul Hausmann in the *Synthetic Cinema of Painting* in 1918. "People are tired of the peasant dipping colour à la Gauguin and van Gogh. Enough of the Dionysian whitewashers" are the opening sentences of a 1922 pamphlet written by Einstein, one of the most original art critics of those years, who dealt with Dix's work in particular.

Dix, too, became a Dadaist. He, too, "recognized his real situation in this way" or aspired to do so, at least.

51

Dresden 1919 – 1921

Dix lived in Dresden from 1919 to 1922. As Otto Gussmann's master pupil, he had enjoyed having a studio at the State Academy of Fine Arts on Brühl terrace at his disposal. Felixmüller, who also painted a portrait of Dix (p. 54), took quite an interest in the artist. He persuaded him to join the "Group 1919" artists' association of the Dresden Secession, of which Will Heckrott, Lasar Segall, Otto Schubert, Constantin von Mitschke-Collande and Hugo Zehder were also members. Felixmüller acted as a go-between, arranging Dix's first contacts to Düsseldorf art patrons and art dealers, and gradually helped him to establish the basis for material livelihood. He described Dix's Dadaist phase in a 1920 edition of the Düsseldorf journal *das Ey*. Stimulated by the work of the Berlin Dadaists and particularly his friend Grosz, "Dix in those days pasted pictures together out of paper, glass, fabric, wood, fur, lace, seashells, iron, upholstery, family albums, in a naturalistic and highly objective style". He produced works such as *Sailor Fritz Müller from Pieschen*, *Match Vendor I* (p. 51), the *Altar for Cavaliers* (p. 60) and *Remembering the Halls of Mirrors in Brussels* (p. 67). Works such as *Skat Players* (p. 49) and *Prager Strasse* (p. 52), all of which date from 1920, portray the war as buffoonery, as a sarcastic farce. They resemble derisive dedications to man the beast, whose malicious social games provide further confirmation of the theory of *homo homini lupus*. After all, what other form of pictorial expression than that of cynicism was there for those who had come through?

Dix added the spice of his own morbid and grotesque sense of humour to the Dadaist *Zeitgeist*, which had nothing but contemptuous disdain for any and all values and ideals. The card players and cripples on the Prager Strasse, one of the elegant shopping streets in old Dresden, have been transformed into wind-up marionettes and jumping jacks that look as if they had been mechanically assembled. They are nothing more than a mass of spare parts thrown together, left-over pieces of bodies. In *Prager Strasse* Dix ingeniously parallels the prosthetic figures of war cripples and the plaster torsos and busts of store-window dummies arranged behind them. Both are incomplete, although one of them is the tragic result of human arbitrariness.

Dix's attitude during those years was one of self-ironic, somewhat disgusted and highly bored nihilism. In a 1920 pen-and-ink drawing

The Street, 1920
Die Straße
Engraving, 24.8 x 22.3 cm
Albstadt, Walther Groz Foundation,
Städtische Galerie Albstadt

Prager Straße, 1920
Oil on canvas and collage, 101 x 81 cm
Löffler 1920/7
Stuttgart, Galerie der Stadt Stuttgart

Conrad Felixmüller:
Portrait of Otto Dix, 1920
Oil on canvas, 75 x 60 cm
Wuppertal, Von der Heydt-Museum

entitled *Dadaistic Self-portrait* various signs are sprinkled in the picture, as well as the large painted word "Ahoi" (Ahoy) and the sentence "Das ist Dix, d.h.A+O zeit+raumlos" ("That is Dix, i.e. A+O time+spaceless"), which adorns the grinning profile of the artist. And the back is inscribed with the line: "I will avenge myself for the sins and virtues of my ancestors. Dix." In other words, as Dix saw it, the programme for the post-war years was attack or, as Carl Einstein put it in 1923: "…attack, sobrely and without being dressed in the impudent imposition of that well-loved false personality, which always smugly sells puns instead of facts…Dix dares

to produce kitsch as called for by the subject matter, that is, the ridiculous world of the cannily stupid bourgeois who wades thickly in suffocating commonplaces."

Dix, the rebel, Dix, the self-appointed "outlaw", Dix, the lonesome soul, as Felixmüller, still his patron and friend, soon came to realize. Felixmüller was saturated personally, artistically, and economically. He was six years Dix's senior, and a committed pacifist. He explained the drastic quality of Dix's pictures as follows: "One has to have seen the bad side of life and remained solitary. Like Otto Dix…Otto Dix is lonely, desperate and poor."

That was easy for Felixmüller to say. His life followed a well-ordered course to the same degree that Dix's was chaotic. Dix was disturbed most by the lack of artistic recognition for his work. In this context, Felixmüller recalled something Dix said: "I just can't seem to make it; my paintings are unsaleable! Someday I'll either be famous or infamous!" The discord between the two artists became increasingly apparent. Before the two finally went their separate ways, Felixmüller gave Dix some last friendly words of advice, namely, that he should work in graphics. As if that were not enough, he also instructed him in the techniques of etching, dry-point etching and lithography. Dix found "great pleasure" – in Felixmüller's words – in the newly learned procedure. Thus, all of the important etchings done in 1920, including *Match Vendor, Sex Murderer, Billard Players, Butcher's Shop*, were produced within a minimal amount of time. By the summer of 1920 Dix was already able to send the first of these works to the Ey Gallery in Düsseldorf, where they quickly sold. It was the beginning of a new, decisive period in Dix's life. A feeling Dix had sorely missed now elated him in a way he had never anticipated. He announced his intentions of renting a studio in Düsseldorf.

Painter Otto Pankok, who was also living in Düsseldorf, as well as Gert Wollheim and "Mother Ey", the legendary art dealer Johanna Ey, helped in the search. However, before Dix finally set out for Düsseldorf on 21 October, 1921, loaded down with paintings, he travelled to Hamburg, in pursuit of new sources of inspiration. "I no longer remember where I lived, nor how long I stayed in Hamburg", said the elderly Dix, in retrospect, attempting to reactivate his memory. "But I do recollect the harbour, the sailors, the women, the pubs, the Reeperbahn and the Herbertstrasse" (Hamburg's famous red-light district).

Otto Dix with Conrad Felixmüller in Dresden

Düsseldorf 1922 – 1925

Dix had been invited to Düsseldorf by Johanna Ey, and also by Hans Koch, a doctor, art collector and first husband of Mrs. Martha Koch, who was later to become Dix's wife. Thus, in a sense, the city where Dix lived and worked from 1922 to 1925 became his "destiny".

In her memoirs Johanna Ey describes Dix's arrival in Düsseldorf with an oft-cited anecdote: "All of the delicacies and liqueurs I could muster were there to greet him. He soon arrived with a flapping cape, large hat, and greeted me with a kiss of the hand, something very unusual for me in those days. In the morning he unpacked his box, revealing: patent-leather shoes, perfumes, nothing but beauty care items..." Dix's dandy-like appearance, his pomaded hair combed straight back, the "American-style" suits, again disprove the myth of Dix the "proletarian". At that time, Dix was the arrogant barfly, the charmeur, the ladies' man, and a superb dancer. His charisma made impression on Martha Koch, née Lindner. Her marriage to Koch was already in a serious crisis at the time. Martha ran a graphics gallery with Koch, which traded under the name "von Berg Art Dealers". It had been set up after the Flechtheim Gallery closed in 1917 because, as the later Martha Dix put it, people "felt that something was missing". Martha and Hans Koch dealt above all in French art, in works by Georges Braque, Maurice de Vlaminck, Marie Laurencin, but also sold works by August Macke, Georg Schrimpf, Paul Adolf Seehaus and Emil Nolde. Martha Dix also writes in her memoirs that "our boom-time came with Nolde. Nolde was expensive, and that drew the people in." The "art dealing" episode lasted until 1920.

The affair between Otto and Martha, on the other hand, was guided by the laws of passion. Koch, whom Dix had brought his paintings to look at, immediately bought two of them, *Salon I* (p. 79) and *Salon II*, both done in 1921. In addition, Koch commissioned Dix to do his portrait, which gave the painter unrestricted access to the Koch household. Martha describes her first encounter with Dix: "I imagined Dix would be a young man with pimples and blond hair. He really did have blond hair, and above all he was very lively. It turned out that he could dance extremely well. Hans found this silly and made things even worse. Horrible. I was just always crazy about dancing and it was decided that we would buy a gramophone. So we danced while Hans drank. We drank, too. From

Portrait of Martha Dix, 1920
Bildnis Martha Dix
Pencil, 36.2 x 34.5 cm
Vaduz, Otto Dix Foundation

Two Children, 1921
Zwei Kinder
Oil on canvas, 96 x 76 cm
Löffler 1921/10
Brussels, Musée Royaux des Beaux-Arts
de Belgique

Cats (dedicated to Theodor Däubler), 1920
Katzen (Theodor Däubler gewidmet)
Oil on wood, 47 x 37 cm
Löffler 1920/3
Vaduz, Otto Dix Foundation

Baccara glasses. They held a quarter litre of wine." Unlike Martha, Dix could not take his drink.

Be that as it may, the two proved a perfect match, at least on the dance floor. They even made plans to enter dance competitions as a way of "improving their financial situation", according to Frau Dix's account. Dix's favourite dance was the shimmy, as well as the Charleston, one of the most popular American steps in vogue at the time. After the war Europe was literally swept off its feet by dancing fever. Jazz, imported from the American South, had swept the world. Americanism was the fashion of the day. America was considered the Promised Land, at least among artists and intellectuals. The model of the American entertainment industry, mass culture, with its grandiose showgirl reviews and lavish spectacles, boulevard theatre and Charlie Chaplin films gradually

took hold in Germany as well. Dix's passion for dancing the shimmy earned him the nickname of "Jim" or "Jimmy". In his own ironic manner, Dix was a fan of Americanism, not as an ardent enthusiast, but with the distance of a man who had enjoyed life's pleasures with gusto and was now cultivating a certain decadence.

In 1921 he drew a self-portrait, signed "Toy in November 21". The profile with the finely aquiline nose, the jutting chin and daring look from slightly squinting eyes reveals a thirst for action and love of conquest,

Suleika, the Tattooed Wonder, 1920
Suleika, das tätowierte Wunder
Oil on canvas, 162 x 100 cm
Löffler 1920/4
Italy, private collection

Altar for Cavaliers, 1920
Altar für Cavaliere
Middle panel with open shutters
Oil on wood. Dimensions unknown.
Löffler 1920/5
Berlin, private collection

mixed with that "certain something" of self-irony and melancholy. One month earlier, he had characterized his future wife (affectionately called "Mutzli") in a pencil drawing. With a few fine lines and shading he evokes the elegant appearance of this woman with the large expressive eyes and an almost magical, fascinating charisma. At the time, in this carefree climate of being in love, the two made a "nice couple", and they savoured their public appearances to the full.

Nevertheless, from the very beginning Martha saw her relationship with Dix in a rather matter-of-fact light. In her memoirs she comments on this period in the following terms: "He was living at Frau Ey's. Of course, she also had her doubts about the matter, as it went on. And it did keep going, on and on. And in the end it went wrong. (Martha's definition of marriage.) I always told him, it's no use. It's enough for me if he comes to visit once in a while. But Hans Koch insisted on a divorce." However, another year passed before this could be effected. In February 1923, Otto Dix and Martha Koch were finally married at the registry office. They

The Sex Murderer (Self-portrait), 1920
Der Lustmörder (Selbstbildnis)
Oil on canvas, 170 x 120 cm
Löffler 1920/12
Whereabouts unknown

married – without any wild artists' party – in the closest circle of friends and relatives. "We bought something or other at the store, made a punch, and that was that," Martha Dix later remembered.

Unlike Dix, Martha came from a wealthy, upper-middle-class background. Born on 19 July, 1895 in Cologne, she grew up in Mannheim and Frankfurt, surrounded by governesses and servants, and was educated by private tutors in several languages and in music. Her father, Bernhard Lindner, was the director of an insurance company. Together with two older brothers and her sister, Maria, to whom she was very close, she enjoyed a carefree childhood and adolescence in liberal, cosmopolitan surroundings. The latest literary and cultural trends were subjects of interest. Maria, who sympathized with pacifist ideas, subscribed to Franz Pfemfert's politically leftist newspaper *Die Aktion.* Martha dismissed as ridiculous any reservations about her relationship to Otto based on supposedly irresolvable class differences. It was not at all uncommon in the 1920s for couples to be from different social backgrounds, and usually

Seated Nude, 1920
Sitzender Akt
Pencil, 58.4 x 48 cm
Vaduz, Otto Dix Foundation

these involved self-confident, emancipated women from wealthy families who did not hesitate to marry working-class men. Dix had found in Martha a woman with a strong personality of her own and the ability to think critically – a match for his difficult, extreme nature. Moreover, she also liked to lead her own life, was an excellent pianist and passionate reader, an outstanding connoisseur of the great works of world literature. She was, therefore, able to accept her husband's frequent absences without feeling lonesome or resentful. Martha Dix was intelligent and self-assured enough to allow her husband the freedom he needed.

Before Otto and Martha Dix finally settled down in Düsseldorf in the autumn of 1922, the couple spent another, short period of time in Dresden. This was the beginning of a period of untroubled, inspired work for Dix. The atmosphere was optimistic, despite constant financial worries. Dix drew a number of sketches of himself and his "Mutzli". These drawings, as well as the letters and cards to Hans and Maria Koch (Hans Koch had in the meantime married Martha's sister, Maria, and they all got along together spendidly), reflect the cheerfulness and boisterous happiness of the young couple.

One of Dix's most significant works originated in the early 1920s: the *Portrait of the Artist's Parents I* (p. 84). Mother Ey, Dix's successful art dealer, acquired it and exhibited it in her gallery. According to her, the general public had no understanding for it and reacted with a perplexed and defensive attitude: "The people laughed about it and commented 'Hm, really nice parents.'" As always in Dix's portraits, the hands and faces of the persons are emphasized in the painting. The two old people are sitting at an angle next to each other, wearing simple work-shirts, trousers and an untied apron. Their arms are resting heavily, but relaxed, on their knees. The large hands are marked by physical labour. The two old people stare ahead, somewhat reflective, a bit tired, but at one with themselves and their destiny. Not a trace of exploitation of the "lower class" went into the painting; instead, Dix conveyed in pictorial terms a stock-taking, perceived with a sensitively attentive view, of two lives marked by a shared concern in achieving a bearable existence.

Dix's major theme, however, continued to be Eros and Thanatos. In those years he devoted himself primarily to the social outsiders, portraying the milieu of anti-bourgeois, exotic worlds such as fairgrounds, brothels, and circuses, or took up taboo themes such as sex-murders, sado-masochism, old age and sexuality. His exposing, liberating sense of humour came into its own when he tackled things which, from the bourgeois standpoint, were "disreputable", forbidden. One of the most telling examples of Dix's savoury-grotesque sense of humour is the 1920 oil painting *Suleika, the Tattooed Wonder* (p. 59). Unfortunately, its whereabouts are not known. According to his wife, Dix was "very interested in tattoos at the time; he bought a book of models with primitive pictures from a master of the trade..." Yet the book did not serve as a model for the painting, as Dix did not buy it until some time after having completed work on it. The woman whom Dix portrayed actually existed. She performed as "Maud Arizona" in German ports and in the Orient.

Working-class Boy, 1920
Arbeiterjunge
Oil on canvas, 86 x 40 cm
Löffler 1920/19
Stuttgart, Galerie der Stadt Stuttgart

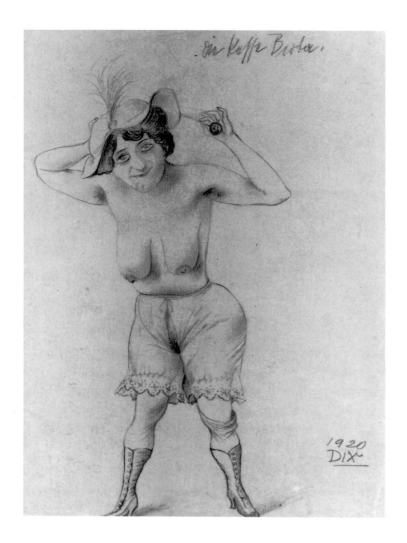

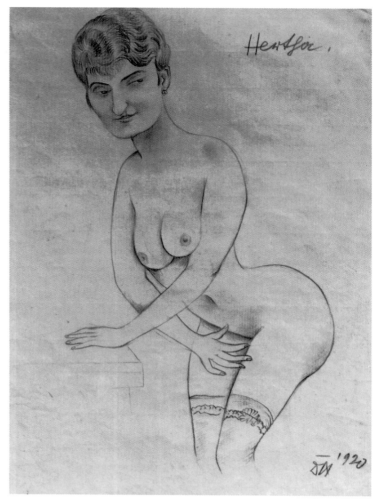

Until the First World War, and even during the war, people greedy for shows and sensations were enormously fascinated by tattooed figures. "It's the fashion of the day!" wrote L. Stieda in 1911. "Many people are getting tattooed in order to make a living." Since tattooed figures, above all women, had begun displaying themselves for money at fairs, these exotic, charming and, at the same time, displeasing people who presented themselves as works of art captivated the interest of the man in the street and scholars alike. They had two main effects: on the one hand, they were quite erotic, something which, as can be gathered from reports of the day, was hardly ever admitted, however; on the other hand, there was a much more widespread tendency to look down on them. People experienced their own fascination as a threat that had to be warded off, which, of course, made the abnormality, the outsider status and the otherworldliness of these decorated bodies all the more manifest. Generally the tattooed figures were considered criminal elements living on the periphery of society. "The threshold to criminality determines the definition of the tattoo as a European phenomenon", was Klaus Oettermann's summary of the situation in his book *Drawing on Skin.*

"Suleika's" tattoos transform her into an ornamental work of art, turn her skin into a vehicle for a lavish abundance of pictorial motifs. On Suleika's body Dix presented the entire arsenal of the art of tattooing,

The War Cripples (with Self-portrait), 1920
Kriegskrüppel (mit Selbstbildnis)
Oil on canvas, 150 x 200 cm
Löffler 1920/8
Formerly Dresden, Stadtmuseum
(confiscated in 1937, whereabouts
unknown; presumably destroyed in Berlin
in 1942)

"imitating" the popular style and related motifs both ironically and with gusto. We can see emblems rich in allusion, such as the imperial eagle on the globe, with various flags of European countries hanging down on the sides, an Iron Cross, the cross on a soldier's grave as well as the view of a soldier from the back equipped with the spiked helmet and death's-head. In addition, there are a female circus rider, a tightrope walker and other acrobats, a sailing ship, a couple embracing, frequently used symbols of good luck such as the sun, little angels of glory, a rose, a pierced heart, a wheel of fortune (helm), and astrological and animal symbols, including a snake, butterfly and horse's head. The motifs selected not only possess the charm of incunabula taken from trivial mythology, but also reveal a kind of private Dixian mythology.

Eloquent symbols, such as the rose, moon, sun, angel's wings, skull or wheel of fortune, repeatedly appear in early self-portraits, and we can infer certain things about Dix's image of himself. With Suleika, Dix was paying homage to a physicality emphasized with relish and also to a prime example of pictorial comedy. This self-enamoured coquette show-attraction stands in a delicately contrived pose on a low, round, white pedestal. She turns her body slightly upward, with her fingers spread out in all directions: a body become ornamental artwork.

The feeling of her own magnificence exudes from every pore of her

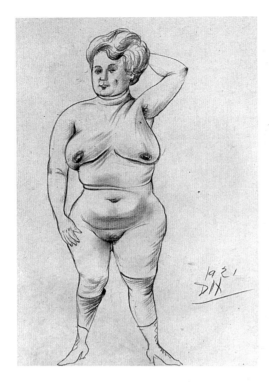

Nude in Stockings and Shoes, 1921
Akt mit Strümpfen und Schuhen
Pencil
Vaduz, Otto Dix Foundation

Remembering the Halls of Mirrors in Brussels, 1920
Erinnerung an die Spiegelsäle in Brüssel
Oil on canvas, 124 x 80.4 cm
Löffler 1920/11
Hamburg, Poppe Collection

body; and this boastful self-satisfaction is also the source of the figure's visible comic quality. This was precisely the pictorial effect that Dix so revelled in, knowing full well that comedy and pleasure belong together: "Yes, of course, it's also a kind of pleasure in the grotesque, just as everything in this world is dialectic! The way the opposites stand side by side! Here the *ceremonial* – and alongside it the *comic.* The fact that it seems to be so closely related, why, that's a kind of…mm, it's not exactly a discovery I myself made, but it seemed to absolutely belong together. No, it was a pleasure for me to find that life is that way, that's it, that not everything is sugar-coated and wonderfully beautiful."

Humour and comic effect were fundamental to Dix's view of the world. The fact that opposites invariably "stand side by side", that the "comic and the ceremonial belong together", was not something that provoked anxiety in him; on the contrary, this insight enabled him to rid himself of anxiety. In two cycles of etchings completed in 1922, *Circus* and *Death and Resurrection,* Dix again pays homage to the beloved creations of a counter-world. Maud Arizona, the model for "Suleika" in his painting, reappears in two versions of *Circus,* which also includes "theatrical sketches", acts of illusion and riding acts; the *Defiers of Death* (cf. water-colour painting, p. 97) proudly expand their chests, adorned with a skull, and in a highly absurd "balancing act" a young woman transports a lavishly decked table on the bridge of her nose. The six etchings in the *Death and Resurrection* cycle, which includes *The Suicide Victim* (p. 101), *Pregnancy, The Barricade, Dead Soldier* and *Burial,* do not shun confrontation even with extreme forms of death. Dix walks a fine line between horror and comedy in *Sex Murder* (p. 71), which shows two small dogs mating in front of a woman's ravaged body. The two extremes converge, life and death mutually determine one another.

Dix devoted several works to the theme of sex murders. He even portrayed himself as the *Sex Murderer* (p. 61) in a 1920 painting. In 1922 he produced another painting entitled *Sex Murder* (p. 70), the whereabouts of which are no longer known, but which will be discussed here in greater detail because of the "grotesque" features of its design. According to Martha Dix, themes such as sex murder were fascinating in those days. Jack the Ripper, for example, was a subject of conversation, just as Frank Wedekind's play *Pandora's Box* (1902) was acclaimed in the theatre. The painting *Sex Murder,* 1922, is an artistic product borne of Dix's power of imagination, a painted vision. It is composed of a number of minute, precise observations which do not necessarily belong together in terms of the time or place, yet are all taken from reality, and Dix pays the greatest attention to detail. The process involved in the picture's creation is comparable to the method employed by a director who transforms a scene that haunts his imagination as precisely as possible into the media of theatre.

The corpse is lying on its back and is about half, in other words roughly up to the waist, draped over a narrow bed with lathed bed-posts and a carved headboard. The legs are spread wide open, in the "classic" position for the sexual act, and slightly bent. Her torso hangs down over the

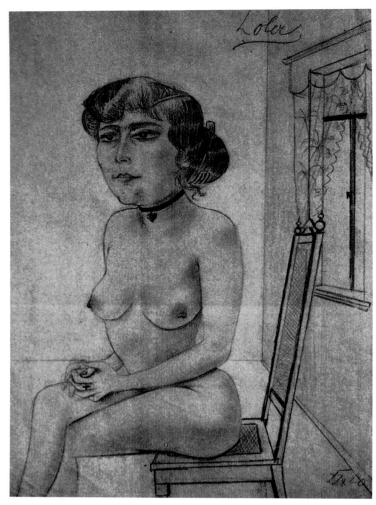

ABOVE LEFT:
Seated Nude, around 1920
Sitzender Akt
Pencil, 43.5 x 31 cm
Private collection

ABOVE RIGHT:
Lola, 1920
Pencil, 44.1 x 31.7 cm
Munich, H.G. Brück Gallery

Portrait of Max John, 1920
Bildnis Max John
Oil on paper, 63 x 43 cm
Löffler 1920/16
Freiburg, Augustinermuseum

side of the bed. Her body is completely wasted, suggesting that the perpetrator exhausted himself in his surge of violence. A pool of blood is painted in front of her head, which is nearly touching the floor – astonishingly, this puddle is nearly rectangular, with a few, "artfully" applied thicker or thinner rivulets of blood trickling from it. The exposed upper part of her torso, on which the left breast can be seen while the right breast is covered by a sheet torn off the bed and hanging onto the floor, also bears traces of blood, but is not "smeared" with it; Dix distributes the blood in artistically contrived arrangements of thin lines and somewhat thicker stripes on the body. Around the throat, on the other hand, thick dark scabs of blood are visible, arranged in three parallel bands along the folds of the neck. The woman's throat has obviously been cut. Rivulets of blood also run down her face, and from her nose, mouth, and right eye. The left eye of the corpse has rolled slightly to one side, and is open, whereas the right eye is closed. The mouth is open and distorted. One tooth is smeared with blood. The corpse has no unique features; it is intended as a prototype for the lower levels of the brothel milieu. The fact that the figure is intended to portray a prostitute can be seen from her clothing with the lace-frilled corset that has slipped down, the stockings decorated with bows and incidentally with holes in places at the toes, and the knee-length, wide, white bloomers edged with silk ribbons. The most

Sex Murder, 1922
Lustmord
Oil on canvas, 165 x 135 cm
Löffler 1922/2
Whereabouts unknown

severe ravishing was committed in and around her pelvis, a conclusion which follows logically enough from the theme that Dix has so meticulously rendered. The lap is shown as a dark, gaping wound, bloody and torn open. The thighs are also covered with streaks of blood. The blood is repeated in blots on the wall.

The concept of sex murder is the very ultimate in paradox, fusing two seemingly irreconcilable, radically opposite poles. Dix was able to depict this theme through the media of the grotesque. The grotesque is not interested in the muted surface that rounds off and marks the body as an isolated phenomenon. This is why a grotesque figure reflects not only an external, but also an internal view of the body. To understand this grotesque figure we must grasp that its definition is blurred in such a way as to permit thoughts of fornication, pregnancy, and so forth. The principle that Dix perceived is innate to this body: "The body of non-official and intimate speech is inseminating-inseminated, bearing-borne, embracing-embraced – a body drinking itself, emptying itself, infirm, dying."

The manner in which Dix painted the victim of this sex murder is a demonstration of the grotesque created through alienation achieved with the media of painting. This body is open, marked by the result of sensual pleasure fuelled by a destructive drive. Its positioning is exaggerated, the legs are spread apart to a degree that is out of proportion to the length of the bed. The face is rendered as a grimace, and the body's whole pose is distorted. The artificiality of the traces of blood as well as the arrangement of the torn-out covers and bed-sheets parallel to the body provoke a strong sense of alienation.

Each and every detail is arranged to fit the others, and this harmony of alienation is in turn almost decorative. Such artistic twists at least make it possible to approach the truly horrific in the first place. In the right foreground, parallel to the position of the body, one sees a chair that has been knocked over, with a wickerwork back and seat. It further intensifies the grotesque effect of the corpse, for the chair's four outstretched legs "imitate" the body in such an exact, provoking manner as to degrade

Sex Murder, 1922
Lustmord
Etching, 27.5 x 34.6 cm
Albstadt, Walther Groz Foundation,
Städtische Galerie Albstadt

71

the once living being. Both the chair and the corpse are suddenly placed on the same level. This breaks the initial shock impact, giving way to a comical-grotesque effect on the observer.

The mirror provides a reflection of the most abused part of the corpse's body. The cheap, peeling wallpaper in turn corresponds with the destructive atmosphere of the scene. In the background one sees – in crass opposition to the chaos in the foreground – a traditional German-style round table with curlicued legs standing in front of a sofa with thick armrests set along the wall to the right. Both pieces of furniture look conspicuously "respectable" in relation to the desolate scene in the foreground of the painting. A narrow lace doily is neatly spread over the

John Penn, 1922
Watercolour, 73 x 50.5 cm
Vaduz, Otto Dix Foundation

Farewell to Hamburg, 1921
Abschied von Hamburg
Oil on canvas, 85 x 59 cm
Löffler 1921/1
Munich, Galerie Gunzenhauser

At the Mirror, 1922
Am Spiegel
Etching, 35.1 x 28 cm
Albstadt, Walther Groz Foundation,
Städtische Galerie Albstadt

table, and the back of the sofa is "beautified" by almost diamond-shaped pieces of checked cloth. The oil lamp hanging from the ceiling is much too extravagant compared with the decor of the room as a whole. Through the narrow, high window one sees the ugly, plain facades of cheap tenement blocks.

The techniques that Dix uses in this picture – parallelism, contrast, reflection, distortion, disproportionality and the care with which he uses and balances them – indicate that alienation is nothing other than a matter of gaining perspective on a radical theme and is, therefore, at least the first step towards coping with it.

Dix had never shied away from being provocative, and in those years he attempted more adamantly than ever to be so. True to his motto "I'll either become famous or infamous", in 1922 he produced the etching *At the Mirror* (p. 74) which caused a scandal. To be exact, the painting *Girl at the Mirror* (p. 76) had already provoked the scandal in 1921. This painting, which is so intimately bound up with the portrayal in the etching that even many of the details are the same, was placed on the Index of works banned from public exhibition or sale for disseminating an obscene reproduction. Charges were brought against Dix.

Arthur Kaufmann describes how Dix prepared himself for the trial: "The evening before the court session we played judge-and-jury at Mother Ey's...I was the state prosecutor and asked Dix: 'Why did you, the accused, paint the *pars media* in such disgusting clarity?' To which Dix replied: 'But those are simply the lady's tools.' We laughed resoundingly, but made it clear to Dix that he would inevitably be convicted if he answered a question of that kind in that way. We advised Dix to explain that he had wanted to warn male youth against vice."

Partly because of an affidavit furnished by his friend Lovis Corinth, Dix was finally cleared of the charges and the state had to cover the costs. Dix encountered similar reactions many times in the course of those years; one such case took place the same year, in 1923, with a trial in Darmstadt involving his painting *Salon II*. This also was decided in the artist's favour. Dix was not particularly troubled by such interludes, as he was able to continue painting without interference. For *Girl at the Mirror* Dix chose a motif that had exerted a strong fascination repeatedly through-out art history and in literature ever since classical antiquity, a motif that brings the bivalency of categories such as beautiful-ugly, youth-age, health-decline, being-appearance forcefully to mind. It is the mirror which first exposes the real physical condition of the woman who, when seen from the back, could very well be a "girl", as Dix ambiguously calls her in the title. An old whore is trying to sell herself as a young woman, forced for reasons of survival to continue playing a role the requirements of which she no longer physically fulfils. This is why she has adorned her body, with its sagging breasts, the way she once did in her youth. She is standing, bent slightly forward, before a large full-length mirror with a pompous frame and base; busy making up her face, she is just raising her right hand to the level of her temple, perhaps in order to readjust a wave of her hair, which is carefully wound over her head in a twist. She is

wearing a corset striped lengthwise and with lace on the plunging decolleté which, owing to the forward inclined pose, clearly bares to the mirror
her breasts, which have pitifully withered with age. The exposure of her
body from the front nullifies any erotic expectation which might have
been aroused by the view of her back, covered as it is in lace and the criss-
cross hooking of her corset. The mirror, which makes a harsh mockery of
her pathetic figure, thus points all the more dramatically to another,
more attractive past. The picture is doubly challenging: not only the

The Woman Sadist's Dream II, 1922
Traum der Sadistin II
Watercolour and pen, 49.5 x 39.9 cm
Rome, Galleria Giulia

taboo subject of an old body, but also the other, more or less also taboo subject of prostitution are considered worthy of portrayal. The mirror, thus twice divested of its conservative function, exposes "ugliness", and is abused, so to speak, by ugliness.

Dix was and remained one of the few modern painters who dared to depict the decaying body. He later had the following to say about this painting and others that dealt with similar themes: "Before the early pictures I had the feeling that one side of reality had not yet been portrayed at all – ugliness." He supplemented this view shortly before his death in 1969 with the comment that "I was not so much concerned with portraying ugliness. Everything I have ever seen is beautiful." Such statements again reveal his underlying insistence on unbiased perception. The usual values attached to the categories of "beautiful" and "ugly" did not mean anything to Dix.

One of the most important paintings of 1922, which was such a productive year for him, was *To Beauty* (p. 81), generally regarded as the

Girl at the Mirror, 1921
Mädchen vor dem Spiegel
Oil on canvas. Dimensions unknown.
Löffler 1921/8
Destroyed during the war

76

forerunner of the big-city triptych he completed in 1927/28. The picture, of which a carefully detailed pencil study has been preserved, depicts the carefree nonchalance of refined *salon* culture to a far greater degree than does the triptych – with its analytic dismantling of the fraudulent promises of luxury and pleasure. Dix himself is placed squarely in the centre of the painting, a cool, stylish dandy, with one hand in his jacket pocket, a telephone receiver in the other hand, impervious to the beauty of the people and the classicist ambience around him, unimpressionably beautiful. The trophies, indeed the stimulants of the age, form the decorative setting for this Twenties go-getter: a couple dancing the Charleston, a black drummer, a "lady" with corsage and a head of curly locks fresh from the hairdresser's. The atmosphere of frozen aestheticism is dosed out to the maximum; the cult of external appearances is administered in shrewd measure. The world and money are in the firm

Woman with Red Hat, 1921
Frau mit rotem Hut
Oil on cardboard, 44 x 41 cm
Löffler 1921/11
Hamburg, private collection

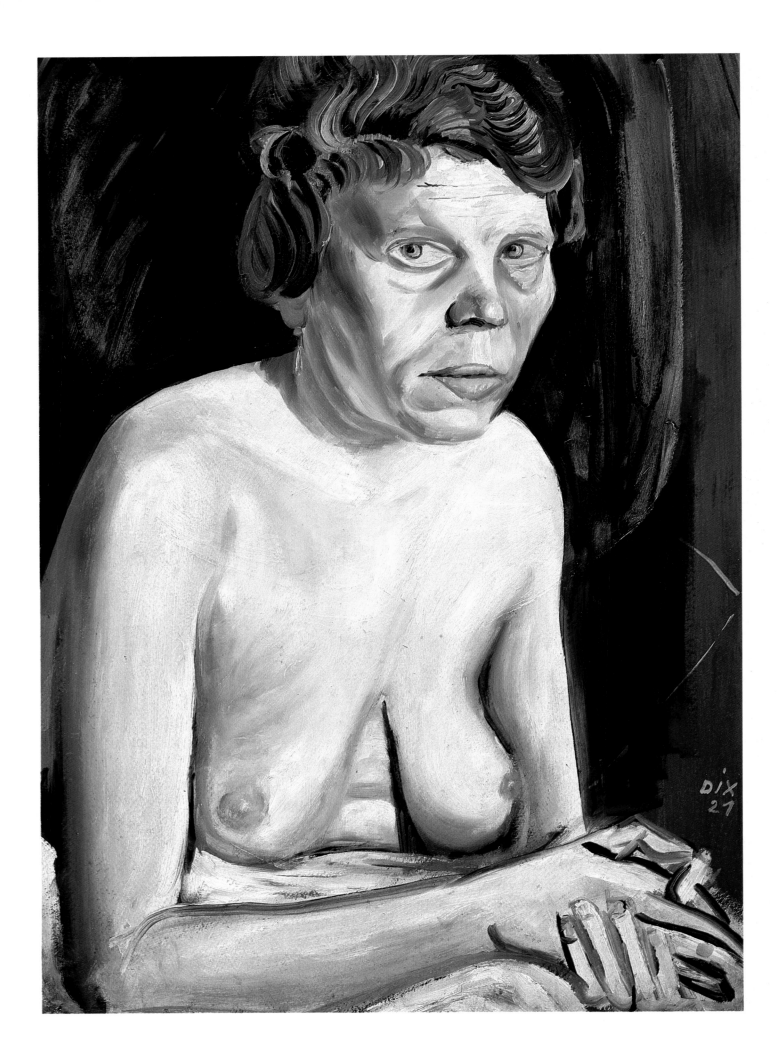

grip of the telephone receiver. Dix could not have evoked more aptly the gulf between having and being, which was masked in those days by a self-assured bearing.

And the manner in which he cast himself in the role of director of the entire scene, as the grand "untouchable", could hardly have been better. Dix produced self-portraits throughout the many periods of his work. When asked why he did so, he replied: "Self-portraits are confessions of an inner condition...I am surprised again and again to discover that 'I don't look like that at all'. There are so many sides to a person..." In those years Dix especially liked to adopt the airs of a cool voyeur, to don the outfit of the elegant lounge lizard and bon vivant or the role of the technoid researcher in the uniform of a surgeon. He repeatedly presented himself in self-portraits and sketches as being surrounded by semantic signs of a private and associational nature and trivial in structure. Dix employed such symbols as a means of indirect self-disclosure as well as of disguise. Thus the sun, moon and stars, for example, appear in his 1918 painting *Longing*. And on a few occasions Dix also embellished his signature, as in the case of *Portrait of the Dancer Anita Berber* (p. 131), painted in 1925, and in the 1920 etching *Sex Murderer*: the 0 in both is shaped like a snake.

The Salon I, 1921
Der Salon I
Oil on canvas, 86 x 120.5 cm
Löffler 1921/17
Stuttgart, Galerie der Stadt Stuttgart

Half-nude, 1921
Halbakt
Oil on cardboard, 65.5 x 48.5 cm
Löffler 1921/6
United States, private collection

Old Woman in Corset, 1922
Alte im Corsett
Oil on canvas. Dimensions unknown.
Löffler 1922/15
Whereabouts unknown

The use of such motifs strewn around the pictures is more or less limited to the years immediately following the First World War, and becomes increasingly rare in his works after 1923. Perhaps these symbols helped Dix to regain his inner balance. Apparently their value, some of which almost attained fetish-like significance for Dix, lay in the protective and defensive function they had. Dix's personality, like the works he produced in the 1920s, is ambivalent. It cannot be considered as having been an integral identity with a clearly describable charisma during this period. One cannot get at Dix's "essence" because it cannot be defined in terms of precise characteristics. In his case, individuality and role presentation are always mixed, and each role is marked by a unique personality which ultimately, however, can only be grasped as something ambivalent.

The pictures which reflect Dix's relationship to women are revealing in this connection. Two studies for self-portraits, graphite drawings dating from 1921, one of which is painted over in water-colours, may provide some insights in this respect. His carefully drawn head is the focal point of both drawings, whereas his elegantly clad torso, in tie and suit, as well as the women's faces and parts of their bodies, are all sketched in a rather more fleeting, inchoate manner. His face is turned away from the women, and under close-knit brows his eyes are focused on some indefinite object. The expression on his face betrays an attentive, sceptical and distanced reflectiveness. The head is strikingly shaped, the stance tense and inclined slightly forward. The cigarette hanging casually from the right corner of his mouth indicates, in addition to the above-mentioned alertness of his view, a certain feeling of satiety, mixed with a touch of melancholy. Dix's head is framed by rapidly sketched women's faces, the faces of prostitutes and similar figures from a whole collection of erotic and sexual sketches all drawn just as hastily. One can make out female bodies on the coloured drawing – a "sex murder" next to Dix's face, for example; a nude's back covered in festering sores behind Dix's head; a vulva between the two women's faces; a "chopped-off" penis next to the snakehead with its flickering tongue on his shoulder; and his sarcastically and sadly placed heart, which is pinned to his suit like a cheap badge.

In addition to women's heads and parts of the body, the second drawing depicts angel wings – ironically "mounted on" the bodies – as well as a skeleton, a broken wheel, a canon and the letters A and O. The picture clearly manifests a state of extreme tension in his relationship to women. Desire and yearning for them and, beneath the surface, the fearful wish to ward them off intermingle. The signs of life and death, which combine with each other particularly in the watercolour drawing, in a sense recapitulate the poles of the Dixian cosmos. Eros and Thanatos, the central theme of his pictures, was also closest to his own heart.

In another drawing, *Me in Brussels* (p. 96) from 1922, also in watercolour, Dix portrays himself in a soldier's uniform, staring – with the inevitable cigarette in the corner of his mouth – with a sharp, lascivious and assessing glance at a young woman passing by. She walks past him

To Beauty, 1922
An die Schönheit
Oil on canvas, 140 x 122 cm
Löffler 1922/6
Wuppertal, Von der Heydt-Museum

Antwerp, 1922
Antwerpen
Etching, 35.2 x 31.2 cm
Private collection

upright, with a self-assured expression, deliberately flaunting the charms of her behind by lifting her skirt up with her left hand. In this picture the focus is on the woman as a seductress, indeed as one who knows her business and makes a pitch at the man's sexual wishes.

The water-colours Dix painted in those years (roughly 400 in number, some of which have, however, disappeared) are among the most beautiful works he ever produced, owing to the breathtaking feel for nuances and tones of colour. Most of these works again show life at the edge of society, prostitution in the harbour district, sex crimes – scenes in the force field of Eros and Thanatos. Dix painted many water-colours of women in the oldest profession, such as *Ellis, Brothel Madame* (p. 109) or *Whore with Red Cheeks* (p. 107). All of the water-colours possess a brilliant, intuitive sense for colour qualities. The spontaneity and transparency of the application of the paint successfully capture the scintillating atmosphere of this dubious shady world. An amusing variation on this flashy glamour is the water-colour *Girl with Rose* (p. 106). The pretty coquette is sitting on a plush armchair in her frilly underwear. Wide-eyed, she smiles at the observer from under her broad-rimmed hat, with the rose, signal of love, enticingly held between her fingers. *Girl with Rose* gives the impression of being Dix's homage to "his" women.

Living in Düsseldorf, Dix was part of the avant-garde scene of the time, which was closely associated with the names of the "Young Rhineland" and art dealer Johanna Ey. Frau Ey used to own a coffee-house near the art academy, and the artists came to her because they could eat "on tick" there. "The Ey" (= the egg), as she was affectionately called, regularly accepted works on a commission basis, exhibiting them in her display window. In this way her coffee-house gradually became the nucleus of a group of young artists, which included Gert Wollheim, Otto Pankok, Hermann Hundt, Arthur Kaufmann, Adalbert Trillhaase, Karl Schwesig, Jankel Adler, and the writers Herbert Eulenberg and Adolf Uzarski. They all belonged to the artists' association, "Young Rhineland", founded in 1919. In 1916 Johanna Ey decided to sell her café and devote herself exclusively to art. From then on she exhibited the works of young, unknown talents in her storefront gallery on the Hindenburgwall; "Dadamax" Max Ernst was one of them. Frau Ey later sold his famous painting *The Beautiful Gardenerwoman* to the Düsseldorf Art Museum.

Dix was especially good friends with Wollheim, Pankok and "Männe" Hundt, also with Kaufmann, president of the "Young Rhineland" between 1921 and 1925. Kaufmann often helped Dix out with money since he was always "down on his luck" in those days. According to Martha Dix's memoirs, he bought "the painting *Little Girl* on his first visit to Düsseldorf, had his portrait painted and gave Dix one of his suits so that the latter would look presentable, instead of walking around with a hole in the seat of his trousers which were mended every night by Frau Ey, in whose house Dix was still living, but were just as inevitably worn through again during the day by Dix's lean bones."

His living conditions progressively improved, however, and in 1923 Dix and his family moved into a house with a balcony and large rooms at

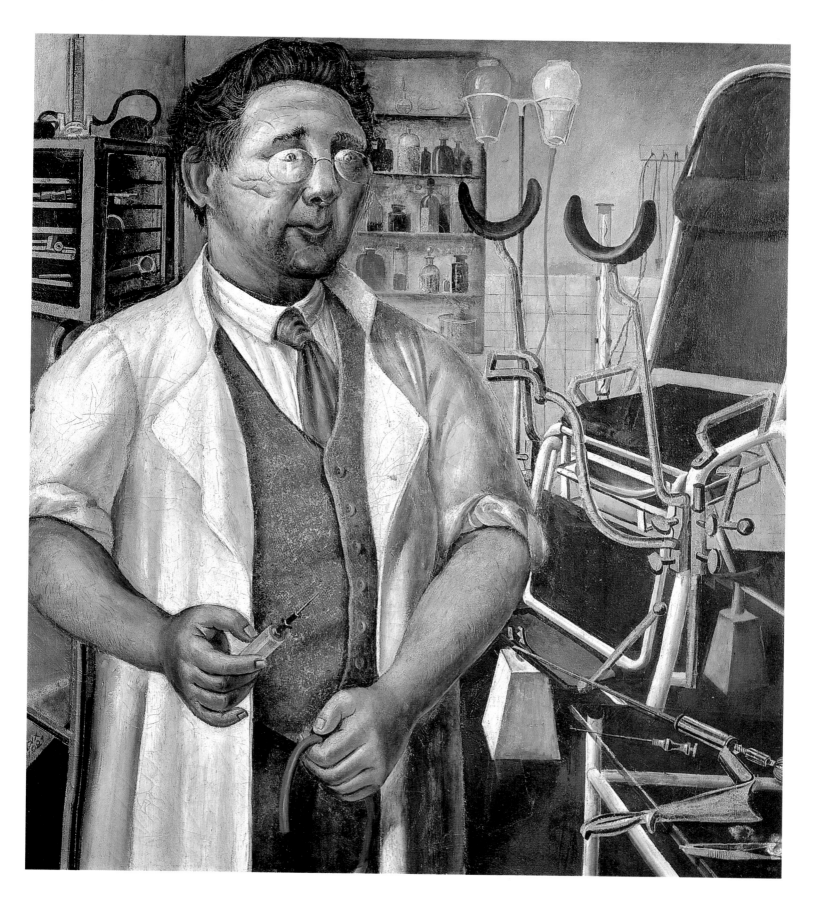

Dr. Hans Koch, the Dermatologist and Urologist, 1921
Der Dermatologe und Urologe Dr. Hans Koch
Oil on canvas, 100.5 x 90 cm
Löffler 1921/13
Cologne, Museum Ludwig

Portrait of the Artist's Parents I, 1921
(Franz Dix and Louise Dix, née Amann)
Bildnis der Eltern I
Oil on canvas, 99 x 113 cm
Löffler 1921/12
Basle, Öffentliche Kunstsammlung,
Kunstmuseum Basel

Hindenburgwall 3, which belonged to art patron Trillhaase. After temporarily sharing a studio with Wollheim, Dix was granted a master-pupil's studio at the art academy where he was studying under Heinrich Nauen. It was not Nauen, however, but Wilhelm Herberholz, who was teaching techniques in graphic printing, who was to play an important role in Dix's development. He helped him to acquire additional experience "by trying out all kinds of techniques" in lithography as well, not only in etching. Between 1922 and 1925 Dix created a series of masterful portraits of his colleagues and friends. The portraits of Jankel Adler, Adolf Uzarski (p. 116), Arthur Kaufmann or the Trillhaase family (p. 114) and of the minute Karl Schwesig attest to Dix's ability to bring out not only the individual, but also the typical, characteristics of a person.

Dix made many statements about the art of portrait painting: "Every

Portrait of the Artist's Parents II, 1924
Bildnis der Eltern II
Oil on canvas, 118 x 130.5 cm
Löffler 1924/4
Hanover, Niedersächsische
Landesgalerie

good portrait is based on show. The essence of every human being is expressed in a person's external appearance; the outside is the expression of the inside; i.e. external and internal are identical. This is true to such an extent that even the folds of the clothing, the person's posture, his hands or ears, immediately tell the painter something about the model's inner being; the ears often more than the eyes and mouth." Similar insights can be inferred from other remarks: "The outside of things is important to me, because depicting external appearance allows one simultaneously to capture the inner being at the same time. The first impression is the right one and has to be preserved in all its freshness. The other, the inner nature, then follows as a matter of course." By concentrating totally on external appearance, Dix eliminated interpretative factors as much as possible. All that was wanted was analysis, dissec-

Standing Nude III, 1922
Stehender Akt III
Pencil
Vaduz, Otto Dix Foundation

Portrait of Dr. Heinrich Stadelmann, 1922
Bildnis Dr. med. Heinrich Stadelmann
Oil on canvas, 90.8 x 55.5 cm
Löffler 1920/18 (!)
Toronto, Art Gallery of Ontario,
W. Landmann Collection

ting everything razor-sharp down to the very last pore of the skin. Regardless of who the subject was – be it the early portrait of Heinrich Stadelmann, M.D. (p. 87), that of art historian Dr. Paul Ferdinand Schmidt (p. 91) dating from 1921, or the afore-mentioned portraits – the main criterion was to turn, to fix the eye on the person's physiognomy. The way the arm, hands and face are held is reproduced in a particularly telling manner with an unmistakable streak of mimicry. At the same time, Dix places his models in front of pointedly "attractive" settings. Uzarski, the biting satirist of all things petty-bourgeois, is depicted with bony and wildly gesticulating hands right in front of a baroquely profusive, lavish facade, stony testimony to German power and money. The Trillhaases sit like marionettes, stiff as boards, with hypnotized eyes, crowded around a tiny table, the son as a transfixed figure-head seated between them, "dull fools" waiting for their Redeemer. Trillhaase was a dreamer out of touch with the world, a Bible-reader, for whom otherworldliness was closer than this world. Dix alludes to this with his skillfully perfidious rendition of somnambulity lodged in clouded consciousness. In 1924 Dix painted Johanna Ey, mother-hen of the artists (p. 126). She is standing – a figure that impresses by its fullness, and with a stern, penetrating, yet benevolent look in front of a heavy, theatrically draped curtain of bright reddish fabric. In her violet dress trimmed with fur, a Spanish ivory comb in her wavy hair, she reigns as the undisputed queen of sweet delights and bitter art products. The boisterous wit, the *esprit* that are a distinctive mark of these paintings, for all their trenchant and incisive characterization, remained a thing of Dix's time in Düsseldorf, which was apparently particularly happy. On 14 June, 1923 Nelly, first daughter of Martha and Otto Dix, was born – this, too, an event that contributed to Dix's inner harmony and equilibrium. Dix naturally painted his daughter, for example in 1924, standing in the midst of flowers (p. 120). The stylistic borrowings from Philipp Otto Runge, the 19th century children's painter, are unmistakable, but as was often the case, they were deliberate on Dix's part. At the same time, he worked from photographs, which he did for a few other paintings. Dix's habit of employing various stylistic media in service of his talent for exact observation is, no doubt, one of the primary reasons for the unmistakable quality of his portraits. Realism of detail, the varnishing technique, and compositional borrowings make his works of the 1920s, especially the portraits, inimitably multi-layered in texture.

A few other major works date from the Düsseldorf period, notably the *Self-portrait with Muse* (p. 123), 1924, and *Three Whores on the Street* (p. 133), completed in 1925. The first painting is part of a series of pictures on the theme of the painter and his model. In this case, Dix (whose preference for enigmatic self-portrayal is by now familiar to us) depicts himself as the cool researcher in his painter-doctor's smock. Impervious to the charms of the luscious, dark-haired beauty before him, he applies the finishing touches to her beauty with his brush. Amused self-irony flickers and sniggers behind the pose of the analytical-dissecting observer.

The picture *Three Whores on the Street* again provides a vivid example

PAGE 88:
The Widow, 1922
Die Witwe
Watercolour, 44 x 28 cm
Zurich, Roswitha Haftmann Modern Art

PAGE 89:
Circus, 1922
Zirkus
Watercolour and opaque white,
50 x 35 cm
Rome, Galleria Giulia

Portrait of the Art Historian Dr. Paul Ferdinand Schmidt, 1921
Bildnis des Kunsthistorikers Dr. Paul Ferdinand Schmidt
Oil on canvas, 83 x 63 cm
Löffler 1921/14
Stuttgart, Staatsgalerie Stuttgart

of Dix's unique way of evoking the grotesque. Three dolled-up ladies of the demi-monde are strolling in front of a luxury store-window display. Each of the three women is marked by significant attributes as a type in her "vice-ridden" milieu. With her huge leather-gloved fingers, the figure on the left, wrapped in a gold-coloured dress and decked out with a helmet-like hat covered in strass, is pressing a tiny dog to her prominent bosom, neck inclined forward, lips pursed with a look squinting to the side. The middle figure, with her syphilitic mouth and hollowed look, shows off her gaunt body; she has decorated her bony decolleté with a pearl necklace. The demi-mondaine to the right, wrapped in a bordeaux-red coat with a grandiose fur collar, and a green capot hat with a huge, oversized bow on her head, is holding an umbrella with a handle shaped like a penis close to her body: an obscenely comic pointer to her role.

The marbled luxury facade in the background with an advertising logo consisting of the high-heeled leg of a woman standing on a globe, of all things, adds additional density to the illusionary feel of the scenery of a false world of consumer pleasures. The bodies, employed as sexual commodities for good profit, and the world of commodities for purchase correspond with one another. The sexualization of the body which becomes a commodity and the sexualization of the commodity merge at this point. Dix conveys this message most effectively by means of grotesque media, in other words, through the media of alienation, distorted proportions, exaggeration, omission; at the same time, they are all also elements of dramatic presentation.

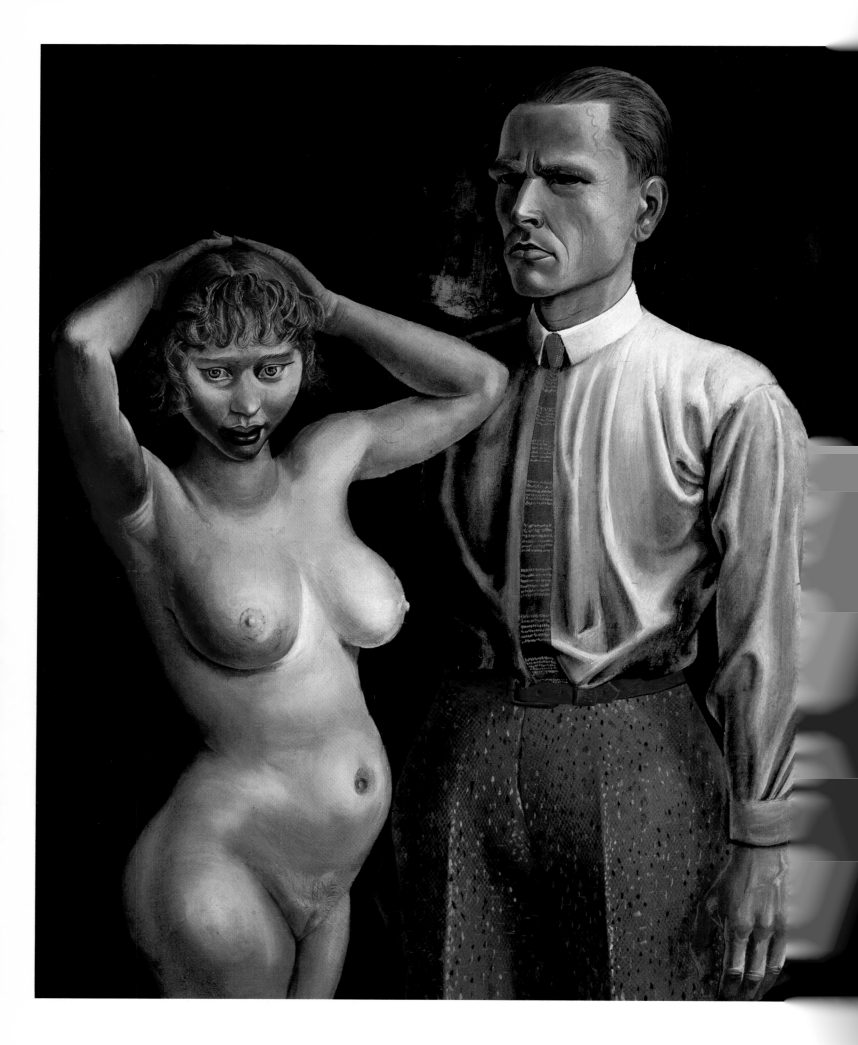

Berlin 1925 – 1927

The Düsseldorf period came to an end in 1925 with the dissolution of the "Young Rhineland" group. Dix went to Berlin for two years. Gallery-owner Karl Nierendorf had set up business there. In 1922 he had already made Dix the attractive offer of a contract with a most-favoured clause. In a letter dated 14 April he made a firm offer modelled on the "Genoa example" (the representatives of the major industrial nations met at the conference of Genoa in 1922): "You agree to send me first all of your works for me to look at & also to make me the most favourable prices; I, for my part, agree to represent your business interests in every respect, to arrange to exhibit your work, to send on approval works to collectors & art dealers, to have plates made of your work, to arrange for articles on your works to appear in art publications & above all also to conclude purchases so that you will not have to have anything to do with sending them back and forth, with business correspondence, etc., and instead only need to keep working away. I think that this will be a very convenient arrangement for you – think it over & write me about it soon." Dix did not think for long. Always short of cash and determined to become famous, he agreed to Nierendorf's proposal. The "Nierendix" era had begun.

As the artist's sole authorized representative, Nierdendorf actively promoted Dix's *oeuvre*. As early as 1922 he sold water-colour paintings, drawings and etchings by Dix. After 1923 he arranged most of the portraits commissioned, and in the same year had already sold the sensational *Trench* picture to the Wallraf-Richartz Museum in Cologne, a painting that was destroyed during the Second World War. Nierendorf also published all of the lithographs that Dix had produced in Düsseldorf, including portraits of Paul Westheim, editor of the magazine *Das Kunstblatt* (The Art Newsletter), and of Otto Klemperer, musical director of the Cologne City Theatre at the time. In 1924 Nierendorf handled the publication of the *War* cycle of etchings in a seventy-copy edition (five portfolios of ten sheets). Despite enormous publicity costs on the gallery-owner's part, the response was disappointing. Museums considered the prices of 700 and 1,000 Reichsmarks to be too high, and private buyers were not quite willing to "take the risk". The gallery-owner unwaveringly and staunchly represented his artist, irrespective of the periodic

Reclining Nude from the Back, 1923
Liegender Rückenakt
Pencil
Vaduz, Otto Dix Foundation

Self-portrait with Naked Model, 1923
Selbstbildnis mit nacktem Modell
Oil on canvas, 105 x 90 cm
Löffler 1923/3
New York, private collection

Self-portrait with Cigarette, 1922
Selbstbildnis mit Zigarette
Etching, 34.9 x 27.5 cm
Albstadt, Walther Groz Foundation,
Städtische Galerie Albstadt

PAGE 96:
Me in Brussels, 1922
Ich in Brüssel
Watercolour and pencil, 49 x 36.8 cm
Vaduz, Otto Dix Foundation

PAGE 97:
Defiers of Death, Two Artists, 1922
Verächter des Todes, zwei Artisten
Watercolour and pencil, 56.5 x 46.5 cm
Vaduz, Otto Dix Foundation

differences of opinion which are surely inevitable in any such community of interests.

Dix could be highly sensitive when it came to money matters. When it took a bit longer than usual for him to receive payment for the *Trench*, he dispatched an angry letter to Berlin, ranting among other things against the "big mouth", and bitterly complaining in the following vein: "Thanks to you dragging your feet and thanks to my blind trust in you! I don't even have the money to give my parents something for Christmas this year... So what good does your big mouth do me! What good is telling me to write if I need money, when all I get then is a few lousy marks...I'm just beginning to see that you are gradually turning into what they call a capitalist art dealer." The letter ends on this note: "You have no damned reason to be insulted if I get nasty once in a while. But you seem to be so much into playing the art-dealer by now that you don't understand this anymore... I've had just about enough! Regards Dix."

Nierendorf stayed cool; he knew his star-artist. In his reply dated 29 December, 1923 he reminds Dix how persistently he has taken care of procuring money for the latter and recommends that he read Emile Zola's *Letters to my friends*, which prove "that one can be a great, genuine artist without the airs of a primadonna or a film star". He rejects Dix's allegation that he has not settled accounts with him for three months. "That is also untrue. We went over everything exactly at my place on 2 December based on my very orderly and precisely kept list, and you yourself signed acknowledgement of the calculation sheet therein. Were you drunk or something when you wrote me that derisory letter? Regards Nierendorf." Dix and Nierendorf nevertheless remained "loyal" to each other, although Dix once terminated the contract in 1927 for a time.

In Berlin Dix and his family lived at Kurfürstendamm 232, on the corner of Fasanenstrasse. His father-in-law, Director Lindner, had paid seven years' rent in advance. Dix's studio was initially located in the building that had formerly housed the college of commercial arts on Prinz-Albrecht-Strasse, and later at Kurfürstendamm 190. In this cosmopolitan city of the Roaring Twenties, in the Berlin of the post-war phase of stabilization, Dix and his wife were soon insiders on the cultural scene. Their wide circle of friends in Berlin included the painters Lovis Corinth, Emil Orlik, Max Oppenheimer, known as MOP, and George Grosz. The contacts already established in Düsseldorf with Alfred Flechtheim, the art dealer, of whom Dix made a portrait in 1926 (p. 141), were also strengthened. In addition to his activities as an art dealer, Flechtheim was also the editor of *Der Querschnitt*, a journal of art and literature, from 1921 to 1924. He and Dix frequently got together with actor Heinrich George, preferably in the Romanisches Café, just as much the home of the bohemian scene as it was of the intellectual and artistic elite of the period, and Dix did portraits of the café's most notable regular patrons, including the Baltic poet Ivar von Lücken (p. 139) as a misunderstood, miserable down-and-out poet. The lyrical world of von Lücken's dreams and wishes collided violently with his real, meagre existence – Dix conveyed this by painting a rose in a beer bottle. Another figure who

Sunday Walk, 1922
Sonntagsspaziergang
Oil on canvas, 75 x 60 cm
Löffler 1922/5
Milwaukee, private collection

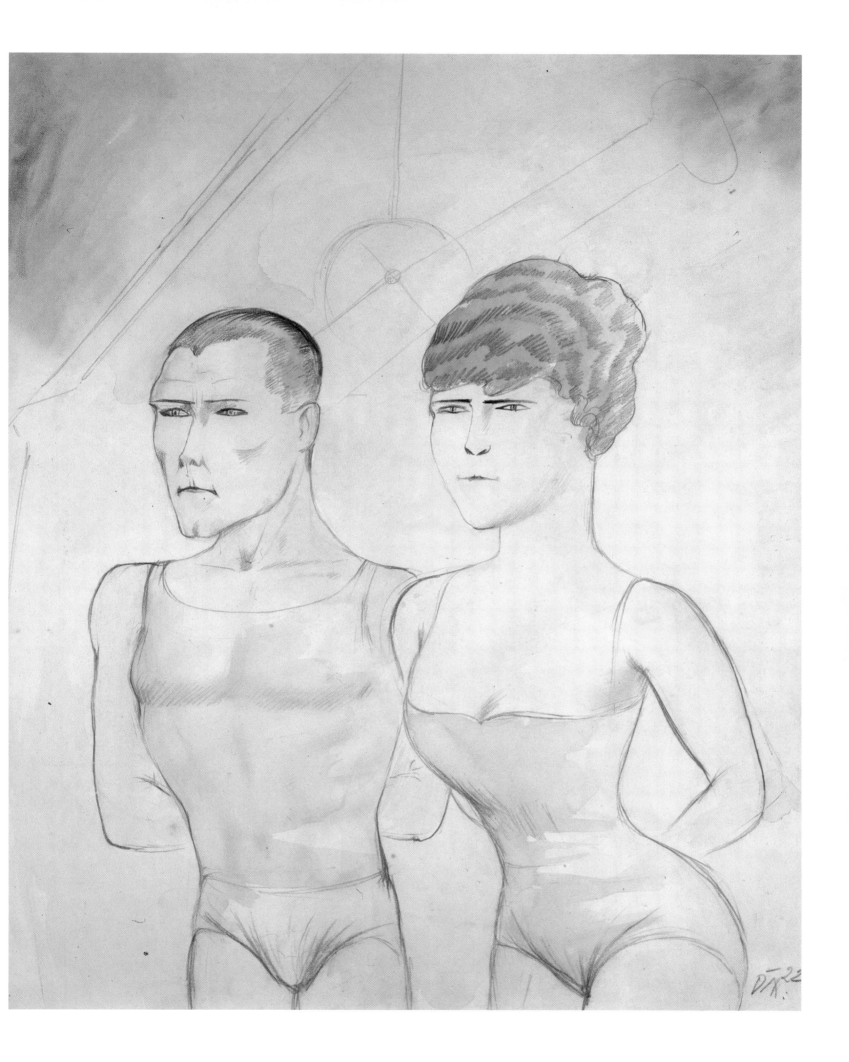

Tropical Night, 1922
Tropische Nacht
Watercolour, 49.5 x 37.5 cm
Ravensburg, Peter Selinka Collection

cannot be overlooked is the bohemian intellectual and writer of romantic love stories Sylvia von Harden (p. 145). Dix painted her sitting at her table in the café with a cocktail, open cigarette case, and the habitual box of matches in front of her. Her hair is done in the boy's cut of the emancipated woman, and she is wearing a loose-fitting checked sack-dress and a monocle on her eye. In her huge bony hand she is holding the cigarette,

the indispensable trademark of the intellectuals and the literary crowd.

However, Dix's most outstanding portrait of a figure from the bohemian world of Berlin was that of the dancer Anita Berber (p. 131), who was a perennial subject of scandal; it is one of his best-known paintings, and rightfully so. He painted it in 1925 while still in Düsseldorf, shortly before moving to Berlin. Anita Berber was born in Dresden in 1899, the

Sailor and his Darling, 1922/23
Matrose und Liebchen
Watercolour, 31 x 24 cm
Private collection

99

Murder, 1922
Mord
Watercolour, 62 x 47.5 cm
Vaduz, Otto Dix Foundation

daughter of a well-known violinist and a singer. After training as a classical dancer with Rita Sacchetto, she gave her first public dance performance as early as 14 February, 1916. After further group performances with the Sacchetto troupe, Anita Berber had her first solo engagement at the Berlin Apollo Theatre in 1919. This was followed by performances at Rudolf Nelson's and at the Berlin Conservatory. Thereafter she rapidly gained a reputation as a nude dancer and show-girl, appearing in all of the nightclubs in Berlin – in the "White Mouse" and in the "Pyramid", for example, an underground club. Both well-known and less well-known contemporaries of Anita's still have vivid memories of her scantily clad and scandal-clad performances. Herbert Pfeiffer recalls in his memoirs: "Anita Berber made the 'White Mouse' her home for awhile. This was also where she had her last dance engagements. It cost ten marks to get in and the 'White Mouse' with its 890 seats and the little boxes was sold out every night. Anita Berber embodied in her life and art the wild flickering and burning of her generation, which distrusted all forms of repression and sublimation and wanted to live life to the fullest,

come what may." Claire Waldoff gives a different account in her memoirs, entitled *Weeste noch?* (*Do you still remember?*): "And sometimes we also disappeared off to places where a very mixed bunch of people got together. Stage artists, Durieux, Paul Cassirer, Gertrud Eysoldt, Paul Graetz, etc., the majority of those present were women with just a very few men, we went to the 'officially registered' association named 'The Pyramid' lottery association...You had to go through three courtyards before you got to the women's secluded Eldorado (a well-known transvestite club in Berlin), 30 pfennigs entrance fee, four musicians with brass instruments were playing the forbidden songs of the association...In the course of the evening the famous Cognac-Polonaise sounded for the umpteenth time – it was celebrated, kneeling on the dance floor, with a glass full of cognac in hand. The unparliamentary lyrics of this Polonaise make my pen quiver... In the meantime the grandes dames of the day – the ravishing dancer Anita Berber, Celly de Reydt and beautiful Susu Wannowsky and her entourage – appeared and were greeted with a big hello."

The Suicide Victim, 1922
Der Selbstmörder (Erhängter)
Etching, 35 x 28.2 cm
Vaduz, Otto Dix Foundation

PAGE 102:
Mother and Child, 1923
Mutter und Kind
Oil on plywood, 82.5 x 48 cm
Löffler 1923/4
Stuttgart, Galerie der Stadt Stuttgart

PAGE 103:
Old Couple, 1923
Altes Liebespaar
Oil on canvas, 152 x 100 cm
Löffler 1923/6
Berlin, Nationalgalerie,
Staatliche Museen zu Berlin

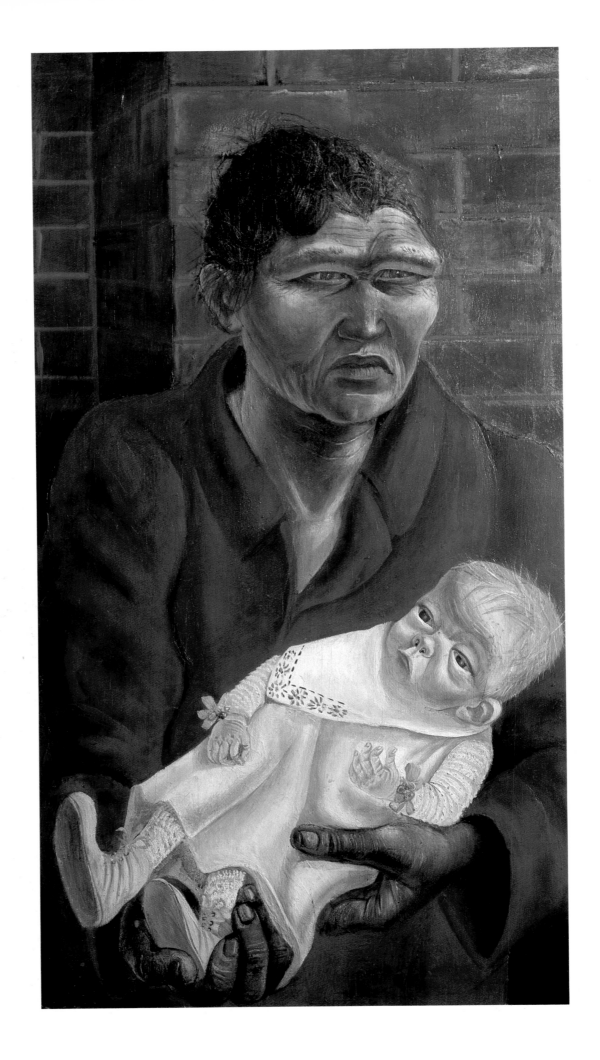

Dix probably did not meet Berber until 1925, the year he painted her. Martha Dix remembers being with Anita Berber before a performance, who "spent an hour putting on her make-up and drank a bottle of cognac at the same time. Yes, and the part about her walking the streets, that was par for the course. We went out for a walk in Wiesbaden (where the Dixes attended one of Anita's performances in a vaudeville show), and she took advantage of every opportunity. Someone would approach her, and she would say: '200 marks'. I didn't find that so very awful. She had to earn money somehow. She had to cover the costs of the expensive costumes that she wore for her performances as a dancer. She couldn't earn very much from that. She was just so charming, so sweet, simply totally natural and delightful."

Dix, however, portrayed Anita Berber in a different light, as the notorious vamp, the way she was viewed by the public. A key figure of the bohemian world, Anita Berber made herself an object onto which others could project their craving for sensationalism as well as the secret pleasure of vicarious participation in something forbidden. Generally speaking, the ambivalence of hiding oneself and exposing oneself at one and the same time are innate in the star as a type, and Dix recognized this as a salient feature of Anita Berber's individuality.

A few statements made by Dix shed light on the uniqueness of his technique of portrait painting: "Usually I made an exact drawing while viewing the model, and, after transferring it to the canvas, I applied the first coat of paint, also referring to the model. And only after that did the actual painting take place: painting *without* a model. I have learned that when the model is present, you start noticing something here and something there and this and that – and gradually everything gets worse and worse and much too complicated – less and less simple and great. That is why I eventually decided to stop doing it that way and complete the work without the model. That's more accurate. That's when the work really begins" (from an interview with M. Wetzel, 1965). This approach – typical for Dix's portrait-work – as well as the technique of applying layers of transparent paint (we shall deal with this technique in more detail when discussing the *Big City* triptych) enabled Dix to achieve the greatest possible precision in producing a replica of his subject. Moreover, the layers of paint that emerged through the long, drawn-out process of varnishing contributed to the intensification of the physical effect.

In the portrait of Anita Berber Dix concentrated exclusively on depicting the body and integrating it into the background variety of different red tones. The tight, high-necked, long-sleeved dress stresses the line of her body. The softness of the breasts and belly is highlighted by admixtures of white which accentuate light and shadow. The very effective line of the folds of the dress, gathered at the right hip, as well as the smaller folds of the fabric under her arms, bring out the provocative agility of the body even more strongly.

Dix once said that "not only the form, but also the colour (are) of the greatest importance and a means of expressing individuality. Every human being has a quite special colour of his own that sets the tone of the

PAGE 106:
Girl with Rose, 1923
Mädchen mit Rose
Watercolour, 61 x 48.5 cm
Private collection

PAGE 107:
Whore with Red Cheeks, 1923
Dirne mit roten Backen
Watercolour and violet crayon,
65.5 x 52 cm
Albstadt, Walther Groz Foundation,
Städtische Galerie Albstadt

picture as a whole." In Dix's painting the colour red specified for Anita Berber does indeed take on a dimension of its own in terms of the body. But the fact that she is wearing a dress made of flowing red fabric that enticingly caresses the form of her body is not decisive. Nor is the fact that her hair is dyed red. What is decisive is the fact that Dix clothed her body in red, or modulated it in various shades of red. The impact of the colour in the most finely differentiated shades of red is so intense that it has to

Old Couple, 1923
Älteres Liebespaar
Watercolour, 39 x 33.5 cm
Private collection

Servant Girls on Sunday, 1923
Dienstmädchen am Sonntag
Watercolour, 54 x 37 cm
Vaduz, Otto Dix Foundation

spread out into the space beyond the body, taking in the entire background of the picture as the continuation and intensification of the red radiance of this body and thus of her very being.

The affinity of red and blue is logical. The aura that surrounded Anita Berber emanated depravity and decadence, Eros and Thanatos. Dix had no other option where colour was concerned. His red composition is a mixture of reddish hues from both sides of the chromatic spectrum – glazing toward the warm colours covering shades of yellow and toward the cold colours mixed with shades of blue. Cold hues are predominant in the dress, created through adding minimal amounts of white and blue, the yellowish-red and reddish-yellow nuances frame the silhouette of

Brothel Madame, ca. 1923
Puffmutter
Watercolour, 50 x 35 cm
Vaduz, Otto Dix Foundation

the body and create a band of light around it, comparable to a halo. Dix's chosen technique of polarizing cold and warm colours in this way is one of the primary reasons for the high level of tension in the picture.

The face and hands are the two features that offer the most precise individual characterization. Anita Berber's bluish-fallow complexion as well as her hands, both painted by Dix primarily using a white incarnadine mixed with a little blue and red, give rise to associations of illness and decay. Her face looks emaciated, the cheeks are sunken, the eyes deep-set, and the thickly lip-sticked mouth is actually thin. The heavy make-up, applied in thick, black lines around her eyes, the false eyelashes and the thin, black lined eyebrows, as well as the eyeshadow

Girl and Death, 1924
Mädchen und Tod
Pencil, 43.5 x 55.5 cm
Private collection

flickering in dark-reddish tones and the mouth, with the fashionable, over-applied fire-engine red lipstick, contribute decisively to the morbidity of this woman's aura. She appears to be marked by addiction. Anita's gaze is fixed, staring into the void. A closer look reveals this expression to be one of desperation and forlornness rather than of superiority and mocking flirtation, the allures she attempts to convey.

Dix characterizes Anita Berber by reproducing the elasticity of her body as a dancer, as someone who learned how to move and pose. The way in which this body displays itself suggests a certain level of dance training. The lack of any and all attributes further contributes to the identification of an extremely physical nature, as in dance. The complete lack of attributes, together with the conspicuous, capricious plainness of the dress, creates the impression of a gleaming, ambivalent aura emanating from Anita Berber's person, lending her a certain quality of rapture. Anita Berber can, in a sense, only be defined by means of her body, the central presence of which contains an element that clearly unsettles the observer, an element conveyed by Anita's notoriety.

Despite its suppleness, which borders on the snakelike, this body creates the impression of being taciturn and aloof. She flaunts her physical charms, yet at the same time remains aloof. Anita Berber had the reputation of being a femme fatale. She nurtured it, and at the same time herself fell prey to it. Immoderation, which was her principal trait, can be positively defined as giving oneself over unconditionally, and a capacity for devotion. Her addictions can also be understood as forms of "negative religiosity". There are, in fact, structural links between addiction and dance. Both strive for a dissolution of boundaries, both seek to mingle or join the body with other bodies, both seek intoxication, ecstasy.

The painting *Unequal Lovers* (p. 125) and a water-colour study for it (p. 124) also appeared in 1925. Desire and futility collide here in the encounter with the carnal "vice" of luscious femininity. The painting depicts the tragedy of denying the constant, inevitable presence of death in the realm of love and eroticism. The allegorical content is in its reference to the taboo placed on death, old age, and decay in the sphere of sexuality, eroticism, life. *Three Women* (p. 134), completed in 1926, could be called a "homage to ugliness". The realism of detail is taken to an utter extreme here and becomes a phantasmagoria. And an inverted, perverse new type of beauty arises, the beauty of anarchy.

Dix also painted several still lifes during his time in Berlin, many of which contained allegorical references. Dix had a very broad understanding of the term 'still life'. Once, for example, he commented on the polemical attacks levelled by art historian Meier-Graefe against his *Trench* picture: "But I have only painted still lifes". The pictures that Dix expressly referred to as such, for example, *Still Life in the Studio* (p. 117) or *Still Life with Widow's Veil* (p. 138), thematize the presence of death in life and ironically quote still-life genre conventions in the dramatic arrangement of skulls, fruits, flowers, dead fish or birds and carcasses. In the painting *Still Life with Widow's Veil* objects with a well-established traditional semantic context, such as the half-filled jug with two lilies, are

Harbour Scene, 1922
Hafenszene
Watercolour, opaque and pencil,
58.3 x 47.9 cm
United States, private collection

110

intended to yield quite opposite meanings through the elaborate use of allusions. The white lily, for example – a symbol of virgin purity in Christian iconography – is a black iris. On the other hand, the widow's veil tends to evoke associations of bridal trains rather than of mourning. It is hanging over a clothes-rack "embellished" with a skeleton – a grotesque-comical ersatz for a body. A plaster mask on the wall portrays a young woman's face, and the artful drapings of the white, heavy cloth clearly follow the lines of the female genitals. The whole picture is built on the principle of a game of reversal; every attribute means its opposite. Dix imagined the bride as a widow. At the same time, one cannot over-look the subdued humour of this portrayal; it would appear to be a parody of the imagery of traditional memento mori painting. In a certain sense nearly all paintings of the 1920s do, in fact, have the character of still lifes. They are noteworthy for a peculiarly static quality in the subject matter. This, in turn, is not least the result of the long, drawn-out process of applying the various layers of glaze, a technique that allowed the artist to establish distance to the subjects of his paintings.

One of Dix's major portraits of the Berlin period is that of art dealer Alfred Flechtheim (p. 141). Dix made notes about this on the back of a letter to photographer Hugo Erfurth. They provide further insights into Dix's technique, indicating that he applied coats of transparent glaze over an imprimatura: "All layers of paint very thin, add very little white scamble. The layers have to be kept thin in the light places, stronger in the shadows, the last layer has to be the most colourful. (Flesh has to be painted, not spread on. Paint from the palette, don't use a lot of binder. A face has to be painted from top to bottom, bit by bit, until it is finished.)" Dix composed his models with an architect's attention to a precise plan. Flechtheim, the prominent Berlin gallery-owner, looks like one of the precious objects he traded. By the same token, they surround him like living things, Juan Gris on the wall, Braque and the Picasso drawings on the table. Dix always handled the ambivalence of things masterfully.

Dix's time in Berlin ended with his almost being commissioned to do the portrait of Hans Luther, the Chancellor of the Reich. He was estab-lished; his art was considered socially acceptable, especially his por-traits. In the end, Luther got cold feet, probably on account of Dix's unconventionally incisive style of portrayal. Harry Graf Kessler, writer and long-standing president of the German Peace Society, whom Dix had probably met through Nierendorf, remarked on this in his diary as fol-lows: "He (Luther) thought, well, it would get around, but the matter was not at all as sure as all that. If it were only a question of Dr. Luther, he would not hesitate for a minute to have himself painted by Dix. But he had his doubts about whether it would come out looking like the Chancellor of the German Reich." Kessler did not have himself painted by Dix either; it would indeed be intriguing to conduct a study of society based on Dix's portraits or, better still, the portraits that were never painted.

Dix was also able in that successful year of 1926 to make his works known abroad, owing to his participation in the International Art Exhibi-tion in Dresden.

Two Browns, 1922
Zwei Browns
Watercolour and pen, 51 x 41 cm
Private collection

Dresden 1927 – 1932

Dix was induced to return to Dresden in 1927 by a professorship at the Dresden Art Academy. He declared his willingness to fill the post left vacant by Otto Gussmann. The fact that he was not granted tenure for life as a civil servant was to plunge him into severe economic plight in 1933, when the Nazi regime ordered that he be dismissed. He could not have foreseen this at the time, any more than he could have guessed that the move to Dresden, an artistic backwater, would hamper his own career rather than further it. But Dix was always attached to Dresden. On the whole, the years up until 1933 were marked by friendship and continued success. On 11 March, 1927 his first son, Ursus, was born, and on 10 October, 1928, his second son, Jan. Both occasions gave rise to forceful drawings as well as the painting *Newborn Baby on Hands* (p. 142). A family portrait also dates from that year – an overly harmonious idyll somewhat eased by the figure of the proud father, who is beaming with joy and gritting his teeth at the same time.

In Dresden Dix belonged to the *Hirsche* ("Stags") Monday club centred round Fritz Bienert, a collector who was the son of art collector Ida Bienert. The *Hirsche*, a group of various intellectuals and artists without any political credo, met regularly in the town hall wine-cellar in Dresden. The men-only club (Martha Dix and Bianca Segantini, daughter of the Italian painter, were the only exceptions) discussed the social and aesthetic problems of the day. Unfortunately, the minutes of the society were confiscated by the Gestapo in 1933. The *Hirsche* organized a juggling and entertainment festival every year, and Dix was crowned king of the entertainers in 1930. He documented the event with a drawing in which he is portrayed with a crown on his head.

It must have been amusing and instructive to hear Dix teach at the academy. One of his students, Gussy Ahnert, told a series of anecdotes which give an impression of the atmosphere in Dix's classes. When one of the models once said she thought she was too fat, Dix demanded: "Turn around, you're beautiful all the way round, you can bet your ass on it." When one student painted a "Negro" portrait that Dix did not like at all, his criticism was "Just painting things black will get you nowhere." And one last anecdote passed on by Fritz Löffler in his catalogue of Dix's paintings, published in 1981, may give some idea of the artist's native wit.

The Family of the Painter Adalbert Trillhaase, 1923
Die Familie des Malers Adalbert Trillhaase
Oil on canvas, 119 x 95 cm
Löffler 1923/8
Berlin, Nationalgalerie SMPK

PAGE 116:
Portrait of the Painter Adolf Uzarski, 1923
Bildnis des Malers Adolf Uzarski
Oil on canvas on pressed fibre-board,
110 x 76 cm
Löffler 1923/12
Düsseldorf, Kunstmuseum Düsseldorf

PAGE 117:
Still Life in the Studio, 1924
Stilleben im Atelier
Oil and tempera on canvas,
146 x 100 cm
Löffler 1924/1
Stuttgart, Galerie der Stadt Stuttgart

*Machine-gun Column Advances
(Somme, November 1916),* 1924
Maschinengewehrzug geht vor
Sheet 1 of Folio V "War"
Etching, 24.5 x 30 cm
Vaduz, Otto Dix Foundation

In 1932, on the day the last King of Saxony, Friedrich August III, was laid to rest in the court church with the condolences of the entire country, Dix said good-bye to his class with the following words: "You can do your dirty work without me." The king is said to have uttered precisely those illustrious words on abdicating his throne. Dix was the most popular teacher at the academy.

In 1927 a second version of the *Match Vendor* appeared (p. 146), which, compared with the 1920 version, was stripped of all derisive aggressivity. Now the youth (no longer a war cripple) leans shamefacedly against a classicist pillar. Poverty during the "phase of stabilization": subdued, humble, resigned.

In 1927 Dix also produced the large-format painting *Street Fight* (p. 147), which depicts civil war. Unfortunately, it was destroyed in 1954 in the storage rooms where it was housed (it had also been confiscated as "degenerate" art). And Dix also painted the portrait of poet Theodor Däubler in 1927 (p. 150), showing him as a massive, bearded Wotan-like

Dead Man (St. Clément), 1924
Toter (St. Clément)
Sheet 2 of Folio V "The War"
Etching, 29.9 x 25.9 cm
Vaduz, Otto Dix Foundation

figure sitting on a chair in front of his neo-classicist temple – an allusion
to his poetry. Surely the most important portrait painted by Dix prior to
1933 was the *Portrait of Actor Heinrich George* (p. 177) completed in 1932.
Dix was a friend of George's and portrayed him in the painting in the
sailor's outfit he wore in the film *Terje Wiggen*. George's widow, Berta
Drews, described from memory how the picture came about. Dix, who as
the Georges' guest watched the filming on Bornholm Island, did not
strike Berta Drews as being exactly "conversational. I liked his reserve.
The sailor Terje Wiggen seemed to set his imagination alight. He was
highly inspired... We were hardly home when, with his phenomenal
talent for hand-drawing, he began making a large charcoal sketch of the

Nelly with Flowers, 1924
Nelly mit Blumen
Oil on canvas, 81 x 55.5 cm
Löffler 1924/5
Private collection

120

portrait he had in mind. George was totally enthralled, and that is how in a space of three weeks, painted on wood using the technique of the old masters, a suggestive, darkly smouldering painting emerged. Visually powerful, broad and forceful."

Beneath the surface, Dix's conception of image-work now began to undergo a transformation in reaction to the insidious change in conditions of the day. Early in the 1930s he again produced a large number of nudes. Some of the works are studies in milieu. In part they place more emphasis on the aesthetic side of portraying the body (this was new in Dix's work) in an attempt to visualize a particular ideal of beauty. Variations on the theme of the pregnant woman are noticeably frequent, as for

Portrait of the Jeweller Karl Krall, 1923
Bildnis des Juweliers Karl Krall
Oil on canvas, 90.5 x 60.5 cm
Löffler 1923/9
Wuppertal, Von der Heydt-Museum

PAGE 122:
Picture with Mirror (with Self-portrait),
1923
Bild im Spiegel (mit Selbstbildnis)
Watercolour, opaque and collage,
48.5 x 32.5 cm
Vaduz, Otto Dix Foundation

121

example in two versions of *Pregnant Women (seated)* from 1930 (p. 164) and *Pregnant Woman (half-nude)* from 1931 (p. 166). Both of the women portrayed come from the underprivileged strata of society, their condition is not one of fulfilled fertility, but rather reflects a draining, added burden. They gaze in submissive joylessness, their bodies look swollen. The pregnant woman painted in half-nude, whose head is turned away, also seems to feel her state to be an imposition, rather than joyful. Whereas the 1919 painting *Pregnant Woman* was still a hymn to femininity and fertility, was still a glorification of the erotic essence of life, it is now procreation, determined by chance and fate, that is the focus of the picture: apparently a fatalistically meaningless reproduction of eternal injustices and disadvantages.

The 1930 painting *Melancholy* (p. 163) is one of a group of pictures with allegorical or mythological allusions with an iconographic recourse to

Karl zur Pfaffenröslein geführt
Vivat crescat floriat!

traditional topoi, for example, the motif of *vanitas*. Works such as *Venus with Gloves* (p. 178) and *Vanitas* (p. 174), both dating from 1932, are variations, again ironically coloured, on favourite classical fine arts themes. Dix's Venus, with black gloves reaching up to her elbows, is a young girl. Her charms clearly lie in the sense of girlish chastity that emanates from her. She embodies more of an anti-type to Venus, the initiated goddess of love. Dix evokes the *vanitas* motif, portraying the transience of youth and beauty, which are subject to the irreversible process of physical decay, by emphasizing the opposite poles of youth and old age. A young woman bubbling with vitality, sensuousness and *joie de vivre*, smilingly conscious of her physical flowering, has stabbed her alter ego in the back, metaphorically speaking. The figure of a grimacing old woman with sagging breasts, bony body and gout-ridden hands stands behind the beautiful girl – a variation on the traditional portrayal of Vanity with the woman in front of the mirror as a personification of the vain creature, whose back is decomposed and riddled with snakes and worms. It would seem to be impossible to bridge the gulf between the worlds of youth and old age, since youth apparently excludes any reflexion on physical decay, aging, dying, death.

On the other hand, Dix's painting *Melancholy* is a deliberate reference to an historical model, Albrecht Dürer's copper engraving *Melencolia I*, dating from 1514. This is part of a set of master engravings by Dürer including *Knight, Death and the Devil* and *St. Hieronymus*. Dürer's *Melencolia* is an allegorical embodiment of the theories and treatises of the four temperaments based on the doctrine of the four fluids. Generally speaking, the melancholy temperament was interpreted as being a depressive inertia, and in Dürer's work this characteristic is given a novel interpretation for the age, namely, that inertia results from excessive rumination and brooding.

The common factor in Dürer's and Dix's respective portrayals lies primarily in the very personal backgrounds that gave rise to the pictorial representation of the theme. Beyond the similarity in terms of the brooding, aimless gaze of the women, there is no explicit pictorial connection. In Dix's work we see a couple sitting in a dramatic pose, turned away from each other. The man, depicted as a peculiarly chimeric figure viewed from the back, is staring through a window over the stormy, turbulent sea. His torso slowly dissolves the further downwards the observer's gaze travels, blending into the wall of the room, although a foot and calf protrude from behind a chair. The extension of his body, however, seems to be more of a wavy cloth that flows down onto the floor. It blends with a shell-like form that prompts associations with a skull. The woman is sitting naked on a chair, with dishevelled hair and a sinister brooding gaze, her legs stretched defensively, with the left arm pointing in the direction of the male figure. However, she is not holding onto him; rather, her arm blends into the man's shoulder. The picture, with its atmosphere of melancholy, despair, and macabre unreality, conveys, as do most of those painted by Dix after 1930, a state of increasing personal and artistic ambiguity and a growing sense of futility.

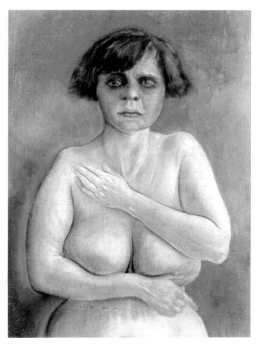

Half-Nude, 1926
Halbakt
Tempera on wood, 79 x 55 cm
Löffler 1926/2
Essen, Museum Folkwang (on loan)

Portrait of the Art Dealer Johanna Ey, 1924
Bildnis der Kunsthändlerin Johanna Ey
Oil on canvas, 140 x 90 cm
Löffler 1924/8
Düsseldorf, Kunstmuseum Düsseldorf
(On loan from private collection)

The "Big City" Triptych 1927/28

Before turning to the Nazi period, let us turn our attention to the *Big City* triptych that was done in 1927/28 (pp.152-157). Along with the *War* triptych, begun in 1929, it is Dix's other great masterpiece. The three-part painting describes how the body was represented in urban society in the Weimar Republic. It is thus also a record of the social structure of the time and Dix's visual remembrance of those years – so important for his development after the First World War. The following approach to the picture focuses on the manner and technique of publicly presenting one's body.

Put more precisely, we shall examine the homogeneity with which women's bodies are represented in public – it is women who predominate in all of the picture segments. In the picture they are so blatantly trying to grab the limelight, and to externalize and thus sell themselves, that we can assume the existence here of an underlying mechanism of glorifying one's own body as a commodity – typical of modern prostitution. What is apparent is the strict distinction between private and public body, with the former vanishing behind the latter. This, too, is a feature of all three segments of the triptych, and implies that a functionalistic attitude to the body was predominant at that time.

Let us first turn to the central panel. It shows high society at play, a milieu of money, luxury and extravagance: the leisure class, comprised of a mixture of Bohemians and the rich, having fun. A jazz band is playing strident rhythms. The "bachelor girl" covered with pearls and pleated frills is waving her pink feather fan, a couple is stepping out to the Charleston, a second couple looks on impassively. These people are the very personification of conspicuous consumption, the principle of enjoyment and extravagance. The luxurious women of the picture's central section have in a sense become precious commodities. They aspire to create as perfect an illusion as possible of happiness based on wealth. They are able, by means of money, to display themselves as exquisite "inalienable goods". The emancipation of women could only express itself in this form of statuesque unapproachability, for it was rigorously tied to the principle of consumption.

The group of women on the right panel, in a clear sequential order, underlined by the baroquish, ornamental architecture rising parallel to

Girl's Head: "Saxon Maiden", 1929
Mädchenkopf "Sächsin"
Mixed media on canvas on wood,
37 x 24 cm
Löffler 1929/6
Private collection

*Portrait of the Photographer Hugo Erfurth
with a Lens,* 1925
Bildnis des Fotografen Hugo Erfurth mit
Objektiv
Mixed media on wood, 75 x 60 cm
Löffler 1925/10
Munich, Bayerische Staatsgemäldesamm-
lungen, Staatsgalerie moderner Kunst

them, on the whole convey the sense of an abstract decorative pattern. The women are moving up or down an imaginary staircase in military formation. They are bejewelled high-class prostitutes offering their sexual favours in line with market developments – in other words, they can be classified as belonging to the demi-monde with its zeal to imitate the monied classes. In this scene Dix crassly stresses the brutal commodity-like character of sexuality by including the fur and red cape of the woman in the foreground as the unmistakable insignia of the female genitals. With her more or less bared breasts the woman behind her embodies the second sexual stimulant. The breasts seem to become part of the monstrous puffs of material at her wrists, which, as far as one can tell, no longer serves any real purpose as clothing or ornamentation. The two women at the head of the row demonstrate the sexualization of the body, so to speak – obscene as a form of physical objectification, marked by the loss of shame. Emancipation is straggling here, since it involves relinquishing physical identity in favour of a profitable sexual commodity value. The female procession clearly has the effect of a border pattern. Dix quite obviously quotes the "living mass ornaments" of girlie-culture which, like the Tiller Girls, for example, had been imported from America and were extremely popular in the "Swinging Berlin" of the time.

Impassively the column of women moves past the war cripple hunched on the ground, saluting them. Dix paints him in his greenish-yellow camouflage uniform as if he were an ornamental outgrowth of the buildings. Two seemingly irreconcilable realities collide: the one, the economic principle which promises consumers an illusory world of pleasures, and the other, the disillusioned reality of physical ruin.

The "low-class" brothel milieu is aptly characterized on the left panel by an alley with cobblestones, the arch of a bridge made of red brick, behind which business can be conducted, and the pseudo-glamour of the prostitutes' cheap flimsy dresses. In this scene the sexualization of the body is shown most blatantly, reduced as it is to a cheap commodity. (In the right and middle wings, the price tag is higher.) At the same time, the mechanism of purchasability that can be discerned in all three picture segments comes best to the fore in its simplicity here.

Feelings of impotence are the response to the signals of enticement. A war cripple stares after the women with a facial expression of craving and powerless hatred; a second man lying on the ground peeks under the women's skirts – a victim, of both the war and his lust.

In other words, the left panel shows the body quite nakedly reduced to an object. The right panel shows a manner of using the body which is already "refined" – to the point of sex becoming an opulent leisure-time pleasure – and it then finds most subliminal representation in the centre section of the painting at the level of absolutized pleasure.

A few remarks on the genesis of the triptych would seem in order. It is important to note that many preliminary sketches were made for the individual objects in the pictures, such as the lion's head or the saxophone. Dix did preparatory studies for the cloth drapings, the clothing, and the legs.

Portrait of the Dancer Anita Berber, 1925
Bildnis der Tänzerin Anita Berber
Tempera on plywood, 120 x 65 cm
Löffler 1925/6
Stuttgart, Galerie der Stadt Stuttgart
(On loan from the Otto Dix Foundation)

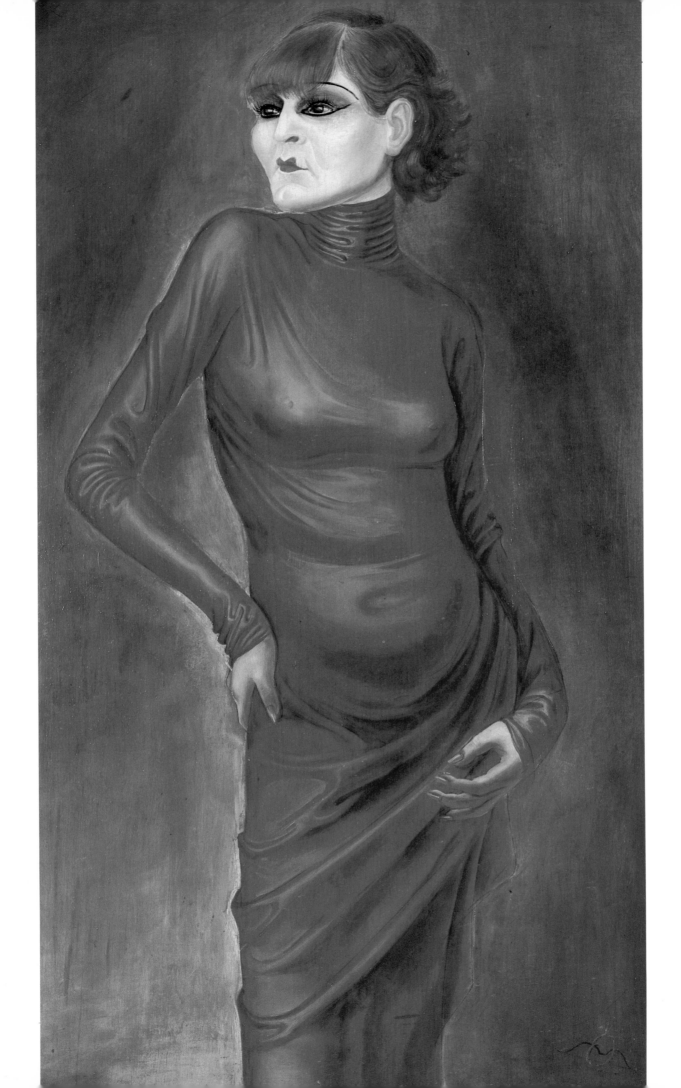

In addition, he devised three cartoons made to the scale of the final picture (pp. 158/159), exact drawings which determined the final composition right down to the details. The layering of tempera and oil paints, a technique involving complicated stages, was the reason for these long-drawn out preparations. Dix was fascinated by this technique because of the transparent effect of the colours it produced. In this connection, he examined the complementarity of colour perception, and also studied Goethe's theory of colour. He was primarily concerned with the diversity of colour values, depending on how they corresponded to and interacted with other colours:

"In other words, if I now put a red here, which is cold, and set blue

Three Whores on the Street, 1925
Drei Dirnen auf der Straße
Mixed media on plywood, 95 x 100 cm
Löffler 1925/2
Hamburg, private collection

The Lunatic, 1925
Der Irrsinnige
Tempera on wood, 120 x 60 cm
Löffler 1925/4
Mannheim, Kunsthalle Mannheim

133

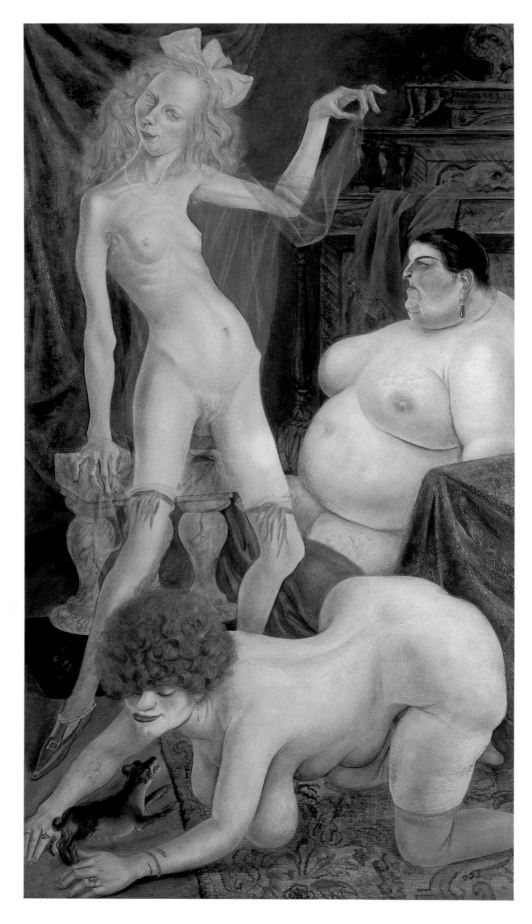

Three Women (Drei Weiber), 1926
Mixed media on wood, 181 x 101.5 cm
Löffler 1926/1
Stuttgart, Galerie der Stadt Stuttgart

Self-portrait with Easel, 1926
Mixed media on plywood, 80 x 55 cm
Löffler 1926/4
Düren, Leopold-Hoesch-Museum der Stadt Düren

Portrait of the Philosopher Max Scheler, 1926
Mixed media on plywood, 100 x 69.5 cm
Löffler 1926/6
Cologne, Philosophische Fakultät, University of Cologne

Portrait of the Manufacturer Dr. Julius Hesse with Paint Sample, 1926
Mixed media on wood, 100 x 70 cm
Löffler 1926/7
Düsseldorf, Ernst O. Hesse Collection

*Portrait of the Art Dealer Alfred
Flechtheim,* 1926
Mixed media on wood, 120 x 80 cm
Löffler 1926/10
Berlin, Nationalgalerie SMPK

against it, then the cold red becomes warm, you see. Like this. And this phenomenon, this change in the colour itself, that's not something that is constant or anything, but something that keeps changing all the time. And now look at the red all by itself – all of a sudden, the red is completely different, you see. It involves a continuous process of fluctuation. The eye is what actually creates the colours." In the triptych Dix again assigned a great value to the fluctuation of the colours: "…so that it has this very fluctuation, this indefinite quality. It oscillates."

This technique distinguishes the colours from one another to an astonishing degree, for Dix is able to depict the transparency and reflection of light in every single bead on the fabrics and on the necklaces and earrings; every hair in the fur boa, every feather is reproduced with utmost precision. The message and content of the big-city triptych are a function of the pictorial structure and technique used to a much greater degree than one might perhaps assume at first glance. The work is extremely complex in terms of both form and content; its multiplicity of levels, however, results from the composition and not from symbolism. The choice of the triptych form was decisive, as was Dix's familiarity with the simultaneous stage techniques of Erwin Piscator, and the technique of using various temporal levels that James Joyce developed in *Ulysses,* revolutionizing the modern novel. In this way, Dix took extremely heterogeneous elements and created a magnificent synthesis, an epic of modern consciousness.

It would seem obvious to consider such a pivotal work as the *Big City* triptych in a broader context: why did Dix choose to paint it as a triptych? What account does it give of big-city life?

According to Dix himself, Joyce's *Ulysses* was a significant stimulus. A copy of the first German translation, published in Basle in 1927, was to be found in the library of his house in Hemmenhofen. The novel unleashed a scandal in Paris after it appeared there on 2 February, 1922, and immediately became the subject of heated debates among literary circles at the time. Dix was probably most fascinated by the compositional arrangement of the novel. Joyce had spliced numerous levels of consciousness, experience and reality and integrated them in a highly artistic compositional scheme by means of a multi-layered use of language.

In this context, we can compare Joyce's technique of reflecting consciousness from many angles and various temporal levels with Sigmund Freud's description of the specific qualities of the system of the unconscious. For the modern novel, and especially *Ulysses,* employed the features of the unconscious that were revealed by psychoanalysis as a revolutionizing new medium of representation. Above all, such novels incorporate the relativity of time and space which marks the unconscious.

In principle the triptych form enabled Dix to divide up the surface of the picture in a particularly multi-facetted way. He was able, for example, to unite temporally and spatially distinct levels of reality in one picture. In addition, he was then in a position to portray the various layers and overlaps in his memory as well as the impulsive nature with which they

140

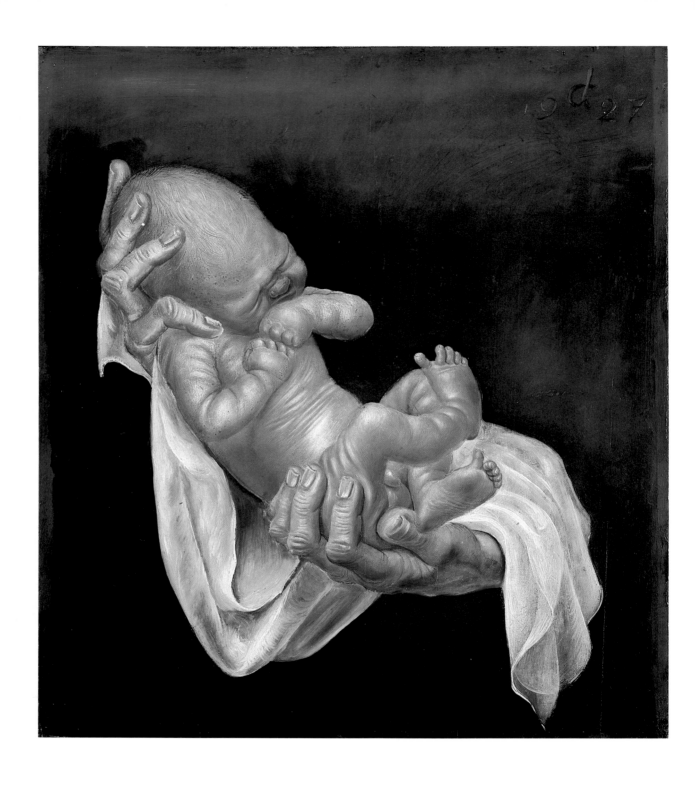

Newborn Baby on Hands
(Ursus Dix), 1927
Neugeborenes auf Händen(Ursus Dix)
Mixed media on plywood,
50 x 43.5 cm
Löffler 1927/5
Stuttgart, Galerie der Stadt Stuttgart
(On loan)

surfaced abruptly and discontinuously in his mind through association. At the same time, Dix was thus able to portray the unique quality of these movements in his memory. The triptych appeared to him to be the aptest pictorial system to make complex subjective processes and objective contents generally understandable. There is no linear, progressive narrative structure in the big-city picture; the point was to evoke subjective, complicated processes of consciousness and to induce reflection.

The three panels of the picture allow the various experiential levels of events to be depicted simultaneously – a factual, itemizing approach, the manner in which they are registered by the person experiencing them, and the reflective bringing to mind of the way in which each came about.

Nelly with Toy, 1925
Nelly mit Spielzeug
Tempera on wood, 54 x 39.5 cm
Löffler 1925/12
Vaduz, Otto Dix Foundation

The portrayal of the synchronicity of actions and events was also one of the major discoveries of epic theatre in the 1920s. Erwin Piscator was the prime mover in epic theatre. He saw it as a reaction to Expressionism and defined it in the following terms:"It is like a novel, in which not only is the dramatic plot portrayed, but also the social and political conditions which determine modern life are described." The parallels to *Ulysses* are evident. It was no longer a matter of portraying a plot, but at the same time also of "clarifying, commenting, analysing, reporting". The "dramatic processes, the action, the plot, became simultaneous juxtaposed actions, the drama became epic" (Piscator) on stage. New techniques had to be found with which to portray the expanded intentions, as is outlined by

Portrait of the Photographer Hugo Erfurth with Dog, 1926
Bildnis des Fotografen Hugo Erfurth mit Hund
Mixed media on wood, 80 x 100 cm
Löffler 1926/14
Castagnola, Thyssen-Bornemisza Collection

Reclining Woman on Leopard Skin, 1927
Liegende auf Leopardenfell
Mixed media on wood, 68 x 98 cm
Löffler 1927/2
Herbert F. Johnson Museum of Art, Cornell University

Piscator in connection with his project for the "total theatre" developed in 1927 in collaboration with Walter Gropius: "But if we were to bring the totality of the world onto the stage, then we needed new media of expression. So I introduced film into theatre, for example, as the most important means of enhancing expression. Moreover, technical innovations such as conveyor belts and hydraulic ramps were adopted as the basis for dramatic functions to a degree that had not been seen since the Baroque.

The stage of *Hoppla, wir leben!* (*Hoppla, Such Is Life!*), was a transparent tiered stage, and in *Rasputin*, the dramatization of Alexei N. Tolstoy's novel, it was a stage built like a segmented globe."

It is not known how much Dix concerned himself with the theatre of his time. However, he evidently had a similar inclination to link dissynchronous events and spatially separated occurrences by means of formal techniques. The mixture of heterogeneous forms of acting within one

Portrait of the Journalist Sylvia von Harden, 1926
Bildnis der Journalisten Sylvia von Harden
Mixed media on wood, 120 x 88 cm
Löffler 1926/9
Paris, Musée National d'Art Moderne,
Centre Georges Pompidou

Street Fight, 1927
Straßenkampf
Mixed media on canvas
Löffler 1927/1
Destroyed at warehouse in 1954

play, the combination of otherwise disparate media of style and expression is the same in approach to that which Joyce also achieved by means of the multi-dimensionality of the language he deployed. In this connection we must remember the roles of the intricate constructions, the ability to render scenes in minute detail. Joyce moves on the most diverse levels of language, which he does not connect in a logical, causal sequence. Instead he establishes an interactive relation between sensuality, emotionality and intellectuality, re-creating the world out of his head with magnificent associative intuition. Dix does the same.

One finds parallels between Dix and Joyce, not only with regard to the composition of the book, but also notably in terms of the links between their lives and their work. Just as the "events" of Stephen Dedalus's life, the novel's main character, reflect those of Joyce's Dublin years (as Hugh Kenner has reminded us), thus showing that the novel contains strongly autobiographical qualities, Dix's big-city picture is also a summary of personal experiences, of his years in Berlin in particular. The two artists have another important trait in common: their sense of humour. Ezra Pound called attention at a very early stage to the fact that this was a key element in *Ulysses*. As an old man he still remembered how Joyce had reacted to reviews and interpretations of his novel: "If only someone

The Match Vendor II, 1927
Der Streichholzhändler II
Mixed media on wood, 120 x 65 cm
Löffler 1927/11
Mannheim, Kunsthalle Mannheim

147

Ellis, 1922
Watercolour and opaque, 38.2 x 27.6 cm
Albstadt, Walther Groz Foundation, Städtische Galerie Albstadt

Couple, 1926
Paar
Watercolour, opaque and pencil, 68.5 x 50.5 cm
Vaduz, Otto Dix Foundation

would finally say that the book is so damned funny." And Joyce himself provides us with one final clue to the affinity between the book and the picture: "Among other things, my book is an epic of the human body...In my book the body lives and moves in space and harbours a fully developed human personality. My words are used in such a way that they first express one bodily function and then another. In the 'Lestrygonians' the stomach dominates, and the rhythm of the episode corresponds to peristaltic movement." For Joyce, as for Dix, "body and soul are a unity. If they (the figures in the novel) did not have bodies, they would have no soul", as Joyce put it.

Critics often refer to the influence of the old German masters – above all, Hans Baldung Grien, Albrecht Dürer, Matthias Grünewald and Lukas Cranach – on Dix's art. These influences refer primarily to the formal innovations of these painters. Dix admired their technical perfection and the principles of their painting technique, which he adapted in his own paintings of the 1920s and 1930s. As a student in Dresden from 1919 to 1922, Dix had ample opportunity to study the paintings of Grünewald, Dürer and Cranach in the Dresden art gallery. He became familiar with Baldung's paintings from other sources, possibly through reproductions, since the catalogues show that the gallery did not house any Baldung works between 1916 to 1923. The use of translucent layers of colour as well as certain similarities in the treatment of colour and the choice of bright, highly contrasting colours may be regarded as results of Dix's interest in the painting of the old German masters. He shares the stress on subject matter and the passion for precision in the details, too. Like Baldung, Dix focuses on the illustration of figures and in doing so on stressing the physicality through sharply drawn contours, whereas land-scapes and architecture recede into the background. However, Dix's treatment of themes addressed by Baldung, such as those of beauty and death, youth and old age, stemmed from a different attitude. Dix viewed the "objectivity" of his time critically, whereas Baldung painted such themes based on his personal proclivity for the cult of superstition in his time. Any view that claims to have discovered traces of mediaeval sym-bolism in Dix's paintings by projecting them onto his work is thus highly problematic.

There is no concrete evidence to support a comparison such as that made by Conzelmann between the flounces on the women's gowns in the middle panel of *Big City* with "drooping wings" and no reason to speak of a "dance of death" in relation to the couple dancing the Charleston or of "the towers of angels taken from mediaeval painters" when referring to the parade of women on the right panel; and there is certainly no basis for interpreting the painting as the history of the "rich man and the poor Lazarus". It is well-known that Dix knew his Bible very well; however, whenever he wanted to portray Biblical themes, he did so explicitly throughout all the periods of his career. A fundamental distinction has to be made between the use of forms and attributes as symbolic agents, on the one hand, and the way in which they are treated, on the other. In the latter case, Dix differs from the tradition of mediaeval painting, which

Nude seen from the Back on Chair, 1928
Rückenakt auf Stuhl
Pencil, 53.3 x 36 cm
Vaduz, Otto Dix Foundation

Portrait of the Poet Theodor Däubler, 1927
Bildnis des Dichters Theodor Däubler
Mixed media on plywood, 150 x 100 cm
Löffler 1927/9
Cologne, Museum Ludwig, Dr. Josef
Haubrich Foundation

employed pre-determined contents only according to the corresponding attributes. In his book on the old German masters, published in 1909, Ernst Heidrich stresses the "prominence of Calvary as the special underlying tone in the substantive world of old German painting. Beyond the aesthetic impression we have of them, the things portrayed remind us of the most serious and important questions of life, and it is always characteristic of this art that the beholder is meant by viewing external appearances to experience a sequence of thoughts and feelings which goes far beyond the surroundings of the sensual present. An unravelling of the relations of content, a contemplation and brooding clings to German art, even aside from the religious subject matter."

The 1920s, by contrast, with their dogma of objectivity and its key claim to value neutrality, had developed an attitude of the equivalence of possible means to be taken to achieve an end, and therefore made use of all possible historical forms and techniques, often indiscriminately and simultaneously. In formal terms, they used quotations bereft of substance, if considered from the point of view of the original text. The main feature of this reliance on quotation during the post-war period lies in the redundancy of quotations of commodities and consumerism when used to mean nothing but themselves. Emptied of their symbolic power, the attributes were reduced to their character as commodities.

Dix conveyed this consciousness of quotation in his picture. The indiscriminate indulgence in decorativity and externals manifests the redundant element that Dix portrayed when he coupled the "old German" formal quotation with "Baroque" formal borrowings or piled up glorious materials or displayed several drapings at one time.

Dix had thus discovered the only parallel between the state of consciousness prevalent in the Baroque and post-war periods: their common preference for redundancy, engendered by the feeling of a loss of mean-

Big City (Triptych), 1927/28
Großstadt (Triptychon)
Mixed media on wood, 181 x 402 cm
Side panels: 181 x 101 cm each; centre panel: 181 x 200 cm.
Löffler 1928/1
Stuttgart, Galerie der Stadt Stuttgart

PAGE 152:
Big City, 1927/28
Großstadt
Left panel
Mixed media on wood, 181 x 101 cm
Löffler 1928/1
Stuttgart, Galerie der Stadt Stuttgart

PAGE: 154/155:
Big City, 1927/28
Großstadt
Centre panel
Mixed media on wood, 181 x 200 cm
Löffler 1928/1
Stuttgart, Galerie der Stadt Stuttgart

153

Half-Nude with Cloth (standing), 1930
Halbakt mit Tuch (stehend)
Mixed media on canvas over wood
Dimensions unknown
Löffler 1930/5
Destroyed during the war

Big City, 1927/28
Großstadt
Right panel
Mixed media on wood, 181 x 101 cm
Löffler 1928/1
Stuttgart, Galerie der Stadt Stuttgart

ing. However, the Baroque was still able, thanks to its perfected capacity for self-presentation, to develop a style in the sense of homogenization of forms. The 1920s were no longer able to do so. The fundamental loss of substance that resulted from the postulate of value-neutrality made the period decadent. This decadence extended equally to the body, transforming the body itself into a quotation. The body became a figure, Eros was reduced to sexuality, and beauty, now a material quantity, increasingly found expression only in attractiveness.

The decadence of the 1920s was one of nihilism as described by Nietzsche. Nihilism simply reversed the value system that had prevailed until then: instead of absolutizing certain idealistic values, the approach until then, nihilism made valuelessness, i.e. the senselessness of all being, absolute. The same way of thinking is retained, the only difference being that it is given a negative predicate. The non-value of being can be recognized everywhere. This results, among other things, in the decisive retention of the old structures of thought that rely on the either-or, on categorical distinctions. Faith, interestingly enough, is not lost in the process: the nihilist believes in Nothingness, which for him has the highest value, and in this sense behaves just like any other believer whose belief is tied to ideals, the only difference being that, as Nietzsche himself also described it, the consequences of a belief in nothingness are very disappointing, as the 1920s demonstrated in some respects.

This brings us to what life in the big city during the 1920s was like. Dix sought to understand the inner structures of it, as it were, and convey them in his picture. For him the experience of big-city life consisted primarily in the multitude of stimuli that appealed to perception and the senses. In general, the "intensification of the activity of the nerves that results from the rapid and uninterrupted alternation of external and inner impressions", as culture critic Georg Simmel described it, can be considered the main characteristic of modern existence in the big city. It is denoted by an effect akin in its momentary suddenness to an electric shock. The notions of time in the city, where the consumption of goods is raised to a higher power, are characterized in relation to the moment, the result of an excessive supply of stimulants for the senses and body. Unrelated events constantly occur with a disjointed rapidity. "The Berliner never has time ... He always has something to do, talks on the phone and makes appointments, arrives in a tizzy for an appointment or a little late – and has a great deal to do ... The Berliner is a slave to the machinery, a passenger, theatre-goer, restaurant patron and white-collar employee. And less of a human being", was the opinion of Kurt Tucholsky, who was in a position to know.

In terms of content, this sense of time had the qualities of fast erosion, of rapid consumption. A sense of emptiness follows hard upon the short-term pleasure of consumption; a perpetual isolating process of repetition that always serves the same purpose: anaesthetization. The senses dull, and the feeling for continuity and organic growth are also gradually lost in the process. The selective sense of time that lends all occurrences a certain charm is experienced by the big-city dweller as both power and

Big City (Triptych), 1927/28
Großstadt (Triptychon)
Cartoon of the painting of the same
name; charcoal, white chalk, red chalk,
pencil and opaque white on paper over
canvas
Left panel: 180 x 103.5 cm;
Centre panel: 180 x 203 cm;
right panel: 179 x 101 cm
Stuttgart, Galerie der Stadt Stuttgart
(On permanent loan from the Kultus-
ministerium of Baden-Württemberg)

impotence. As power, because he can step into action, at least seemingly,
at any time, and as impotence, because all momentary events necessarily
appear interchangeable to him. The body, employed as the key medium
in a commodity-oriented form of communication, was also affected by
this phenomenon; the value placed on arbitrariness meant that communication ceased to be binding for the persons involved. Gradually the
feelings of impotence increased the more time was experienced as a
discontinuous phenomenon. Further consequences of this development
were the banality of events, and ultimately the neutralization and then
loss of any sense of time whatsoever. A state of indifference became
widespread.

The concepts of continuity/discontinuity and growth also link into the spatial structure of this understanding of time. A feeling of confinement and then of a loss of space corresponds with discontinuity. Spatially, a large city, compared with nature and landscape, is by far the most confining of the three, owing to the masses of people and commodities squeezed into a small area. The big-city dweller develops an ever more "impoverished" awareness of space, which he must additionally split up into inner, i.e. living and "body" space, and outer, i.e. public, space. In the latter he presents his body as a public phenomenon dressed appropriately for the respective occasion, as a figure with an "image", but no longer as a person. The cause of the separation of private and public body

Portrait of Mrs. Martha Dix I, 1928
Bildnis Frau Martha Dix I
Mixed media on plywood, 60 x 59.5 cm
Löffler 1928/2
Stuttgart, Galerie der Stadt Stuttgart (On loan)

behaviour can be seen as the subjectivization in human motivation (as Volker Rittner puts it).

Sometimes one has, as now, to deal with somewhat more abstract issues. Rittner describes the "history of the human body, and thus Western history" as the "process of a severance of needs from the gratification of needs, the dissociation of action and purpose, of person and subjectivity" – in other words, as the history of processes of separation. Traditional society only acknowledged "preordained, unequivocal purposes", tied to "limited possibilities for action" and the "unalterability of meaning", thus excluding an "escape into privacy". The great value attached to subjectivity referred the subject to a private, inner realm which it was initially successful in maintaining vis-à-vis the "non-space" of the public sphere. In the latter it saw itself as being anonymously and futilely exposed to the mercy of the money-based economy. The experience of intensified subjectivity, so highly valued at the outset, was, however, increasingly perceived as something threatening and isolating. The unbounded interior spaces of consciousness were met by the constraints of the public urban space, which the subject sought to adapt to by externalizing its body. The discrepancy between intimate and public body became ever greater. In the end the subject found itself confronted by a lack of shelter not only in the interior of its consciousness, but also in the public space – both correspond to the loss of the "undivided body". The sense of a loss of spatial shelter (interior as well as external space), which can be derived from the loss of a feeling of shelter in the body, and a loss of a continuity in time characterized the disoriented big-city dweller of the 1920s.

Let us cite one last, somewhat abstract passage on the subject of city life in the 1920s, inspired by Dix's painting: "The unique quality of Baudelaire's poetry is that the images of woman and of death mingle in a third, that of Paris." This statement by Walter Benjamin could also have been written as the key to the big-city triptych. The women in the picture function as representatives of one of big-city life's principal sources of attraction – the seemingly unlimited range of pleasures it offers, the vast selection and availability of commodities. The women fulfil a dual function: they are salesgirl and commodity in one. Or, put another way: they have bought their market value as luxury products by hard work. Thus they serve the (ascetic) economic principal in exemplary fashion, for this legitimates itself by pointing to the extravagance that it implies. The girlie-reviews of the 1920s, the dance shows patterned after Broadway, lend themselves best to the study of this peculiar coupling of economy and extravagance. Every single body there was drilled, along lines borrowed from the modern organization of labour, in order to achieve perfect interchangeability of appearance and function. The body was indirectly compensated for the abstinence it had to endure (in being deprived of individual pleasures) by being allowed to participate in an overall stage experience that was one lavish hymn to luxury and money from start to finish. This extravagance was geared not to the body itself, but to the effects that it helped to generate. The aim was a flawless surface, a world of illusion.

Portrait of a Young Girl (Erni), 1928
Bildnis eines jungen Mädchens (Erni)
Mixed media on wood, 34.5 x 21.5 cm
Löffler 1928/7
Vaduz, Otto Dix Foundation

Melancholy, 1930
Melancholie
Mixed media on wood, 137 x 98 cm
Löffler 1930/1
Stuttgart, Galerie der Stadt Stuttgart
(On loan from the Otto Dix Foundation)

Portrait of the Painter Franz Radziwill,
1928
Bildnis des Malers Franz Radziwill
Mixed media on paper, 87.5 x 60 cm
Löffler 1928/12
Düsseldorf, Kunstmuseum Düsseldorf

The extravagance encouraged by the consumer industry was carefully calculated and subject to strict controls, as well as differing fundamentally from the waste that centred on the body itself, in that it always left a sense of dissatisfaction behind (for it always claimed, after all, to be "boundless"). The one-sided fixation of the economic principle of extravagance on the pleasure-value things and bodies negated one further essential quality inherent in the body: the nutritional, substantive value of things. Pleasure as the product of the industrial world of commodities is nothing other than an inadequate surrogate for enjoyment. Pleasure, organized economically when treated as a superficial charm,

Self-portrait with Jan, 1930
Selbstbildnis mit Jan
Mixed media on wood, 119 x 90 cm
Löffler 1930/2
Private collection

The Pregnant Woman (Seated), 1930
Die Schwangere (sitzend)
Mixed media on wood, 93 x 72 cm
Löffler 1930/4
Stuttgart, Galerie der Stadt Stuttgart

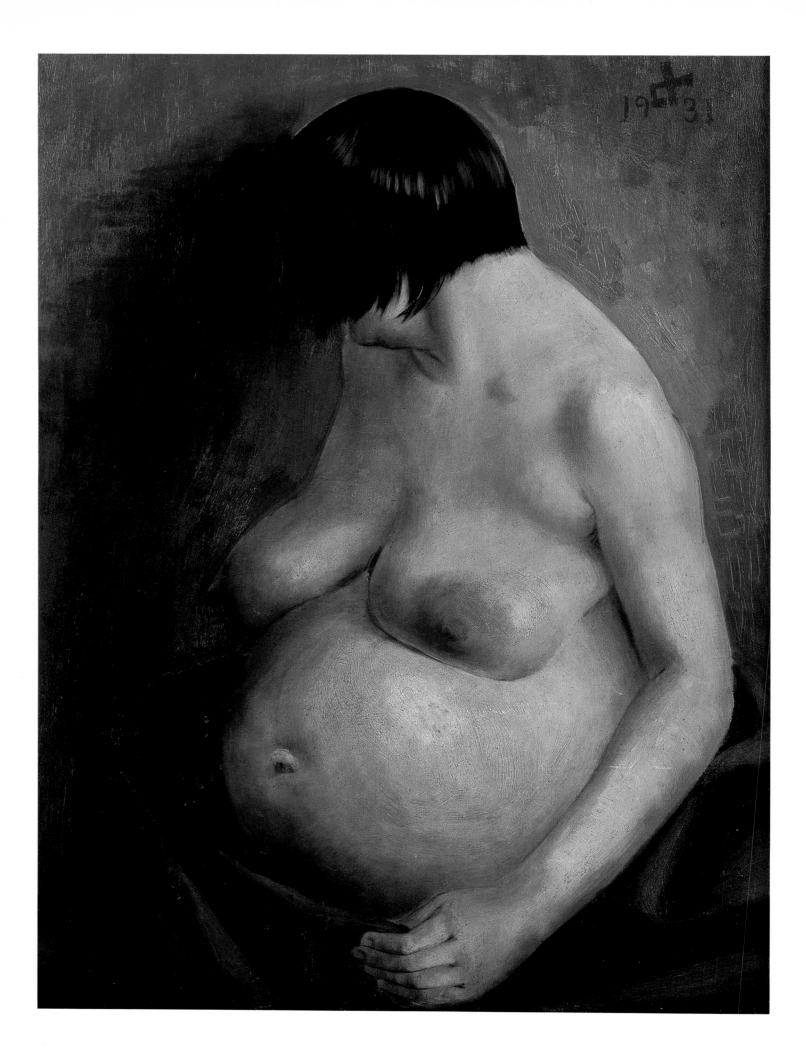

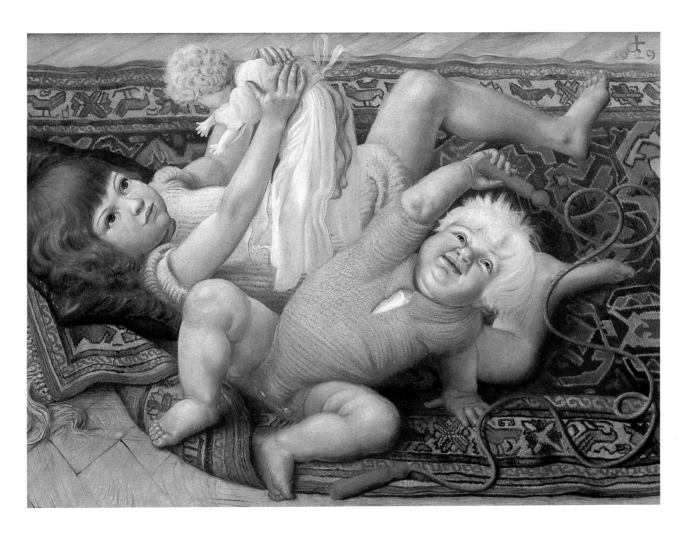

invariably leaves the person bent only on enjoyment "empty", since it is only ostensibly aimed at the person's bodily expression, but actually only serves its own economic preservation.

Benjamin's observation that the images of woman and death mingle in a third image, that of the big city, applies to Dix's picture with respect to the connection between sexuality and death it expresses. By sexuality we mean that form which depends on the mechanisms of commodities. With increasing rationalization, sexuality was progressively reduced to mechanistic genital sexuality and thus ever less able to unfold in the form of an eroticism of the whole body. Sexuality had been degraded to one of the big city's commodities.

Children at Play, 1929
(also known as *Nelly with Doll and Ursus*)
Spielende Kinder (auch: Nelly mit Puppe
und Ursus)
Mixed media on plywood, 72 x 93 cm
Löffler 1929/2
Private collection

The Pregnant Woman (Half-Nude), 1931
Die Schwangere (Halbakt)
Mixed media on wood, 83 x 62 cm
Löffler 1931/2
United States, private collection

The 1930s and 1940s:
Inner Emigration

In 1933, the year Hitler came to power, Dix was dismissed without notice from his teaching position at the art academy in Dresden. He gave up his professorship with a heavy heart, as he had loved the close relationship he had to his students. He even went to Ludwig Justi, who was director of the National Gallery in Berlin at the time, for assistance: "I have never belonged to or sympathized with a political party. I feel myself to be the prototype of a German painter in the best sense of the term", he wrote in a letter dated 12 April, 1933. Many fellow artists who shared the same dilemma, like Kirchner, were completely surprised by the compulsory measures instituted by Nazi cultural policy, and could never quite understand why they, of all people, were suddenly considered "degenerate". Justi, at any rate, responded evasively and thus extricated himself from things: "My antipathy for your portrayals of streetwalkers and the war did not, however, keep me from recognizing and appreciating your unusual talent; I have therefore attempted to provide a visual intimation of your skill in the National Gallery on the more or less neutral level of the portrait." Ultimately, however, Justi submitted to the NSDAP's ideology: "I would regret it if an artist with your talent were to stand by forever, and would welcome it with grateful joy if such a talent would join us in working for a positive form of creative German art". These are the cowardly phrases of a person who wanted to save his own skin. Dix did not make compromises.

The official reason given for finally dismissing him was that some of his pictures "most seriously injure the moral feeling of the German people, and others could dampen the German people's will to defend themselves" – on which Dix commented as follows in 1966: "I was informed that I was no longer to set foot in the academy. But I still had all of my works there. Nevertheless: I had to get out right away! In Saxony, things grew sinister: they're particularly fanatical there, on the one hand; and on the other, they're friendly, as it were."

In the summer of 1933 the New Dresden Secession urged Dix nonetheless to take part in their exhibition. Despite the considerable success Dix had achieved with paintings of children such as *Ursus with Top, Children at Play* (p. 167), *Self-portrait with Jan* (p. 165) or *Portrait of the Dancer Tamara Danischewski* (p. 183), all of which were chosen because they were "inoffensive", the situation for him and his family became increas-

Nelly with Doll II, 1929
Nelly mit Puppe II
Mixed media on wood,
74.8 x 40.5 cm
Löffler 1929/3
Vaduz, Otto Dix Foundation

Self-portrait in Smock with Crystal Ball and Palette, 1931
Selbstbildnis im Malkittel mit Kristall-kugel und Palette
Mixed media on wood, 100.5 x 80.5 cm
Löffler 1931/1
Cologne, Museum Ludwig, Dr. Josef Haubrich Foundation

Red-haired Woman, 1931
Rothaarige Frau
Mixed media on wood, 60.5 x 36.5 cm
Löffler 1929/4 (!)
Munich, private collection

Portrait of the Singer Elisabeth Stüntzner, 1932
Bildnis der Sängerin Elisabeth Stüntzner
Mixed media on wood, 99 x 69 cm
Löffler 1932/17
United States, private collection

ingly dangerous. The first exhibition of "Degenerate Art of the Systems Period" opened in September under the title "Reflections of Decline" in the Dresden city hall's patio courtyard. In the spring of that same year an exhibition had already been held in Stuttgart entitled "The Spirit of November, the Art of Demoralization". At the instruction of the Director for Culture in the Reich's Ministry for Propaganda a second touring exhibition on "Degenerate Art" was set up in 1937 and shown in Munich, Berlin, Leipzig, Dresden and Düsseldorf. A total of 260 works by Dix, who had been banned from exhibiting his work since 1934, had been confiscated from German art collections. These included not only the two paintings *War Cripple* and *The Trench*, but also such "harmless" paintings as the portraits of Theodor Däubler (p. 150), Hugo Erfurth (p. 128) or Max Scheler (p. 136) and *Portrait of the Artist's Parents I*, as well as the *Seated Nude of Ursus as a Child*. A portion of the confiscated works was either auctioned off or sold outright by the Ministry of Propaganda in the Fischer Gallery in Lucerne; the rest of them were burned in the Berlin fire-station.

In the autumn of 1933 Dix and his family moved to Lake Constance. In 1936, after spending almost three difficult years at Schloss Randegg near Singen on the Hohentwiel, he finally settled in Hemmenhofen in his own newly built house. He completed the allegorical painting *The Seven Cardinal Sins* (p. 181) as late as 1933, having already conceived it in 1932. The personifications of the different vices have banded together in a horde to spread moral ruin. On top of the bent figure of the old witch, the allegory of greed, hunches a tiny, dwarf-like figure embodying envy. Naturally Dix did not add the Hitler moustache to its face until after 1945. The usual community of sins is to be seen behind the two: death in the figure of slackness of heart, the devil as anger, the woman, symbol of depravity, pride with a mouth shaped like an anus and a bizarre figure wearing something like a pot on its head, representing gluttony. On a crumbling wall one can make out a sentence from Nietzsche's *Thus Spake Zarathustra*: "The desert grows, woe to him who harbours deserts." Dix was levelling vehement criticism at the times, albeit in coded form. His painting is testimony to resistance. And it is a picture with which Dix attempts to evoke forces which would dispel the forces of evil.

Triumph of Death (p. 185), painted 1934/35, is a truly scintillating lament for times unhinged by intoxication with power. A number of completely different people are assembled before the backdrop of a Romantic German landscape painted in the style of the old masters. A small child is crawling around amongst the meadow flowers, a scene rendered in the manner of Runge. An older woman is bending down to him. A handsome young couple – the woman is naked – is standing entwined in each other's arms in front of a wall. A fat man with a puffed-up face is sitting behind them, and in front of him a little mutt is barking and baring its teeth. The two of them are staring upward, where Death, a gruesome skeleton with a flapping coat, swinging an enormous scythe and wearing a brightly flashing tiara, is plunging towards them. All of the

The War, 1929-1932
Der Krieg
Centre panel
Mixed media on wood, 204 × 204 cm
Löffler 1932/2
Dresden, Staatliche Kunstsammlungen,
Gemäldegalerie Neue Meister

other figures remain untouched by the monstrous phantasmagoria, including the soldier in the steel helmet standing in front of the tree and holding a loaded weapon, gazing steadily ahead. The personification of Nazi terror with its sweeping lust for destruction in the figure of Death is clear. The formal quotations borrowed from various styles of German art of the past as well as the fusion of unrelated figural visual elements create a mood that fluctuates between sentimentality and brutality, vividly reflecting the prevailing insanity of the times.

Two further paintings, the *Temptation of St. Anthony*, 1937, and *Lot and His Daughters* (p. 192), 1939, are intended as socially critical allegories. In both paintings the colours border on kitsch with their "venomous" tonalities. The sickly sweetness of the female figures, and the bombastically exaggerated landscape (reminiscent of the pathos-laden settings of Wagnerian operas) show Dix evoking the megalomania of the period. In the background of *Lot and His Daughters* Dix envisions Dresden in flames: the buildings on the Brühl terrace, the cupola of St. Mary's church and the graceful tower of the court church built by Gaetano Chiaveri are clearly recognizable. Exactly six years later, in 1945, the city would indeed go up in flames. Dix once made the following comment about the *Temptation of St. Anthony*: "Well, I am obsessed with the devil, that is how I know what's up in this world." Disgusting demons, grimacing heads with blood-thirsty mouths and poison-spewing, tooth-baring animals have attacked St. Anthony, who is kneeling on the ground and pleading for help. A buxom, lascivious woman is also holding him down. Anthony finds himself on the brink of an abyss, literally and metaphorically speaking.

Both pictures demonstrate the perverted system of values of the time all the more radically in that they primarily obey aesthetic guidelines in keeping with the state's wishes. Dix deliberately quotes the "international kitsch" of the Nazis, as Paul Westheim aptly put it in 1938. West-

The War, 1929-1932
Der Krieg
Triptych with predella
Mixed media on wood
Side panels: 204 x 102 cm each; centre panel: 204 x 204 cm; predella: 60 x 204 cm
Löffler 1932/2
Dresden, Staatliche Kunstsammlungen, Gemäldegalerie Neue Meister

PAGE 174:
Vanitas (Youth and Old Age), 1932
Vanitas (Jugend und Alter)
Mixed media on wood, 100 x 70 cm
Löffler 1932/7
Friedrichshafen, Städtisches Bodensee-Museum

PAGE 175:
Trench Warfare, 1932
Grabenkrieg
Mixed media on wood, 212.5 x 100 cm
Löffler 1932/4
Stuttgart, Galerie der Stadt Stuttgart

Heinrich George sitting for Otto Dix

heim, the politically active critic who had been living in exile in Paris since 1933, provided a very fitting description of those products of "high-flown German yarns", as he called the effusions of the official Nazi "great artists": "Romantic flight into a pathos-filled, theatrical world of illusion is the real salient feature of Hitlerian art... The fact that it is (albeit to an inconceivable degree) tasteless, kitschy, academically dull and meagre in terms of craftmanship is something it has in common with the lower middle class and philistine creations of producers of kitsch in all countries, called 'pompiers' in France. In this respect, it is simply international kitsch, the least national style that could ever exist in the field of art" (from: *Verlogener Realismus*, 1938).

The 1930s and 1940s represent an exceptional phase in Dix's work. The works he produced during these years reveal an unmistakable inner crisis in his development and work, brought on by political circumstances. Dix's pictures were considered degenerate. In addition to a very few paintings with Biblical themes and isolated commissioned portraits done in loveless fashion, all he produced during those years were landscape paintings, painstakingly and masterfully executed with the transparent coating technique. The fact that Dix devoted himself almost exclusively to the "old German masters' exact manner of painting", as he himself put it, and initially (until 1938) did no water-colours or spontaneous sketches, points to the existential state of emergency he was in at the time. He had no other choice but to take refuge in the landscape. This appeared to afford the only possible means of continuing his work without it being subjected to the constraints of value judgements. The pictures he painted during that period evoke an exceptional intensity of atmosphere, by virtue of their technical perfection and their flawless, impenetrable beauty or smoothness. But they intimate an underlying tension and injuries in the artist. Dix was not politically persecuted (as we have seen, Dix was in principle not interested in politics), but suffered rather more as the result of a certain worldview which, at that time, came closest to the Romantic feeling of life with its sense of a loss of security, but also represented a longing for meaning. Isolated as he was at the time, Dix could only feel secure to an extremely limited extent.

It is important to bear in mind at this point that the National Socialist cultural policy-makers propagated certain epochs of German landscape painting as being "exemplary" for "German" art. They placed the 16th century Danube School centred around Albrecht Altdorfer at the very top of their list alongside Caspar David Friedrich, the demi-god of Romantic landscape painting. The fact that their position was based on two such diverse "prototypes" is in itself amazing.

On the one hand, there was the humanistically enlightened Danube School of the early 16th century, whose influence spread in the area north of the Alps and which has to be understood against the background of the Reformation, the discovery of America, and the projection of the Copernican view of the world. On the other hand, there was the Romanticism of the period around 1800, which advocated a counter-plan to rationalism and classicism, clinging to the subjectivity of the individual.

Portrait of the Actor Heinrich
George as Terje Wiggen, 1932
Bildnis des Schauspielers Heinrich
George als Terje Wiggen
Mixed media on wood, 100 x 85 cm
Löffler 1932/5
Stuttgart, Galerie der Stadt Stuttgart

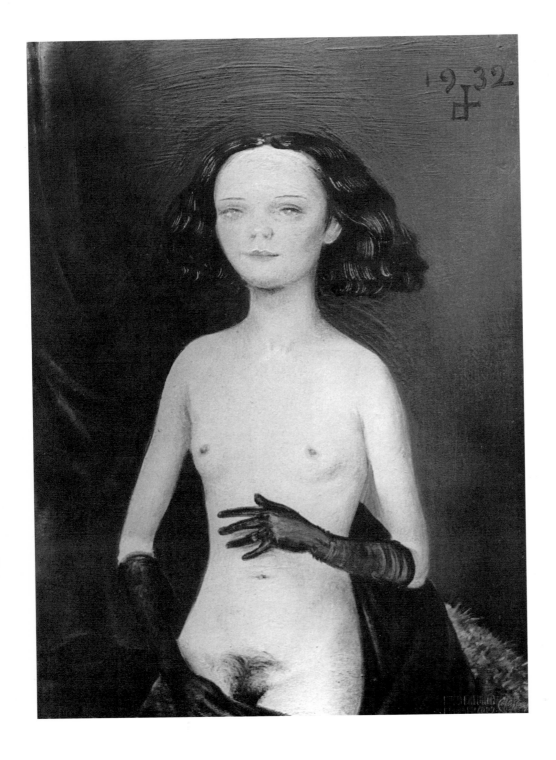

Venus with Gloves, 1932
Venus mit Handschuhen
Mixed media on wood, 25 x 20 cm
Löffler 1932/11
Private collection

The Nazis were thus giving preference to Friedrich, of all people, who had been considered a rebellious outsider in his own day. The motives behind the didactic and ideological promotion of two such heterogeneous ideals were not particularly analytical in nature. Rather they must be seen as part of a very general, rather diffuse effort to elevate the Nazis' status. Landscape and Nature, which can easily be associated with *Heimat* and "the German homeland", lent themselves as vehicles with which to project the German spirit in its "infinitude", "vastness" and "clarity". Wilhelm Westecker, for example, commenting on a portfolio of "German Landscapes" in 1941, asserted: "Landscape portrayals thus dominate the period of Romantic painting, above all the work of C.D.

Lovers with Nasturtium, 1930
Liebespaar mit Kapuzinerkresse
Mixed media on plywood, 81 x 64 cm
Löffler 1930/11
Jörg and Heide Mussotter Collection

Friedrich, which almost exclusively sought a new style of landscape portrayal, which brought the landscape to life as a space between time and eternity. On the wings of the landscape the spirit seeks to merge with the infinite. No one has ever succeeded in imbuing the landscape with living spirit as C.D. Friedrich did."

In other words, Friedrich's one-sided, heroic version of the German soul was no more than *Heimat* sentimentality. Statements such as "the landscapes which the artists of today's Germany paint are also filled with a yearning for vastness and clarity... The reality of a particular landscape is elevated to an (...) ideal German landscape which strives to surmount the reality of particular mountain formations as perceived by

The Seven Cardinal Sins, 1933
Die sieben Todsünden
Cartoon of the painting in Karlsruhe
Charcoal, 178.5 x 118.5 cm
Stuttgart, Galerie der Stadt Stuttgart

The Seven Cardinal Sins, 1933
Die sieben Todsünden
Mixed media on wood, 179 x 120 cm
Löffler 1933/1
Karlsruhe, Staatliche Kunsthalle
Karlsruhe

the eye to arrive at a landscape in which German longing seeks its home" were aimed at reducing a highly complex dialectical conception of landscape and Nature such as that of Friedrich to the level of easily-ingestible genre art – an aim that was achieved.

In fact, a large number of landscape pictures were produced in which motifs from Friedrich's work were rendered in a typified and idyllically harmless manner. What the Nazis demanded of landscape painting – that it promulgate a soulful atmosphere to compensate for the lack of substance – took the form in such paintings of conformist trivialization, of a bland idyll of fields, forests, meadows and sunshine. The more "blemished" the political and social present became, the more "timeless" and untouched Nature and landscape had to appear to be. Landscape-painting in the Third Reich thus became an exact opposite to Friedrich's art, which aimed at integrating contradictions in the picture. When motifs from Friedrich were used, such as the favourite fir trees, mountains, tree stumps and barrows, they were not recognizable as quotations; rather, the poor imitations were even brazenly monumentalized and prostituted. They were atrocious panoramas of kitsch. The tradition invoked was at the same time being destroyed.

The Friedrich cult and the glorification of the Danube School were no secret to Dix. Undoubtedly he knew of Hitler's speech inaugurating the "House of German Art" and the first "Great German Art Exhibition", in which the Führer had referred to "our German Romanticists". Dix's flight into landscape painting has to be seen from two viewpoints in this specific historical context: on the one hand, in terms of tactical, pragmatic considerations that allowed him to work relatively free of interference, provided that he seemingly accepted the official art policy; and, on the other, in terms of a reflective, critical element. Dix was able, owing to the way he designed his pictures – for example, by quoting Romantic or old German formal elements and making them recognizable as such – to convey, if subtly disguised, his unequivocal rejection of the officially sanctioned form of landscape-painting. Unlike the recognized landscape painters of the 1930s, Dix gave the impression, on the surface, of conforming to the demands of National Socialism, especially during the period from 1934 to 1942, by making meticulous use of the transparent coating technique characteristic of the old German panel paintings, and by designing landscapes, invariably devoid of human figures, that were viewed from afar and thus demonstrated "vastness" and "infinity".

In reality, however, Dix made use of the room for interpretation which National Socialist cultural policy had itself created by using flexible concepts of the soul and introspection, to express his own state of mind and his own personal kind of resistance. The very perfection of his technique expressed his opposition. The Nature he depicts does not look harmlessly idyllic and "clean" at all, but instead – quite on the contrary – unapproachable and uninhabitable. It is a haven only for the imagination. Dix's landscapes should be regarded as melancholy quotations of a past and irretrievably lost sense of life (that of Romanticism), the reconstruction of which can be called literary in quality – this also had a

Portrait of the Dancer Tamara
Danischewski with Iris, 1933
Bildnis der Tänzerin Tamara
Danischewski mit Iris
Mixed media on wood, 82 x 64.5 cm
Löffler 1933/2
Stuttgart, Galerie der Stadt Stuttgart

Portrait of the Painter Hans Theo Richter
and His Wife Gisela, 1933
Bildnis des Malers Hans Theo Richter und
Frau Gisela
Mixed media on wood, 100 x 70 cm
Löffler 1933/3
Nuremberg, Germanisches National-
museum (on loan)

comforting effect on Dix, as it provided him with a preserve in which he could make statements without interference.

In Hegau, near Lake Constance, Dix painted, drew and did water-colours together with Franz Lenk, an old friend from his days as a student in Dresden, during the summer of 1934. Lenk, who did not belong to any party, had been appointed President of the Reich's Chamber for Fine Arts in 1933 and now found himself in the difficult situation of having to mediate between the official art policy and the artists who had been branded as "degenerate". The works of Dix and Lenk were exhibited in January, 1935 in the Nierendorf Gallery in Berlin. It was a demonstrative event featuring, on the one hand, a cultural functionary and professor of landscape-painting in Berlin, and someone who was completely ostracized, on the other. In addition to portraits such as those of Ivar von Lücken, Ursus Dix or Nelly in flowers, Dix exhibited several landscape drawings, including the silver-point drawing *Randegg in the Snow* and the pen-and-ink drawing *The Spruce.*

Early in 1935 Dix sent a humorous drawing to Lenk with the telling words: "Our common landscape-painting in the light of criticism Happy New Year to all of you Dix." One cannot help but have the impression that the works Dix was painting at the time were again serving as a grim recapitulation of art history – in the absence of other themes that could be addressed. Paintings done in 1934 – *Randegg in the Storm*, for example – bear remarks such as "painted exactly – Romantic-old German" or, in the case of *Winter in Randegg*, "old German – resembles Breughel" and, of *Randegg with Hohentwiel*, "smooth – exact in the old German style". Dix drew his motifs from the surrounding landscape in the Lake Constance

Triumph of Death, 1934
Triumph des Todes
Mixed media on wood, 180 x 178 cm
Löffler 1934/1
Stuttgart, Galerie der Stadt Stuttgart

Mother and Eva (Louise Dix and Granddaughter Eva Kolberg), 1935
Mutter und Eva (Louise Dix und Enkelin Eva Kolberg)
Mixed media on plywood, 80.4 x 70 cm
Löffler 1935/1
Essen, Museum Folkwang

185

area, which he presented pictorially as it changed according to season
and time of day. What else could he do? Paintings such as *Randegg in the
Snow with Ravens* (p. 187) and *Jewish Cemetery in Randegg* (p. 186), both
completed in 1935, still attest to the unbroken continuity in his work.
Dix's manner of seeing was always highly individual. The detail, the
choice of an unmistakable perspective, and atmospherics such ravens in
the winter landscape, create compositions with great density and a magical aura.

When Dix painted the *Jewish Cemetery in Randegg*, the persecution of
the Jews had already begun. The low gravestones at a remote spot some
distance from the village cluster on the hillside. Pale light covers the
scene, a ghoulish unreality. Dix made two trips to the Engadine valley in
1935 and 1938, returning with silver-point drawings and – after a fairly
long interlude – a large number of water-colours. These studies subsequently provided the basis for no fewer than ten paintings, including
*Valley in Engadine, Valley near Pontresina, Glacier in the Engadine, At the
July Pass.* In a letter written in 1943 Dix describes his feelings about this
landscape: "You should really go up a glacier once or as far as a glacier, it
is truly a great, primaeval experience, and anyone who can look at these
forces and not believe in fate or in God is beyond help. If the earth's axis
shifted slightly for 1,000 years, country that is now in full bloom would
look like this world of ice." Words full of foreboding.

Most of the landscapes of the years up to 1942 show the country in
various weather conditions at different times of year. The view is from
afar, usually across spring fields or corn fields. Otherwise, Dix painted
Lake Constance – again and again, always in a different atmosphere, *In
Stormy Weather*, for example, or in the snow, at the height of summer, or
in the fog. Dix relished all the facets and nuances of landscape painting
with an almost alarming assiduity. Even now the stress on subject matter

and the body, characteristic of his paintings during the 1920s, is unmistakable. An element of theatrical arrangement can always be sensed – a certain reflective distance towards what is perceived. During those years of imposed stagnation Dix even took on decorative tasks. He was asked by F. Niescher, a collector, to decorate the latter's garden pavilion in Chemnitz. Dix chose the theme of Orpheus and the animals. Unfortunately, the summerhouse was completely destroyed by bombs in 1945, but the designs and sketches which have been preserved make it possible to reconstruct the original state of the painting, produced as a secco work in casein, with a fair degree of precision. Orpheus is sitting, surrounded by a backdrop of trees, in an antique cloak before an expansive landscape and is speaking, like a second St. Francis, to the animals gathered around him.

Randegg in the Snow with Ravens, 1935
Randegg im Schnee mit Raben
Mixed media on pressed fibreboard,
80 x 70 cm
Löffler 1935/13
Vaduz, Otto Dix Foundation

Ice Breaking up with Rainbow near Steckborn, painted in 1940, is also a theatrical rendition of Nature, portrayed as the stage of sinister, dramatic events. The blue-green-black feel of the storm on the lake, with ice floes cracking and bursting upwards, is lightened by the rainbow which rises vertically directly above the village in an apocalyptic, visionary manner. Although a natural phenomenon, there is something artistic and contrived about this portrayal with its allegorical components, transcending as it does its subject matter. Light and darkness, the forces of preservation and destruction, are in battle with each other.

During the 1940s Nature in Dix's works increasingly becomes the metaphor of a personal crisis coming to a head. A close-range frontal perspective gradually becomes predominant in his work, focussing on segments of forests, thickets, pieces of wood, broken-off branches, as in the painting *Smashed Tree*. In 1940, well-balanced, harmonious landscape scenes such as *View of the Hegau* (p. 189) stand side by side with scenes done in much narrower perspective. Dix now preferred to observe the forest, trees, entangled heaps of branches, scrubs and under-

"Flanders", 1936
"Flandern"
(after Henri Barbusse's *Le Feu*)
Mixed media on canvas, 200 x 250 cm
Löffler 1936/1
Berlin, Nationalgalerie SMPK

brush, as in the painting *The Protection Forest*, 1942. This is landscape as a landscape of the soul, chaotic, disrupted. This is underscored by the titles of pictures, such as *Dark Day in Sottum*, *Evening Storm*, *Clouds in the Sudeten Mountains* or *Smashed Tree*. Precipitous rock walls (in the Sudeten Mountains), steep cliffs and an ominously low-hanging sky in the years 1940/41 contribute to the impression of conditions which are becoming ever more threatening, not only in the weather and in Nature, but also in society as a whole and in Dix's personal situation.

During these years Dix had an opportunity to get to know the Bohemian mountains south of the Saxon border, and the Sudeten Mountains. Invited by the Silesian industrialist Hasselbach, a relative of the Bienert family who were friends of the Dixes, the painter was able to make repeated visits to the Sudeten Mountains during 1941 and 1942. The paintings *Aupa Valley* and *Small Pond and Large Valley* document those trips. While on one of these visits, Dix was commissioned to paint a series of pictures with peopled scenes of the Sudeten Mountains. This presented the painter with a new and welcome challenge, for all of his landscapes had until then been devoid of human figures.

View of the Hegau, 1940
Blick in den Hegau
Mixed media on wood, 64.5 x 84.5 cm
Löffler 1940/9
Private collection

Dix completed this work with the virtuosity and accomplishment of a master, but without the passion of earlier works. Essentially, Dix had inwardly withdrawn during those years. He seemed instead to be looking for a concept of space and time that could be juxtaposed to the present, and the calming, general validity of which appeared to be guaranteed by the regular change of the seasons. During this time, for Dix landscape was a space for meditation; it functioned as a preserve of personal (religious) needs that could no longer be satisfied in domains customarily accorded them.

The individual had become humble, ready to succumb to Nature as the greater power and at the same time to acknowledge the transitory and futile nature of all intentional action. Dix described the various states of Nature produced by the change of day and of the seasons, states which occur largely independently of human intervention, unburdened by the categories of evaluation, classification or a will to power. These descriptions are accompanied by a certain melancholy, while at the same time a rebellion begins to emerge in the face of the futile effort to find peace within these magical spaces removed from time. It is impossible to find tranquility, for the subject is individual and can never escape its subjectivity, can never merge with the "non-subjectivity" of Nature – a yearning which was a fundamental element defining Romanticism.

Dix summarized the period of the 1930s and 1940s in his laconic way: "I painted scores of landscapes during the Nazi period. That was all there was. So I went out into the countryside and drew trees, a few trees and things like that. I was exiled to the countryside. At first it was new to me. Now I've seen it so often that I don't even notice it anymore. It doesn't really interest me very much. Whereas people, people do." There is a certain undertone of resignation in such words. Dix was never able to shake it off – which comes as no surprise. The period of National Socialism left a wound that never completely healed. The fact that this period was one of crisis is also reflected in a decade's work lacking Dix's typical sense of humour. During those years Dix's *joie de vivre* had seized up.

The painter had the good fortune not to be bothered much by the Nazis. There was only one occasion when things looked critical: he was suspected of being an accomplice to the attempt on Hitler's life in the Munich Bürgerbräukeller on 8 November, 1939. Dix and his friend Friedrich Bienert were arrested in Dresden. Until 1943 Dix travelled regularly to Dresden because of his work. The two were held and interrogated for two weeks in the Gestapo prison before finally being released. Comrades at the front described his bravery during the First World War and so came to Dix's rescue. The fact that the Gestapo even thought of arresting Dix and Bienert resulted from the two men's previous activities in Dresden. Between 1927 and 1933 Dix was a member of the Stag Club founded by Bienert, an influential industrialist. Participants in this discussion and social circle included Count Nikolaus von Seebach, the director of the Dresden city opera, and the poet Paul Adler. Bienert and Dix were on the Gestapo's list of "Leading Men of the Systems Period", which also included the Stag Club.

PAGE 192:
Lot and His Daughters, 1939
Lot und seine Töchter
Mixed media on pressed fibreboard,
195 x 130 cm
Löffler 1939/1
Aachen, Städtisches Suermondt-Ludwig-Museum (on loan)

PAGE 193:
St. Christopher IV, 1939
Der hl. Christopherus IV
Mixed media on plywood, 160 x 130 cm
Löffler 1939/1
Gera, Kunstgalerie Gera

In February, 1945, Dix had to endure tribulations for the last time: at the last minute, he was conscripted into the *Volkssturm*. After the fighting ended a month later, he became a prisoner-of-war in Colmar. A French officer recognized him as the famous painter, Otto Dix. He was subsequently found a place in the camp's artists' colony in the automobile painting workshop, where he was able to paint. This brought forth works, usually commissioned, such as the *Madonna in front of the Barbed Wire*, a triptych he completed for the prison camp chapel.

Self-portrait with Palette in front of Red Curtain, 1942
Selbstbildnis mit Palette vor rotem Vorhang
Mixed media on wood, 100 x 80 cm
Löffler 1942/4
Stuttgart, Galerie der Stadt Stuttgart (on loan)

Self-portrait as a Prisoner of War, 1947
Selbstbildnis als Kriegsgefangener
Oil on pressed fibreboard, 60 x 54 cm
Löffler 1947/2
Stuttgart, Galerie der Stadt Stuttgart (on loan)

The Later Years

Like other people, Dix had problems returning to normal life after the war. In order to provide for himself and his family, he took on portrait work, usually in pastels, painting the women and children of members of the French occupation forces. Small water-colour paintings and landscapes were exchanged for food and cigarettes. Much of this "bread-and-butter" art has recently resurfaced. His art now underwent an important transformation: he broke with the elaborate technique of applying several transparent coats of paint. As early as 1944, Dix had again begun to produce landscape paintings done in the more spontaneous *alla prima* technique he had used in the early years prior to 1919. The brush marks, the painterly action, again become important. As in the early landscapes, line determines the content of the works. There can be no doubt that Dix felt his return to *alla-prima* painting to be liberating: "The change in technique (this is not the right word at all, it is actually a new way of seeing that has taken hold of me) is bringing forth many strange blossoms: what can at any rate be said is that I. The painting has become more spontaneous, the lousy care one had to take with the constant application of the various coats of translucent paint is gone. II. Everything is becoming COARSER, thank God, I have been painting much too much with the tip of the brush over the last twenty years and am now coming back to the period of my first war picture, in other words, I have been unleashed. III. Formal spatiality is giving way to a spatiality of colour and the colours are beginning to form 'sounds'. IV. I throw all ideal compositions, the golden section and all that Renaissance stuff overboard at will and paint unleashed. And as I write this, I realise that none of this can be explained, the paintings have more formal stature despite the freedom from convention."

The optimism of these sentences points to the high expectations which Dix also associated with the freedom he had regained at long last for his artistic development. Only shortly before, at Easter 1946, he had sounded rather downcast in a letter to his son Ursus: "My dear Ursus, I have now been back at home for almost ten weeks, but haven't worked very much. But next week I want to begin painting a few pictures. This morning I pasted canvas on boards with Jan (his second, younger son). I was, after all, somewhat shaken from the long time in captivity. Although I was able

The Temptation of St. Anthony II, 1940
Die Versuchung des hl. Antonius II
Mixed media on pressed fibre-board,
40 x 32 cm
Löffler 1940/1
Oehningen, private collection

to paint in Colmar, everything was forced. On top of it, the studio is full of older, larger panels, and really you feel a sense of obligation to earlier works." It was not long, however, before the old Dixian fighting spirit asserted itself: "I work a lot and you will see some things you'll find interesting when you come back", he wrote to his youngest son in August, 1946.

As had already been the case following the First World War, Dix now found a release from the trauma of the immediate past through his paintings. In particular, the *joie de vivre* around him, the colourful Alemannian carnival antics in southwest Germany, the masked processions and dances seemed to have quite an effect on him. Subjects such as *Masks in Ruins* (p. 197), *Carnival in Ruins*, *Pile of Fools*, *Costume Ball* or *Mask with Quinces* fascinated and inspired Dix, testifying to a hopeful process of restoration.

The continuity with which Dix carried out variations on a few themes during the time up to his death in 1969 is not based on some stylistic experiment undertaken by the artist; rather, it is the result of necessary stabilization. At times, however, one cannot help but have the impression that Dix's creative development had at least in part stagnated. This was true of most of the artists who had been active in the 1920s. Grosz, Wollheim, Schlichter – none of them ever regained the vitality of their previous works.

Still another factor may have had a bearing on Dix's late works, at times at least: Dix was more or less ignored by the art business following the Second World War and during the early 1950s. Abstraction set the tone of the day. Tachism and *art informel* set the European and German scene. The new Expressionism, such as Jackson Pollock's American work or that of Franz Kline, was abstract. On the other hand, Dix found some small measure of comfort in the recognition his early works gradually began to receive in the mid-1950s. Yet the continuing lack of understanding for his late works cut him to the quick. A few years before his death he said: "It's easier, after all, to be fitted neatly under a heading like that, and remain true to it without making any waves. The art dealers and probably the historians, too, would like it if one kept swimming in the same stream. It's the kiss of death for them if all of a sudden something different starts up, it's really deadly. – In those days (the 1920s) people insulted me for painting that way. And now? Now they're running after the pictures and paying fortunes for them, fortunes."

Nevertheless, between 1946 and 1949 Dix was astonishingly creative. Approximately 150 paintings were produced in the space of these four years. The number sank to around twenty per year in subsequent years, and then – with the exception of the prolific year of 1955 – dropped off even further. Dix was just as unable to deal with the lack of success as anyone else. The depressing experiences in this regard began as early as 1947, when Dix held an exhibition in his home-town of Gera. The following letter by him was reprinted in the catalogue, and it is revealing of how his view of art, a view which in essence he remained true to from the very beginning: "I already wrote you not too long ago that I am not willing to

put my pictures up for discussion. In Germany we have heard the voice of the people on artistic matters for years now, and so little about the true nature of art has emerged from it. Discussions are aimed at letting every philistine and every 'blind man' make his little wishes known. Everybody thinks they know what art *should* be. But very few of them have the sense that is necessary to experience painting, that is, the sense of sight, that

Masks in Ruins, 1946
Masken in Trümmern
Tempera and oil on wood, 120 x 81 cm
Löffler 1946/11
Vaduz, Otto Dix Foundation

sees colours and forms as living reality in the picture. What is important in the picture is not the objects, but the personal message of the artist. In other words, not the *what*, but the *how*. The first thing that an artist demands from the observer is not loud discussion but modest silence. For there is little in an artwork that can be explained, its substance can't be explained, it can only be contemplated."

It was precisely this insistence on contemplation that formed the basis of Dix's categorical rejection of abstract painting. He did not like intellectualism and claims to absolute validity. In 1958 he voiced his opinion in the following terms (and what he has to say here was valid for the entire period after 1945): "We don't have to discuss my pictures – we can see them. – I base everything on the visible. – I don't want to invent new themes and don't want to arrange themes as Salvador Dalí does, for example. What I most like to do is see the fundamental themes of humankind with my own eyes in a new light... Art defies any and all definition. You are an empty vessel for a long time, then something grows that you don't want, something creeps into it that you actually cannot do. The God of Chance creates in us. I am emphatically opposed to dogma in art. The fact of the matter is that art is not a science and is not subject to any tangible law. The painter has to work with the living phenomenon. It is his task to form the world and show people that they cannot live on bread alone. I am against the painters without objects, who paint with a broom, shoot at the canvas with a crossbone and let coloured gravy run down it. The successes are pictures that one could continue *ad infinitum*. There is precious little inventiveness in it, and it is suited at most for wallpaper and ladies' skirts. I have been called conservative. And maybe I am; at any rate, I am primitive and plebian, I need the tie to the sensual world, the courage to depict ugliness, undiluted life. The chapel in Vence by Henri Matisse – that is decorative painting without any meat to it. But Picasso is a great master with enormous powers of imagination, a Proteus who knows how to give shape to the problems of his time. No, it is not the task of artists to correct and convert. They are much too small for that. But they must give their testimony. Grace is not at the command of human beings, but it is grace that counts. Endeavours in art require a lot of patience. For a long time I was a nobody, but suddenly one can become something."

These are the words of a man who has grown wise with age, and they also convey strength of character, the greatness of an independent thinker and prominent figure. Dix's art had to remain attached to content, in other words, had to remain "object-ive", because he was totally and completely a man of perception. Nevertheless, there were unmistakable tendencies toward stronger formalization in Dix's late works.

Self-portrait as a Prisoner of War (p. 194), completed in 1947, manifests Dix's new working principles especially vividly. The abruptly halted brushstrokes, shredded and porous-looking colour surfaces, and the adjacent and intersecting lines and surfaces of colour that mark Dix's face evoke the recent period of crisis; he dispenses with the surface-fixated glaze Layering.

Dix's view of the Second World War, in contrast to his youthful euphoria prior to the First World War, was distinctly negative. In 1943 he wrote: "I hope the shit will soon be over ... I hope with all my heart that the puke will be over before it's Dresden's turn, which means most to me as a city, it's my second home. If it doesn't end soon, there would be no reason for the enemy to spare Dresden."

Dix's aesthetic remained constant. As he told the *Tägliche Rundschau*

Self-portrait in Fur Cap against Winter Landscape, 1947
Selbstbildnis mit Pelzkappe vor Winterlandschaft
Oil on wood, 79.5 x 58.5 cm
Löffler 1947/3
France, private collection

Great Crucifixion, 1948
Große Kreuzigung
Oil on canvas, 210 x 150 cm
Löffler 1948/7
Darmstadt, Hessisches Landesmuseum

in Berlin in 1949, he wanted "to get very close to our present, to be strikingly close to the times, without subjecting myself to an artistic dogma." Greater formalization was never allowed to block the emotional access to the picture: "Colour and form alone are no substitute for a lack of experience and deep emotional involvement. I try to create meaning for our time with my pictures. Painting is an attempt to create order, for me art is holding something at bay."

In other words, in his late works Dix consciously linked up to his early period. In the themes that he took up again in his late works (self-portraits, portraits, landscapes and especially religion) he was continuing the work of his early career. This happened in a more relaxed, balanced, and also more sober manner than in his younger years, when his work was laden with the heady intensity of temperament. Dix no longer had to prove his skill, his masterly craftsmanship, his technical virtuosity. He saw no reason to document the current events of the day, and consequently devoted himself (in his art as well) to those who were closest to his heart: his grandchildren, whom he deeply loved and repeatedly painted and made lithographs of; the villagers, whom he made portraits of; and the surrounding countryside, to which he was attached.

After 1944 Dix's landscapes also changed. Gradually, Dix's nature ceases to be charged, metaphorically, with calamitous foreboding. The brush strokes again begin to play a greater role, the line again becomes more significant, as in the earlier years prior to 1919. In the late pictures, as in the early works, Dix also allows formal principles to function to a greater degree as elements of a message; for example, the independent dynamics of the brushwork or the rhythm of the lines are now given more of a role. Nevertheless (and this fact is so crucial that it bears repeating here): although there is a certain shift in the focus of the relation between content and form, neither component is ever sacrificed for the sake of the other. Dix insists on content.

At the beginning of 1955 Dix's beloved daughter Nelly, herself highly gifted artistically, suddenly died. This was an irreplaceable loss for Dix; Nelly's daughter Bettina, born in 1951 and dearly loved by her grandfather, was able to help him get over it somewhat. Dix and his wife eventually adopted the little girl. This, too, was a sign of their affection for their daughter Nelly.

Dix wrote the following in a letter to Dresden about Nelly's death: "We are left speechless in the face of her death. I would gladly have gone in her place, for my life, too, seemed to have ended somehow. It is good that I still have to provide for the living." The year 1955 was so productive because Dix sought to assuage his grief through creative activity.

The portraits, which included numerous self-portraits, formed a extensive set of works in the later years. One of the most important self-portraits that emerged in the Forties is the 1947 *Self-portrait in Fur Cap against Winter Landscape* (p. 199). In it, Dix appeared especially fascinated by the possibilities of conveying the qualities of fabric. The jacket and cap, each of which has the effect of a decorative pattern, dominate

the face and hand(s); an amazing reversal compared with the portraits of the 1920s. The *Portrait of the Painter Erich Heckel* (p. 201), painted the same year, uses colour and spatial qualities to integrate the artist's face into the total organization of the picture. Dix applied the principle of assigning equal value to figure and background down to the very last of his portraits. In subsequent years he was commissioned to do several portraits, but none of them ever matched the brilliance of his early portrait work. Most of these works are conventional, flattering portrayals

Portrait of the Painter Erich Heckel, 1947
Bildnis des Malers Erich Heckel
Oil on pressed chipboard, 40 x 31 cm
Löffler 1947/6
Private collection

The Mocking of Christ, 1948
Verspottung Christi
Pastel, 31.3 x 37 cm
Albstadt, Walther Groz Foundation,
Städtische Galerie Albstadt

that Dix seems to have knocked off without much inspiration. That was routine work and offered no challenge.

It was not until the 1960s that Dix again produced outstanding portraits, such as that of Käthe König (1963) and especially that of Susu (1964), Dr. Fritz Perls (p. 206) and Max Frisch (1967). In Fritz Perl's portrait Dix was again able, as he had been in the 1920s, to convey the aura of a person purely through detail and by concentrating on the unusual in his subject.

Perhaps the most significant and, in any event, most interesting complex of Dix's late works are those devoted to religious themes. Dix had an outstanding knowledge of the Bible and he never tired of sounding the praises of Holy Scripture. In a conversation with friends in December 1963 he commented on it in virtually effusive terms: "You have to read every single word. For the Bible is a wonderful history book. There is a great truth in all of it. Most people don't read the Bible. But reading the Bible, reading the Bible as it is, in all of its realism, including the Old Testament: it's quite a book. Quite a book, you might even say it is the book of books, the Bible is, also in terms of cultural history, social history, a magnificent book in every respect, simply magnificent!" When Maria Wetzel asked him in an interview in 1965 whether his "roots were not in religion after all", Dix replied: "In history. (Smiles) In the history of the Bible. There are such wonderful images in it; when I was a boy, when we had 'Bible Study', I always imagined to myself exactly where that might have happened in my homeland. I knew the exact place – you went into the forest and there were a few hills – and that is where Jacob lay, in other words, I saw Jacob's ladder right there in front of me. And I was familiar with the place where Joseph was thrown into the well by his brothers. A half-hour away from our village the banks of the Old Elster were full of sedge, full of reeds. That was where the king's daughter fished Moses out of the water in his basket…(Laughs.) The images were what interested me – the other part, the moral part, didn't interest me at all."

Although Dix had left the Protestant faith, he nevertheless maintained the best relations to the institutions of both denominations. He did not feel like a Christian in the explicit sense of the term. "Christ said: 'Follow me', something I cannot and do not wish to do". And in 1963 he said: "I don't know whether I believe in God or whether I'm an atheist or whatever. I don't know a thing. Not a thing… At any rate, I am not a believer of dogma, but instead very sceptical. Sceptical."

Be that as it may, after 1943 he produced numerous paintings, pastels and lithographs with religious themes. The central focus was on the Passion of Christ, with its recognition of redemption from the reality of suffering by unconditional acceptance. What apparently fascinated Dix above all else was the physical aspect of this suffering and death: "Then he's hung up there, he's put up there on the cross looking like a ballet dancer, you know, pretty and polished and pretty, wonderfully anointed and pretty, you know. And then when you read a detailed description of a crucifixion, well, that's something that is so horrible, awful. How the limbs swell up, you know. How the person can't breathe. How the face

Ecce Homo III, 1949
Oil on pressed chipboard, 81 x 60 cm
Löffler 1949/2
Munich, Gunzenhauser Gallery

changes colour. How he dies a horrible, utterly horrible death. Then he's portrayed up there as a wonderfully beautiful youth. Well, that's all fraud. All fraud. Instead of seeing everything exactly as it is, completely realistically, to make the miracle of resurrection infinitely greater. No, they had to go and hang him up there like a pretty boy. That is what I really reject, I suspect. That is – the church wants it that way – but I reject it. I reject it. I will always reject it. I see it totally realistically and want to reject it. And if he was a great man, then he was in the most horrible pain. He was tortured so much. He collapsed and fell unconscious, having to carry the cross like he did. And all of that, how is all of that portrayed, how did the preachers portray it? They portrayed it as if it were virtually theatre. It was worse than the way it was in the war. He was completely alone. Nobody helped him. Nobody was with him. Everyone abandoned him. A

Woman and Child, 1958
Frau und Kind
Oil on canvas, 102 x 83 cm
Löffler 1958/3
Jörg and Heidrun Mussotter Collection

magnificent description of the human being who is alone. Magnificent! Of the brilliant human being who is alone. And who understands that. Well, just look at the little people. Then they went and made a big thing out of it, and that is what is revolting. Really revolting. Putrid. Well, I'm against it. I'm completely against it."

The insistence on the humanity and corporeality of Christ is further proof of Dix's much-discussed "realism". This, too, is a factor in his intensive involvement with Biblical themes: "The Christian element is not an idea born in the studio. My life gave me enough occasion to live through the passion of my brother, indeed with my own body."

In 1946 Dix created several paintings and drawings of crucifixions. Dix painted *Gethsemane, Ecce Homo I and II*, a *Flagellation of Christ*, the *Mocking of Christ, Veronica's Veil* and finally one entitled *Great Crucifixion* (p. 200) in close succession and with a similar expressive density. The last painting is extremely powerful.

In 1948 Dix completed a series of extraordinary pastels with religious themes. He used a remarkable technique of multiply re-drawing and painting over linear structures. What emerged was a mesh of linear structures with spatial depth which, because of the transparency of layerings that the observer can reconstruct in his mind, provides a vivid transcription of pain and vulnerability. Above all, the pastel *Gethsemane* demonstrates the creation of figures from layers of lines. Owing to their effects of depth and transparency, these pastels are related in terms of their technique to the paintings employing the transparent coating technique. The pastel *Mocking of Christ* (p. 202) also demonstrates this complexity of content, achieved with formal media.

In 1959 and 1960 Dix was commissioned to do three major works. He made three large stained-glass windows on the subjects of "St. Peter the Fisherman", "Tend to My Flock" and "St. Peter's Denial" for St. Peter's (protestant) church at Kattenhorn am Untersee. The second work commissioned was a fresco to complete the rear wall in the auditorium of the Singen town hall. In 1960 Dix finished it as a "synthesis of what I have tried to do in my work my whole life long", as a variation on the basic theme of Eros and Thanatos. The mural with the title *War and Peace* was five metres high and twelve metres long, of truly monumental proportions. In 1960 Dix also painted the smaller auditorium in the registrar's office in Singen, likewise located in the town hall. Again he painted frescos on three walls arounds the hall, in this case scenes in paradise, including the meeting of Adam and Eve with the animals.

On the whole Dix never achieved the success he deserved after 1945. He exhibited, but usually in smaller regional group exhibitions. Although he had gained fame in the glorious Twenties, he was now virtually ignored, something he could not understand. Both Germanies, the Federal Republic of Germany as well as the German Democratic Republic, held mistaken views of his work: the Federal Republic rejected all objective art of any kind, and as for the GDR, Dix's work did not sufficiently lend itself to the framework of Marxist ideology. He was neither given a professorship in Dresden, nor were his entries for the Third German Art

Winter at the Lake, 1951
Winter am See
Oil on pressed chipboard, 60 x 81 cm
Löffler 1951/17
Vaduz, Otto Dix Foundation

Exhibition in 1953 accepted. It was not until 1956, when he was made a corresponding member of the German Academy in Berlin, and subsequently exhibited, that he was compensated, at least to a small extent.

Dix was also strangely affected by the enormous rise in the prices paid for his early works, whereas no one would buy those produced after 1946. Jean Cassou had initiated the run on Dix's works from the *Neue Sachlichkeit* period by buying the portrait *Sylvia von Harden* (1926) for the Musée National d'Art Moderne in Paris. Still, the Federal Republic hesitated for a long time before finally deciding to accord the painter the recognition he deserved – by purchasing his works. The Stuttgart municipal gallery was one of the first to buy a large number of works by Dix, beginning in the late 1960s. On the other hand, Dix was awarded prizes and distinctions at regular intervals; one suspects that someone had a guilty conscience. In 1959 he was awarded the Cornelius Prize of the City of Düsseldorf as well as the Federal Cross of Merit, First Class.

During the last ten years of his life Dix was veritably showered with awards. Gradually the recognition his work deserved started to grow nationally and to some extent also internationally. At least Dix lived to see the beginnings of this acclaim. He was named an honorary member or citizen in several cities – in 1964 by the Carl Gustav Carus Medical

Academy in Dresden, in 1966 by the cities of Gera and Singen, in 1968 by the State Academy of Fine Arts in Karlsruhe. In 1964 he became an honorary member of the Accademia delle arti del disegno in Florence (Italy had also discovered Dix long before Germany) and in 1966 of the Federation for the Fine Arts in the GDR. He was awarded prizes: in 1966 the Lichtwark Prize of the City of Hamburg, in 1967 the Hans Thoma Prize of the State of Baden-Württemberg, the Lindner Prize of the City of Wuppertal and the Medaglia d'oro del Monte dei Paschi di Siena, and finally, in 1968, the Rembrandt Prize of the Goethe Foundation in Salzburg.

That was all very well. Yet must Dix not have felt he had failed in his late works? If he had not believed in himself, at this late juncture as well, his capacity for artistic creation might have been completely shaken. This way, however, he knew that the distorted perspectives of history have a way of setting themselves straight in the course of time.

In 1957 and 1958 Dix travelled to southern France. In 1962 he was a guest in the Villa Massimo in Rome. Each time he gathered new, fruitful ideas for his work. In the last ten years of his life, city scenes and portrayals of historical buildings took the place of landscapes. In 1955 Dix painted the *Court Church in Dresden*, as he saw it from the Brühl terrace. In 1957, after his first stay in France, he produced the *Church of Arnas*, and in 1958 a view of the town of St. Cyr au Mont d'Or. The two small sheets *Steps of Olevano* and *Olevano* (both completed in 1962) are reminiscent of his stay at the Villa Massimo. The last painting from this "architectural series" was the *Salzburg Cityscape* (1969), with the collegiate church in the middle. The portraits Dix drew during the last year of his life represented a late flowering of his work. Rome, where Dix stayed in 1962, visibly inspired his work. In paintings such as *La Contessa* and *Roman Woman in Blue Dress*, both dating from 1962, and later in the portraits *Fashionable Lady* (1965) and *Eleonore Frey* one senses the impact on them of Dix's late and certainly animated second encounter with that inimitable culture of style and decadence which had also been a distinguishing feature of the Weimar Republic. Actually, it was only now that he had returned to his "old home" – late, too late.

In November 1967 Dix suffered his first stroke. It left his left hand temporarily paralysed. Nevertheless, Dix continued to work, and documented his state of increasing decline in self-portraits such as *Self-portrait after Stroke*, the *Self-portrait with Hand and Drawing Pen*, the *Small Self-portrait* and, most heart-rending, the *Self-portrait as Skull* (p. 248), a lithograph completed in 1968, which he dedicated to Cassou. A further lithograph (created in two versions in 1968) entitled *Self-portrait with Marcella* bears the unmistakable signs of Dix taking his leave from the world. On 19 July, 1969 he suffered a second stroke. His last painting was standing on the easel, a bouquet of flowers. Dix never recovered. He died on 25 July in the hospital in Singen.

The fact is that Dix is indisputably and internationally recognized today as the leading artist of the style known as *Neue Sachlichkeit*. However, it is also a fact that even today, nearly seventy years later, he is to

Portrait of Dr. Fritz Perls (Founder of Gestalt Therapy), 1966
Bildnis Dr. Fritz Perls (Begründer der Gestalttherapie)
Oil and tempera on wood, 93 x 75 cm
Löffler 1966/1
Vaduz, Otto Dix Foundation

La Contessa, 1962
Oil on pressed chipboard, 81 x 54.2 cm
Löffler 1962/3
Essen, private collection

Pregnant Woman, 1966
Schwangere
Oil on pressed chipboard, 107 x 75 cm
Löffler 1966/2
Chemnitz, Städtische Kunstsammlungen

PAGE 210:
*Otto Dix in his studio in
Hemmenhofen,* 1964
Photo: Stefan Moses

some extent misinterpreted owing to the same prejudices that he came up against at the beginning of his work.

Dix is a brilliant artist. He does not deal only in social criticism and accusation, nor exclusively in stylistic purism or an art of quotation. He is more of a chronic adventurer and a painting chronicler of his time. He was not concerned with approximating an absolute ideal; ultimately, he was a sceptical spirit through and through. He was surely more concerned with making vital processes visible. And he was concerned – to a greater extent than perhaps initially meets the eye – with portraying beauty, which to him meant the variety of the world, and the *joie de vivre* this entailed. Like the old masters of the 16th century whom he took as an example, in his "best" years – the 1920s – Dix was a constructor of his subject matter who arranged the material of his perceptions in line with strictly tectonic principles. Dix staged the world as a play, as a grotesque farce. But the form he chose to do so was based on the classical canon of beauty. Dix lived his life and served art, for he adhered to the age-old rule that the American painter Ad Reinhardt put in a nutshell: "Life is life, and art is art."

The editor, author and publisher thank the museums, galleries, private collectors, archives and photographers who have helped us in preparing this book. Our special thanks go to the Otto Dix Foundation, Vaduz, and its president, Rainer Pfefferkorn, for its energetic cooperation in this project, and to the Otto Dix Archives (Northild Eger). We also owe thanks to Alfred Hagenlocher of the City Gallery in Albstadt; Serge Sabarsky, New York, who helped us out with many an exhibit, even under the most severe time pressure; and Suse Pfäffle, Leinfelden, who provided us with useful information. To all, our sincere thanks. – The present interpretation and evaluation of Dix's work by Eva Karcher, who locates the artist in the great cosmic complex of Eros and Thanatos, of waxing and waning, and who believes the roots of his art lay in the philosophy of Friedrich Nietzsche (whom Dix had already read as a young man), is surely one possible interpretation, and one which is accepted by many today. At the same time, however, one should not forget that the pictures by Dix, especially his collages and realistic paintings of the early 1920s or the magnificent series of etchings on *War*, are also a form of political protest and an accusation levelled against the lunacy of war and social injustice, albeit not in the sense of a merely tendentious, poster-like protest, as in some of his contemporaries' works. Precisely for that reason, however, they transcend the setting from which they emerged and still endure as timeless memorials of a moralist who wanted a better world.　　　I.F.W.

Otto Dix 1891 – 1969:
A Chronology

1891 Wilhelm Heinrich Otto Dix is born on 2 December in Untermhaus near Gera in Thuringia, the eldest son of potter Ernst Franz Dix (1862-1942) and his wife Pauline Louise, née Amann (1864-1953) (cf. *Portrait of the Artist's Parents I-II*, pp. 84-85).

1899-1905 Attends school in Untermhaus. His art teacher is Ernst Schunke.

1905-1909 After his apprenticeship as a painter and decorator in Gera he works as a painter in Pössneck. In 1908 he produces his first oil paintings, pastels and chalk drawings.

1909-1914 Enrolls in the Dresden Commercial Art College in autumn, 1909, and attends classes there until 1914. His teachers are Richard Mebert, Paul Naumann and Richard Guhr. Lives on Elisenstrasse. Produces his first landscape paintings in 1909, with motifs of Dresden and Thuringia, such as *Lennéstrasse in Dresden* or *Railway Embankment*. Visits the Van Gogh exhibition in Dresden in 1912. Self-portraits (pp. 6, 11 and 16). Study trips to Austria and Italy in 1913; influence of Futurism (cf. p. 20). Reads Friedrich Nietzsche.

1914-1918 Enlists voluntarily for mili-

Dix as a young man

tary service in field artillery in Dresden. Is trained as machine-gunner in Bautzen in 1915. As of autumn, 1915, volunteers for service as machine-gunner and platoon leader on the front line in Flanders, Poland, Russia and again in France. In autumn, 1918, training as pilot in Silesia. During the war, in 1916, first exhibition of war drawings in Galerie Arnold, Dresden. Numerous gouaches and self-portraits in

oil reflect his wartime experiences (pp. 19, 20, 26 to 39). Returns to Gera at the end of 1918.

1919 Goes to Dresden in January and stays there until 1922. Master pupil of Max Feldbauer and Otto Gussmann at the art academy. Rents studio at Antonsplatz 1. Founding of the Dresden Secession Group 1919; takes part in its first exhibition in Galerie Emil Richter. Meets Hugo Erfurth and Theodor Däubler, of whom he later does portraits (pp. 128 and 150). Expressionist phase (pp. 40 to 47).

1920 Meets George Grosz. Participates with Grosz, Schlichter and Heartfield in the first DADA Fair at Galerie Burchard in Berlin. Period influenced by Dada, collages, first realistic pictures (pp. 44, 49 to 51, 58 to 69). Participates in the "German Expressionists" exhibition in Darmstadt and in that held by the *Novembergruppe* in Berlin.

1921 Travels to Cologne and Düsseldorf. Meets Dr. Hans Koch (p. 83) and his wife Martha. Joins Grosz and Schlichter in opposing the Berlin *Novembergruppe*. Publishes portfolio with wood-cuttings and etchings in Dresden. *Portrait of the Artist's Parents I* (p. 84), *Farewell to Hamburg* (p. 73), *Two Children* (p. 56).

Otto Dix, prior to 1914

Otto Dix (third from left) with parents, brother and sisters in Gera. Around 1916/17.

211

1916, with the field artillery in France. Dix can be seen in the middle of the front row.

With café-owner and art dealer Johanna Ey, known as "Mother Ey" (cf. portrait on p. 126), in Düsseldorf, 1924/25.

1922 Takes part in the exhibition held by the "*Kugel*" in Magdeburg. Galerie Nierendorf in Berlin is his sole representative. Moves to Düsseldorf, where he remains until 1925, and studies as master pupil under Heinrich Nauen and Wilhelm Herberholz at the academy. Associates with the circle around café- and gallery-owner Johanna Ey ("Mother Ey"), of whom he does a portrait (p. 126) in 1924, and the "Young Rhineland" group. Lawsuit over *Girl at the Mirror* (pp. 74 and 76). Self-portrait *To Beauty* (p. 81) and a series of watercolours from the harbour, prostitution and circus milieu (pp. 72, 89, 96 to 100, 111).

1923 Marries Martha, Hans Koch's ex-wife, in February. Birth of their daughter Nelly on 14 June. Participation in the spring exhibition of the Berlin Art Academy and in "German Art 1923" in Darmstadt. The lawsuit ends with Dix being acquitted of charges. *Salon I* (cf. p.

79) is confiscated in Darmstadt. Completes *Trenches* (destroyed), which the Cologne Museum purchases. Trip to Italy as far as Palermo in winter 1923/24. *Self-portrait with Naked Model* (p. 92), *Unequal Lovers* (p. 103), portraits (pp. 114, 116, 120).

1924 Joins the Berlin Secession. *The Trench* is exhibited in the Berlin academy. Participates in the "First All-German Art Exhibition" in Moscow, Saratov and Leningrad. The portfolio sheafs *War* with fifty etchings is published by Nierendorf in Berlin (pp. 118ff.). Employs techniques of old masters in oil paintings (tempera, layering, etc.). *Still Life in the Studio* (p. 117), *Portrait of the Art Dealer Johanna Ey* (p. 126).

1925 Settles in Berlin, where he lives until 1927. Travels to Paris. Is offered a teaching position at the Dorpat Art College. Takes part in collective exhibitions

in Berlin and Munich as well as in the Mannheim exhibition, "Neue Sachlichkeit". Meets art dealer Alfred Flechtheim, paints his portrait in 1926 (p. 141). Series of large, representative portraits until 1928, including the *Portrait of the Dancer Anita Berber* (p. 130).

1926 First relatively large solo exhibition at Neumann-Nierendorf's in Berlin and at the Galerie Thannhauser in Munich. Participation in collective exhibitions in Dresden, Berlin and Zwickau. *Three Women* (p. 134), numerous portraits (pp. 135-139).

1927 Moves back to Dresden, where he holds a chair, succeeding Gussmann, at the art academy until 1933. Lives at Bayreuther Strasse 32, but has a studio on the Brühl terrace. His first son is born on 11 March (p. 142). Takes part in the "European Contemporary Art" exhibition in Hamburg. Works on the *Big City* triptych,

Around 1923

Dix in front of an unfinished painting *Self-portrait with Martha as a Dance Couple* (whereabouts unknown), 1923.

In the garden at the Tusculum, around 1923

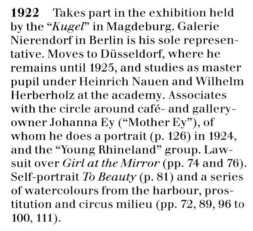

Around 1925

Martha Dix, 1925

Around 1925

which he completes in 1928 (pp. 152-156). *Street Fight* (p. 147), *Portrait of the Poet Theodor Däubler* (p. 150), *Match Vendor II* (p. 146).

1928 On 10 October, birth of his second son, Jan (cf. p. 165). Travels to Alsace. Participates in the 16th Biennial in Venice, the International Exhibition of Modern Art in the Brooklyn Museum, New York, and exhibits *Big City* in "Art and Technology" in the Folkwang Museum, Essen. *Portrait of Mrs. Martha Dix* (pp. 160).

1929 Trip to Danzig. Takes part in "Exposition des Peintres Graveurs Allemand Contemporain" at the Bibliotheque Nationale in Paris and "Exhibition of Modern German Prints" in Detroit. Begins with the *War* triptych, which he completes in 1932 (pp. 172ff.). Series of children's pictures (pp. 167 and 169).

1930 Travels to Paris and Vienna. Exhibits in the 17th Biennial in Venice and in "Socialist Art today" at the Stedelijk Museum, Amsterdam. *Melancholy* (p. 163), *Pregnant Woman* (p. 164).

1931 Becomes full member of the Prussian Academy of the Arts in Berlin. Takes part in "German Painting and Sculpture" at the Museum of Modern Art, New York, exhibition held by the German Federation of Artists in Essen, and for the last time in that of the *Novembergruppe*. *Pregnant Woman* (p. 166), *Self-portrait in Smock with Crystal Ball and Palette* (p. 168).

1932 Exhibits the *War* triptych at the Prussian Academy. Mural at the Museum of Hygiene in Dresden (chiselled off by the Nazis in 1934). *Trench Warfare* (p. 175), *Portrait of the Actor Heinrich George* (p. 177), *Vanitas* (p. 174).

1933 Loses his chair at the Dresden academy; his students are also reprimanded. In May, exclusion from the Prussian Academy of the Arts. Defamation of his works in the exhibition "Reflections of Decay" in Dresden and Stuttgart. Paints *The Seven Cardinal Sins* (p. 181).
Moves in the summer from Dresden to Schloss Randegg near Singen, where he remains until 1936. Begins landscape painting. *Portrait of the Painter Hans Theo Richter and His Wife Gisela* (p. 182).

1934 The Nazis ban the "degenerate" Dix from exhibiting his works. He visits his former Dresden home every year (until 1945). Takes part in "New German Painting" in Zurich. Paints *Triumph of Death* (p. 185).

1935 Travels to Switzerland and Venice.

Dix and Heinrich George (cf. portrait on p. 177), 1932.
Photo: Hugo Erfurth

The Dix Jazz Band: Otto Dix with daughter Nelly and his sons, Ursus and Jan

At an art exhibition in Dresden, October 1947

With daughter Nelly in St. Goar, 1929

Taking a break in the studio, Hemmenhofen, 1948

Last exhibition in Germany before the end of the war, at Nierendorf's in Berlin. Participates in "Modern Works of Art" at the Museum of Modern Art, New York, and in "International Exhibition of Paintings" at the Carnegie Institute, Pittsburgh. Landscapes such as *Jewish Cemetery in Randegg* (p. 186), *Randegg in the Snow with Ravens* (p. 187).

1936 Moves to Hemmenhofen near Radolfzell on Lake Constance, where he will live until his death. Paints *Flanders* (p. 188).

1937 Goebbels orders that 260 of Dix's works be confiscated by Ziegler. In July eight paintings, including *The War Cripples* (pp. 65/66), are shown at the "Degenerate Art" exhibition in Munich. He is accused of "sabotaging the spirit of defence". Hitler says: "It is too bad these people can't be locked up."

1938 Recuperates in a Swiss sanatorium after car accident.

1939 Arrested and temporarily detained in Dresden for alleged complicity in Munich attack on Hitler's life. More than 1,000 "degenerate art" works are burned on 20 March in Berlin, including Dix's works *The Trench* and *The War Cripples*. Some of the paintings confiscated are auctioned off by the National Socialists during the summer in Zurich and Lucerne.

1940 Trip to Bohemia. *View of the Hegau* (p. 189).

1942 Trip to the Sudeten Mountains and the Bohemian Mountains. Turns down contract to paint portrait of the Foreign Minister of the Reich, Joachim von Ribbentrop. *Self-portrait with Palette in front of Red Curtain* (p. 191).

1943 Visits Dresden for last time before the end of the war. Begins "one-coat-only" painting. Dix's father dies on 27 July.

1945 Dix, now 54 years old, is conscripted into the *Volkssturm*. Taken prisoner by the French forces at Colmar. Paints triptych for the chapel of the prison camp.

1946 Returns to Hemmenhofen. Begins works on religious themes, such as *Job* and *Christ on the Cross*. Again begins to exhibit in numerous galleries in Germany and abroad.

1947 Visits Dresden every year. Portrait of his fellow painter Erich Heckel, who also lives in Hemmenhofen (p. 201). *Self-portrait as a Prisoner of War* (p. 194).

1948 Renewed work on lithographs. Participation in the exhibition "Painting

Otto and Martha Dix eating pork knuckle at "Hanne's Place" in Berlin, 1963

His parents, Ernst and Louise Dix. Easter, 1941

In his studio

As the "King of Thule" on his 75th birthday with the wreath and goblet, gifts from his son Jan, 1968

Otto Dix with his wife Martha

and Sculpture" at the Museum of Modern Art, New York.

1949   Takes part in numerous collective exhibitions, e.g. in Hagen, Düsseldorf, Flensburg, Hamburg, Dresden, Gera and Cologne.

1950   Participation in "International Exhibition of Paintings" at the Carnegie Institute, Pittsburgh.

1951/52   Numerous exhibitions marking his 60th birthday.

1953   Travels to southern France. Dix's mother dies on 26 August.

1954   Becomes president of the Upper Swabia-Lake Constance Secession. Exhibits in "Reality and Fantasy 1900-1954" in Minneapolis and in "German Arts" in Dublin.

1955   Dix's daughter Nelly dies on 11 January. He becomes a member of the German Academy of the Arts in West Berlin. Travels to southern France. *Portrait of the Artist's Parents II* is exhibited at the "documenta" in Kassel.

1956   Becomes corresponding member of the German Academy of the Arts in East Berlin.

1957   Appointed honorary senator of the Dresden College of Fine Arts. Trip to southern France. Participates in "German Art of the Twentieth Century" in New York.

1959   Travels to southern Italy. Awarded

the City of Düsseldorf Cornelius Prize and the Federal Cross of Merit, First Class. Publication of the first major work on Dix, by Otto Conzelmann.

1960   Murals in the town hall of Singen.

1962   Guest of the Villa Massimo Foundation in Rome.

1964   Honorary member of the Accademia delle arti del disgeno in Florence. Honorary member of the Carl Gus-

tav Carus Medical Academy in Dresden. Awarded the Carl von Ossietzky medal. Exhibits in "documenta III" in Kassel and in "20th Century Master Drawings" in New York, Minneapolis and Cambridge, Mass.

1966   Last visit to Dresden. Dix receives numerous honours in both East and West to commemorate his 75th birthday. Lichtwark Prize of the City of Hamburg. Martin-Andersen-Nexö Prize of the City of Dresden. Honorary citizen of Gera, his home-town. Honorary member of the Federation for the Fine Arts in Berlin. Awarded the honorary ring of the City of Singen. Documentary film on Dix's life shown on West German television. Numerous exhibitions.

1967   Travels to Greece in the summer. In November he suffers his first stroke, resulting in paralysis of left hand. Receives Hans Thoma Prize of the State of Baden-Württemberg. Lindner Prize of the rbk Group of the City of Wuppertal. Honorary member of the Art Association of Constance. Medaglia d'oro de Monto dei Paschi di Siena.

1968   Honorary member of the Karlsruhe Art Academy. Rembrandt Prize of the Salzburg Goethe Foundation. *War* is purchased by the State Art Collection in Dresden. Participation in "L'art en Europe 1918-1968" in Strasbourg.

1969   Donates drawings to the Dresden gallery collection of copperplate-engravings. Second stroke on 19 July. Dies on 25 July in the hospital in Singen. Buried on 28 July at the cemetery in Hemmenhofen.

Bibliography

Bibliography:
Löffler, Fritz: *Otto Dix. Leben und Werk.* Dresden, 5th ed., 1982 (pp. 399-416: list of literature and exhibitions until early 1982)

Memoirs, interviews:
Selbstzeugnisse. Schriften, Briefe, Gespräche, Erinnerungen. In: Diether Schmidt, *Otto Dix im Selbstbildnis.* Berlin, 1978, pp. 199-253.
Dix selbst (conversations, letters, interviews). In: Catalogue of Museum Villa Stuck Exhibition, Munich, 1985, pp. 273-292.
Wetzel, Maria: *Professor Otto Dix. Ein harter Mann dieser Maler (interview with Otto Dix).* In: Diplomatischer Kurier 14 (1965), pp. 731-745. Reprinted in: Catalogue of Museum Villa Stuck Exhibition, Munich, 1985, pp. 284-290.

List of works:
Karsch, Florian: *Otto Dix. Das graphische Werk 1913-1969.* Hanover, 1970.
Löffler, Fritz: *Otto Dix 1891-1969. Œuvre der Gemälde.* Recklinghausen, 1981 (not complete).

Biographies, monographs, studies and books with works by Otto Dix:
Barton, Brigid S.: *Otto Dix und die neue Sachlichkeit 1918-1925.* Michigan, 1981.
Conzelmann, Otto: *Otto Dix. Handzeichnungen* (drawings). Hanover, 1968.
Conzelmann, Otto: *Otto Dix – Weiber* (women). Frankfurt/M., 1976 (special edition published by 2001).
Conzelmann, Otto: *Der andere Dix – Sein Bild vom Menschen und vom Krieg.* Stuttgart, 1983.
Fischer, Lothar: *Otto Dix, ein Malerleben in Deutschland.* Berlin, 1981.
Karcher, Eva: *Eros und Tod im Werk von Otto Dix* (doctoral thesis, Munich, 1982). Münster, 1984.
Karcher, Eva: *Otto Dix.* Munich, 1986.
Kinkel, Hans: *Otto Dix – Protokolle der Hölle.* Frankfurt/M., 1968.
Löffler, Fritz: *Otto Dix. Leben und Werk.* Dresden, 1960, 5th ed., 1982.
Löffler, Fritz: *Otto Dix. Der Krieg.* Leipzig, 1986.
Löffler, Fritz: *Otto Dix. Bilder zur Bibel.* Berlin, 1986.
Lüdecke, Heinz: *Otto Dix.* Dresden, 1958.
McGreevy, Linda F.: *The Life and Works of Otto Dix, German Critical Realist.* Michigan, 1981.
Otto, Gunter: *Otto Dix, Bildnis der Eltern. Klassenschicksal und Bildformel.* Frankfurt/M., 1984.
Pérad, Rudolf: *Otto Dix – Religiöse Gemälde* (religious paintings). Darmstadt, 1961.

Schmidt, Diether: *Otto Dix im Selbstbildnis.* Berlin, 1978.
Schmidt, Paul Ferdinand: *Otto Dix.* Cologne, 1923.
Schubert, Dietrich: *Otto Dix in Selbstzeugnissen und Bilddokumenten.* Reinbek bei Hamburg, 1980.
Wolfradt, Willi: *Otto Dix.* Leipzig, 1924.

Essays and catalogue commentaries:
Barr, Alfred H., Jr.: *Otto Dix.* In: The Arts 17 (1931), pp. 235-271.
Barth, Peter: *Otto Dix und die Düsseldorfer Künstlerszene, 1920-1925*, in catalogue of the exhibition held at Galerie Remmert und Barth, Düsseldorf, 1983.
Beck, Rainer: *Krieg*, in catalogue of the Museum Villa Stuck exhibition, Munich, 1985, pp. 11-21.
Cassou, Jean: *Otto Dix*, in catalogue of the exhibition held at Galerie Erker, St. Gallen, 1962.
Conzelmann, Otto: *Der Fall Otto Dix* (Special edition published by the Hans Thoma Society), Reutlingen, 1971.
Conzelmann, Otto: *Otto Dix. Sammlung der Galerie der Stadt Stuttgart* (special publication on the Galerie der Stadt Stuttgart, Stuttgart, 1979.
Conzelmann, Otto: *Das "Kriegstagebuch"* (war journal) – *Ein Merkbuch der Erkenntnisse*, in exhibition catalogue of the Rupertinum, Salzburg, 1984, pp. 32-36.
Conzelmann, Otto: *Otto Dix der Menschenbildner*, in catalogue of exhibition held at Palais des Beaux-Arts, Brussels, 1985, pp. 18-21.
Däubler, Theodor: *Otto Dix*, in: Das Kunstblatt 4 (1920), pp. 118-123.
Dix, Ursus: *Die Maltechnik*, in Museum Villa Stuck exhibition catalogue, Munich, 1985, pp. 259f.
Dix, Ursus: *Mein Vater*, in catalogue of exhibition held at the Kunsthalle Berlin, 1987, pp. 33-40.
Dokumente zu Leben und Werk des Malers Otto Dix (1891-1969), in the Archiv für Bildende Kunst, Germanisches Nationalmuseum, Nuremberg, 1977.
Fischer, Ilse: *Der Dadaist (Otto Dix)*, in: Das junge Rheinland, H. 9/10, 1922, pp. 23-28.
Fischer, Lothar: *"Ich habe das gemacht, was ich wollte." Otto Dix – Bemerkungen zu Leben und Werk*, in the catalogue to the exhibition held at the Kunsthalle Berlin, 1987, pp. 22-31.
Hagenlocher, Alfred: *Otto Dix – Zeuge und Chronist*, in exhibition catalogue of the Rupertinium, Salzburg, 1984, pp. 9-14.
Karcher, Eva: *"Alle Kunst ist Bannung"*, in exhibition catalogue of the Rupertinum, Salzburg, 1984, pp. 15-30.
Karcher, Eva: *Eros und Tod*, in Museum

Villa Stuck exhibition catalogue, Munich, 1985, pp. 149-154.
Karcher, Eva: *Landschaft*, in Museum Villa Stuck exhibition catalogue, Munich, 1985, pp. 201-206.
Karcher, Eva: *Das Phänomen Otto Dix*, in catalogue of the exhibition held at Palais des Beaux-Arts, Brussels, 1985, pp. 8-17.
Kinkel, Hans: *Begegnung mit Otto Dix*, in: Stuttgarter Zeitung, Nov. 11, 1961 issue. Reprinted in Hans Kinkel, Vierzehn Berichte, Stuttgart, 1967, pp. 69-78, and in Kunsthalle Berlin, exhibition catalogue 1985, pp. 15-21.
Löffler, Fritz: *Otto Dix*, in: Zeitschrift für Kunst 3 (1949), pp. 173-193.
Löffler, F.: *Die letzten Selbstbildnisse von Otto Dix und sein religiöses Schaffen*, in: Das Münster 25 (1972), H. 5/6, pp. 373-380.
Löffler, F.: *Das christliche Thema*, in Museum Villa Stuck catalogue, Munich, 1985, pp. 229-238.
Rathke, Ewald: *Der Maler Otto Dix – Ehrlichkeit statt Schönheit*, in: Artis 2 (1967), pp. 18-22.
Sager, Peter: *Otto Dix, der allzeit unbequeme Realist*, in: Zeitmagazin No. 50 (1981), pp. 30-38.
Schmidt, Diether: *Krieg und Frieden – Bekenntnisse zum Humanismus in Wandbildern von Pablo Picasso und Otto Dix*, in: Dezennium 1 (1962), pp. 234-250.
Schmidt, Diether: *Der souveräne Poet. Zu einigen Selbstbildnissen von Otto Dix aus den zwanziger Jahren*, in the almanach of Henschel (publishers), Berlin, 1975, pp. 203-208.
Schmidt, Diether: *Selbstbildnis*, in: Museum Villa Stuck exhibition catalogue, Munich, 1985, pp. 61-70.
Schmidt, Paul Ferdinand: *Otto Dix*, in: Die Horen 4 (1927/28), pp. 865-872.
Schmidt, Werner: *Rede auf Otto Dix* (speech commemorating the awarding of the 1968 Rembrandt Prize of the Goethe Foundation), Salzburg, 1969, pp. 9-21.
Schubert, Dietrich: *Die Elternbildnisse von Otto Dix aus den Jahren 1921 und 1924*, in: Städel-Jahrbuch 4 (1937), pp. 271-298.
Schubert, Dietrich: *Rezeptions- und Stilpluralismus in den frühen Selbstbildnissen von Otto Dix*, in: Beiträge zum Problem des Stilpluralismus, W. Hager and N. Knopp, eds., Munich, 1977.
Schubert, Dietrich: *Otto Dix und der Krieg*, in: Pazifismus zwischen den Weltkriegen, D. Harth, D. Schubert and R.M. Schmidt, eds., Heidelberg, 1985.
Wentzel, Hans: *Otto Dix zum Gedächtnis*, in: Kunstchronik 25 (1972), H. 1, pp. 1-10.
Wolfradt, Willi: *Otto Dix*, in: Der Cicerone 16 (1924), pp. 945-954.
Wolfradt, W.: *Ein Doppelbildnis von Otto Dix*, in: Der Cicerone 15 (1923), pp. 173-178.

·Pictures of the Mind·

THE ILLUSTRATED
ROBERT LOUIS STEVENSON

·Pictures of the Mind·

THE ILLUSTRATED
ROBERT LOUIS STEVENSON

John Scally

CANONGATE

in association with

THE NATIONAL LIBRARY OF SCOTLAND

Acknowledgements

The publisher has taken all reasonable steps to obtain from their copyright holders permission to reproduce the images which appear in this volume. Thanks are due to: Checkerboard Press for permission to reproduce illustrations from *A Child's Garden of Verses* (Chicago: Rand McNally & Co., 1919); The Limited Editions Club for permission to reproduce illustrations from *Treasure Island* (New York: Limited Editions Club, 1941) and *The Strange Case of Dr Jekyll and Mr Hyde* (New York: Limited Editions Club, 1952); the estate of Mervyn Peake for permission to reproduce illustrations from *Treasure Island* (London: Eyre & Spottiswoode, 1949); the estate of Mervyn Peake and The Folio Society for permission to reproduce illustrations from *The Strange Case of Dr Jekyll and Mr Hyde* (London: The Folio Society, 1948); Ralph Steadman for permission to reproduce illustrations which first appeared in *Treasure Island* (London: Harrap, 1985); Harry Horse for permission to reproduce an illustration from *The Strange Case of Dr Jekyll and Mr Hyde* (Edinburgh: Canongate, 1986); Bantam Doubleday Dell for permission to reproduce illustrations from *The Master of Ballantrae* (New York: Heritage Press, 1965); The Stewartry Museum and the E. A. Hornel Trust for permission to reproduce an illustration from *Memories* (London: T. N. Foulis, [1912]). Illustrations from *Treasure Island* by Robert Louis Stevenson, illustrated by N. C. Wyeth, are reprinted with the permission of Charles Scribner's Sons, an imprint of Macmillan Publishing. Copyright 1911 Charles Scribner's Sons; copyright renewed 1939 N. C. Wyeth. Illustrations from *Kidnapped* by Robert Louis Stevenson, illustrated by N. C. Wyeth, are reprinted with the permission of Charles Scribner's Sons, an imprint of Macmillan Publishing. Copyright 1913 Charles Scribner's Sons; copyright renewed 1941 N. C. Wyeth. Illustrations from *David Balfour* by Robert Louis Stevenson, illustrated by N.C. Wyeth, are reprinted with the permission of Charles Scribner's Sons, an imprint of Macmillan Publishing. Copyright 1922 Charles Scribner's Sons; copyright renewed 1950 Charles Scribner's Sons and Carolyn B.Wyeth. Illustrations from *The Black Arrow* by Robert Louis Stevenson, illustrated by N. C. Wyeth, are reprinted with the permission of Charles Scribner's Sons, an imprint of Macmillan Publishing. Copyright 1916 Charles Scribner's Sons; copyright renewed 1944 N. C. Wyeth. Illustrations from *The Strange Case of Dr Jekyll and Mr Hyde* by Robert Louis Stevenson, illustrated by W. A. Dwiggins, are reprinted by permission of Random House, Inc. Copyright ©1929 and renewed 1956 by Random House, Inc. Illustrations from *The Strange Case of Dr Jekyll and Mr Hyde* by Robert Louis Stevenson, illustrated by Barry Moser, are reprinted by permission of the University of Nebraska Press. Copyright © 1990 by Pennyroyal Press, Inc.

The author gratefully acknowledges the support of his colleagues in the National Library of Scotland, and in particular the assistance of Mr Graham Hogg and Dr Kenneth Gibson. Thanks are also due to Dr Andrew Noble of the University of Strathclyde.

Reproductions of book illustrations are taken from copies in the collections of the National Library of Scotland

Book design by Ann Ross Paterson

Photography by AIC Photographic Services & Steve McAvoy

British Library Cataloguing in Publication Data
A catalogue record for this book is available on request from the British Library

ISBN 0 86241 492 X

Front cover: 'The Treasure Cave', by **Ralph Steadman**, an illustration for Robert Louis Stevenson's *Treasure Island* (London, 1985)
Half-title: Illustration by **Edward A. Wilson** from *Strange Case of Dr Jekyll and Mr Hyde* (New York, 1952)
Frontispiece: Illustration by **Jessie Willcox Smith** for 'Picture Books in Winter' from *A Child's Garden of Verses* (New York, 1905)
Title-page: Robert Louis Stevenson, drawn by **Fairfax Muckley** from 'The South Seas: A Record of Three Cruises' in *Black and White* (London, 1891)
Illustrations on this page by **Jessie Willcox Smith** for 'The Land of Nod' and 'To My Name-Child' from *A Child's Garden of Verses* (New York, 1905)
Contents page: 'Long John Silver', by **Ralph Steadman**, the cover illustration for Robert Louis Stevenson's *Treasure Island* (London, 1985)
p.7: Photograph from a collection in the National Library of Scotland, Adv.MS. 21.6.10.
p.14: Illustration by **Jessie Willcox Smith** for 'The Wind' from *A Child's Garden of Verses* (1905)

CONTENTS

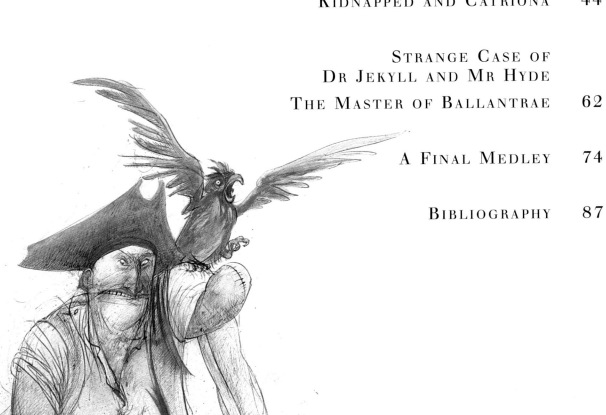

FOREWORD

For just over a century Robert Louis Stevenson has delighted youngsters and the young at heart all over the world with his stories, poems and essays.

Indeed, the world will have grown older and, I think, a little sadder if readers cease to thrill at that splendid tale of derring-do that whisks us with young Jim Hawkins from the Admiral Benbow public house to a treasure island aboard the *Hispaniola*. *Treasure Island, Kidnapped,* its sequel *Catriona,* and the sombre-hued *Strange Case of Dr Jekyll and Mr Hyde* are for me not only the very stuff of enchanted hours, but wonderful truth of the triumph of will and ability over the physical frailty which dogged Stevenson in his all too short life.

Stevenson himself was also something of an artist. Certainly his words can burn very bright pictures into their readers' minds and it is this strong pictorial quality in his best writing which has appealed so much to the many illustrators of his books and, far more importantly, to their readers.

The potency of the link between text and famous illustration is perhaps inseparable for most readers of Stevenson. How appropriate, then, is a book which brings together a great many of the wonderful illustrations over the last century enabling us to indulge our nostalgia or re-kindle new enthusiasm for the books themselves.

Stevenson himself, aware as he was of the commercial benefits of well illustrated books, would doubtless have smiled at the thought of a book 100 years after his death in which words were subsidiary to the pictures; but I am sure he would have approved.

I would also like to think Stevenson would have endorsed support from The Post Office for this delightful publication. If anything, the role of The Post Office in the business and social life of Scotland's many communities is more pervasive and certainly more diverse than in Stevenson's day; and our success in handling 10 million letters and parcels every day in this country underpins modest support such as this for the 'belles lettres' of which Stevenson was such an elegant adept.

The back cover of this book illustrates a pictorial airletter dedicated to Robert Louis Stevenson which is our own small tribute to a man whose travels and fame have made him truly international.

KENNETH GRAHAM
Chairman, Scottish Post Office Board

INTRODUCTION

In the early evening of 3 December 1894, an emaciated Scotsman, standing on the balcony of his home at Vailima, Samoa, suddenly put his hand to his head and exclaimed to his wife, 'Do I look strange?'. A blood vessel had burst in his head; he fell to his knees and was dead within a few hours. He was one of the most beloved of late Victorian writers, not only a successful author, essayist, poet, letter-writer and polemicist, but a real-life traveller and adventurer. A sparkling storyteller, whose initials – R.L.S. – were recognised throughout the world, had died at the age of forty-four. An appropriate epitaph for this remarkable man would have been 'never a dull moment'.

Robert Louis Balfour Stevenson was born on 13 November 1850 at 8 Howard Place, Edinburgh. He was the only son of Thomas Stevenson, a third-generation member of a respected family of engineers, and Margaret Isabella Balfour, daughter of Lewis Balfour, minister at Colinton village, south-west of Edinburgh. Louis, or 'Smout' as he came to be called by his doting parents, was the product of two powerful influences in Scottish society: science and religion.

Within three years of his birth the respiratory ailments which dogged Stevenson throughout his life began to appear. Considerable periods of his first ten years were spent in bed fighting one illness after another. During this time his devoted nurse, Alison Cunningham, or 'Cummy', was his constant companion. A staunchly Calvinist woman, she imbued the child with tales from Scottish history and the Bible, of Covenanter heroes who upheld the Protestant faith against Popery, and punctuated these with laments on the devil's corrosive influence on society. More tales, together with bedside games, came from Stevenson's father, though these stories, unlike Cummy's, were largely an attempt to distract the ailing child from interminable periods of confinement in bed. From very early on, Stevenson's imagination became an important area through which he could be transported from illness to a world of adventure, romance and history. In his own words:

> I have three powerful impressions of my childhood: my sufferings when I was sick, my delights in
> convalescence at my grandfather's manse of Colinton, near Edinburgh, and the unnatural activity
> of my mind after I was in bed at night.[1]

In January 1853 the family, in a vain attempt to escape the pervasive dampness of the Water of Leith, moved across the way to Inverleith Terrace, and thence, four years later, to the damp-free splendour of 17 Heriot Row in the heart of New Town Edinburgh. Although these moves were prompted by a need to find a congenial environment for the sickly family, they were also an index of the success of Thomas Stevenson, engineer to the Board of Northern Lighthouses.

Although a frail child, Louis, when his health permitted, was a most active and imaginative playmate. He spent much of his time at Colinton and there enjoyed the fresh air and the company of his numerous Balfour cousins. It was to these memories that Stevenson returned in his collection of poems, *A Child's Garden of Verses*, in which the child's world is presented as a mixture of isolation in bed with adventure just out of reach, and a glorious sequence of energetic games with other children.

With long periods during which he was incapacitated in bed, it is hardly surprising that Stevenson's formal education was affected. From about 1859 he had short, interrupted, periods at local schools, one in Canonmills, the other in India Street, and this was supplemented by a string of domestic tutors in Edinburgh and elsewhere. Some time was also spent in boarding schools in England until Louis eventually settled into regular attendance at Mr Thomson's school in Frederick Street, Edinburgh, where he remained until 1867, the year he matriculated at Edinburgh University.

At university Stevenson studied first Science, in anticipation of his joining the family firm of engineers, then switched to Law – a sop to his father – after announcing his determination to be a writer, not an engineer. (Law was considered an appropriate profession to fall back on if the attempt at securing a living from writing failed.) Louis stuck to his side of the bargain and was called to the bar in 1875, though his university days were distinguished more by his eccentric dress, long hair, and mild rebellion against the respectable middle-class society into which he was born. He read Charles Darwin and Herbert Spencer, was a member of the University Speculative Society and the more insidious L.J.R. (Liberty, Justice and Reverence) whose members determined to ignore everything their parents had taught them. His friends, Walter Simpson and Charles Baxter, participated in most of these activities. The trio also explored the Old Town, drank in taverns, and, apparently, consorted with prostitutes. Edinburgh was a city of contrasts, seen most vividly in the seedy, dilapidated, yet warm and inviting, Old Town and the repressed, moralistic cold society of the New Town where Louis lived with his parents. Stevenson often employed themes of social and psychological duality in his writing, most successfully, perhaps, in his *Strange Case of Dr Jekyll and Mr Hyde* (1886).

The family strain created by Stevenson's decision not to train as an engineer was intensified by his confession of agnosticism to his deeply Calvinist father in January 1873. This created a rift that was never fully healed and over which Stevenson was comforted by his English friends Frances Sitwell, his first love, and Sidney Colvin, his life-long friend and adviser, who was to provide invaluable assistance in getting the young writer's name known in London publishing circles.

Illness and travel were dominant experiences in Stevenson's life, the second often necessitated by the first. Excursions and walking holidays in Scotland, England, Belgium and France were commonplace and hardly a year passed in which he did not find occasion to escape the harsh weather and repressive society of New Town Edinburgh. It was on one such trip, to an artists' colony in Grez-sur-Loing, France, in the summer of 1876, that he met his future wife, Fanny Vandegrift Osbourne, a married American woman with two children from Indiana. Over the next two years Stevenson made numerous trips to France to be with Fanny, and when she returned to California in August 1878, Louis, unable to settle, made a hazardous trip across America to be with her. Following Fanny's divorce, the couple married in San Francisco in May 1880. The trip to America and Stevenson's subsequent honeymoon in an old silver miner's cabin were recorded in the superb travel chronicle, *The Amateur Emigrant* (1895), and in *The Silverado Squatters* (1883).

By the year of his marriage Stevenson had published about sixty short essays and reviews, two travel books, one long essay and a play in collaboration with W.E. Henley. His first book, *An Inland Voyage* (1878), which gave an account of his canoeing trip in Belgium and France with Walter Simpson, was followed by his hugely enjoyable double-edged celebration of his native city, *Edinburgh: Picturesque Notes* (1878). Next came *Travels with a Donkey* (1879), featuring Modestine (perhaps the most difficult female that Stevenson ever encountered) and, finally, with Henley (perhaps the most difficult male), his first play, *Deacon Brodie, or, The Double Life* (1880). From his marriage until his death in December 1894, Stevenson published something each year, in most years two or three items. This was less to do with his marriage being a turning point in his literary development, and more with the fact that overnight he had become chief bread-winner for a wife and two step-children. Henceforward, physical illness, financial necessity and literary ambition were the three forces in his life.

Stevenson's early published efforts barely caused a ripple, though the appearance in book-form of

Treasure Island, which was begun on his return to Scotland from America in 1881 and completed in Switzerland in 1883, made a splash. (The book would never be out of print and would go on to be one of the most successful adventure stories ever written.) After spending just under two years on the Continent, in Switzerland and France, the Stevensons settled in Bournemouth, England, from September 1884 to August 1887. This was the most productive phase of R.L.S.'s career and saw the publication of, most notably, *A Child's Garden of Verses* (1885), *Prince Otto* (1885), *More New Arabian Nights* (1885), *Strange Case of Dr Jekyll and Mr Hyde* (1886) and *Kidnapped* (1886). The turning point in all this was undoubtedly *Jekyll and Hyde*, for it was the author's first major British and American success and the increased profile that it brought also meant publicity for Stevenson's previous efforts. The publication of the sublime historical adventure, *Kidnapped*, in July 1886, confirmed his growing reputation.

The death of Stevenson's father, Thomas, in May 1887, removed one of the main reasons for tolerating the harsh British climate (as well as releasing funds) and Stevenson, his wife, mother and stepson, Lloyd, sailed for America in August of that year. On his arrival in New York in September, R.L.S. was followed by reporters, fêted by publishers and lionised by New York society. Within a month, however, the party moved on to Saranac Lake in the Adirondack Mountains, to try out another cure for Louis's respiratory condition. At this time, 1888-89, Louis was producing monthly essays for *Scribner's Magazine*; in addition, *The Black Arrow* (1888) and *The Master of Ballantrae* (1889) were published.

Fanny and Stevenson, with Nantoki and Natakanti, on Butaritari in the Gilberts. 'The South Seas: A Record of Three Cruises', in *Black and White.*
O. Lacour
(London, 1891)

Afflicted once more by the travel bug, the party set sail from San Francisco on board the yacht *Casco*, on the first leg of a three-year journey that would take them around the South Seas and end on the island of Upolu in the Samoan Islands, where Stevenson spent the last three years of his life. In this final phase of his career, Stevenson followed two themes in his writing. He wrote on South Seas topics, in works such as *In the South Seas* (1890), *The Beach of Falesá* (1892), *A Footnote to History* (1892), and *Island Nights' Entertainments* (1893). And, in the last years of his life, though far away from home, Stevenson returned to Scottish themes in the form, principally, of *Catriona* (1893), the long awaited sequel to *Kidnapped*, and *Weir of Hermiston* (1896), the latter being the masterpiece he left unfinished at his death.

•   •   •

Stevenson is the most visual of writers. With a few phrases he can bring to life a character or a scene, creating for the reader a vivid image – a picture of the mind – which is due as much to Stevenson's love of the visual arts as to his better-known skills as a writer. A fusion of these two has created the essence that is Robert Louis Stevenson.

Treasure Island is not only memorable for its characters but for the images and sensations, the thrill of suspense and fired imagination that the story evokes. We are with Jim Hawkins in the apple barrel, terrified, while outside the malevolent, yet magnetic, Long John Silver cajoles another sailor into joining

the mutiny. During the flight in the heather in *Kidnapped* we can almost reach out and touch Alan Breck and David Balfour as they trudge moodily across the wet, inhospitable, landscape of highland Scotland. So, the enduring quality of R.L.S., like that of any great storyteller, is his ability to create characters, sketch scenes and convey moods with an economy of words. Take, for instance, the description of Long John Silver, spoken by Jim Hawkins, in *Treasure Island*:

> His left leg was cut off close by the hip, and under the left shoulder he carried a crutch, which he managed with wonderful dexterity, hopping about upon it like a bird. He was very tall and strong, with a face as big as a ham – plain and pale, but intelligent and smiling.

Later, in the same book, the description of the pirates at breakfast, before they go on the treasure hunt, perfectly conveys the scene with economy and clarity:

> They had lit a fire fit to roast an ox; and it was now grown so hot that they could only approach it from the windward, and even there not without precaution. In the same wasteful spirit, they had cooked, I suppose, three times more than we could eat; and one of them, with an empty laugh, threw what was left into the fire, which blazed and roared again over this unusual fuel.

Stevenson's ability to render character, scene and mood is strong and instant. The picture of Long John Silver, in which the amputated leg is described first, establishes the character's essential difference, but also creates the feelings of repulsion and attraction with which we are meant to view Silver.

It is this ability to establish a character clearly that makes Stevenson's art so distinctive. Each character is always in sharp focus. 'Am I no a bonny fighter?', Alan Breck asks David Balfour after the fight in the Roundhouse in *Kidnapped*; and these six words, especially after the carnage that had just taken place, are enough to show Alan as both brave and conceited. In 'The Land of Counterpane', from *A Child's Garden of Verses*, Stevenson, at his most autobiographical, describes the sick child confined to bed:

> And all my toys beside me lay
> To keep me happy all the day...
>
> I was the giant great and still
> That sits upon the pillow-hill.

Whether it is a highland Jacobite glorying in his fighting prowess or a sick, imaginative child playing with his toys, we remember Stevenson's creations simply because they are so vividly drawn by an author who was also an artist and illustrator.

One of Stevenson's drawings to accompany his first story, *The History of Moses* (Daylesford, PA, 1919).

The first story attributed to Stevenson was the *History of Moses*, his entry for a competition set by his Uncle David on that subject, which young Louis, aged six, dictated to his mother in the last few months of 1856. The child drew and coloured the illustrations to accompany his text. At school, the fifteen-year-old Louis was editor, illustrator and chief contributor to the school magazine. Only one of each issue was produced of the 'Sunbeam Magazine' and it was circulated at a charge of 'one penny per night, the proceeds are to be devoted to the Sealkote Orphanage'.

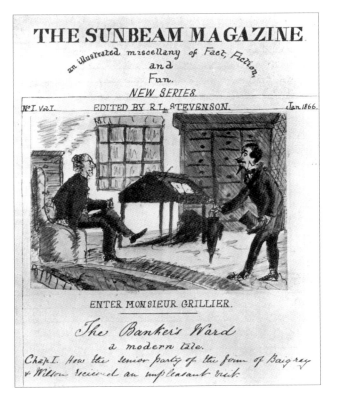

'The Sunbeam Magazine' written and illustrated by Stevenson, reproduced from the sale catalogue of his library (New York, [1914]).

Later, as an adult, Stevenson recalled, 'I was, indeed, always drawing'; and this is borne out in a letter to his friend W.E. Henley, in the summer of 1875, in which he outlines his activities in a typical day while convalescing in France:

I rise between five and six; walk from seven till eleven; at eleven, breakfast; 12 to 3, stroll and the exercise of the initiative outs in a sketchbook – the results are so comic, Henley! – 3 to 5 or so, work; 6, dinner; bed about nine; last night at 8.15, but then I was dead beat.[2]

Just over three years later, in the winter of 1878, during his walking tour of the Cévennes from which came *Travels with a Donkey*, he carried a sketchbook that he filled with pencil drawings and watercolours. Imagine Stevenson, then, as a visual artist as well as a writer, with the sketchbook in one hand and the more familiar pen, ink and paper in the other.

One of Stevenson's lead pencil drawings made in Le Monastier, France, in 1878, reproduced from *The Studio* (London, Winter 1896-97).

Perhaps the most celebrated example of R.L.S.'s attempt to produce illustrations to accompany his own work is the sequence of verses, with accompanying woodcut illustrations, which he produced over two winters in Davos, Switzerland, between 1880 and 1882. The story behind these delightful productions is as interesting as the poems and woodcuts themselves, and is worth the telling. Davos-Platz was a remote health resort in the Swiss Alps where those with tubercular and other respiratory ailments congregated. It was here that Stevenson, his new wife, Fanny, and his stepson, Lloyd, arrived in the winter of 1880 (and to where they would return the following winter). Whilst there, Louis and Lloyd occupied themselves by printing material using Lloyd's miniature printing press; first Stevenson produced woodcut illustrations, and then he composed appropriate verses to go with them. The results were *Moral Emblems. A Collection of Cuts and Verses; Moral Emblems. A Second Collection of Cuts and Verses;* and *Moral Tales.* They were advertised with bills printed on the same press and sold for ninepence at the Swiss resort.

'Rob and Ben or The Pirate and the Apothecary. Scene the First.' *Moral Tales* ([1882]), here reproduced from *A Stevenson Medley* (1899).

'Rob and Ben . . . Scene the Third.' *Moral Tales* ([1882]), here reproduced from *A Stevenson Medley* (1899).

Ostensibly done for the amusement of his eleven-year-old stepson, the Davos publications reveal the child in Stevenson and were composed, revealingly, at the same time as *Treasure Island*. As with most of the literary efforts that Stevenson completed, he was delighted with the results, and, to his cousin Bob Stevenson, he wrote:

I enclose all my artistic works, they are woodcuts – I cut them with a knife out of blocks of wood: I am a wood engraver; I aaaam a wooooood engraver. Lloyd then prints 'em: are they not fun? I doat [sic] on them; in my next venture, I am going to have colour printing; it will be very laborious, six blocks to cut for each picter, but the result would be pyramidal. [5]

Stevenson's efforts as an illustrator advanced little beyond the Davos cuts, coinciding, as they did, with his first success as a writer. Yet time and again, throughout his career, he considered that the success of his publications depended on whether or not they were illustrated. In November 1881, whilst writing the final chapters of *Treasure Island* at Davos, he told Henley, 'with anything like half good pictures, it should sell. I suppose I may at least hope for eight pic's? I aspire after ten or twelve'.[4] A few years later, Stevenson gave detailed instructions about the numerous illustrations he wished to accompany *A Child's Garden of Verses*, confiding to Cummy that without illustrations 'no child would give a kick for it'.[5] In the winter of 1887-88 Stevenson recommended William Hole to illustrate the half-finished *Master of Ballantrae*, and, when his wish was granted, declared it 'one of the most adequately illustrated books of our generation'[6] when it appeared in 1889. In his later career Stevenson continued to be equally anxious about illustrations for his publications, whether for his South Seas stories such as *The Beach of Falesá* or his later Scottish stories like *Catriona*.[7] Indeed, the prospect of *Kidnapped* and *Catriona* appearing in a two-volume work called 'The Adventures of David Balfour', copiously illustrated by William Hole, was something which excited Stevenson's imagination in the last year of his life.

•   •   •

The illustrations in this book span a period from about 1878 to 1985, from Walter Crane's conventional black and white wood engraving for *An Inland Voyage* to Ralph Steadman's explosive colour paintings for *Treasure Island*. In between Crane and Steadman, there is such a wide selection of work; artists of varying styles, using different techniques and grappling with different stories or poems. All of this has been an important element in the publishing phenomenon that is Robert Louis Stevenson.

The illustrator attracted to the nostalgic poems in *A Child's Garden of Verses* would, perhaps, be unsuited to the romance and adventure of *Treasure Island* and *Kidnapped*, or the dark duality of *Strange Case of Dr Jekyll and Mr Hyde*. Thus the black and white drawings of Charles Robinson and the rich colour illustrations of Jessie Willcox Smith, though quite different in style, both respond to the author's simple, evocative verse in *A Child's Garden*. In contrast, the early monochrome engravings by Walter Paget for *Treasure Island*, instantly recognisable for their unerring attention to detail and conventional format, are quite distinct from the paintings of the great American illustrator, N.C. Wyeth, whose work for the same book is unmatched in its power and movement. While even different again are the vivid colour splashes and violence of Ralph Steadman's unforgettable pirates.

Like *Treasure Island*, the popularity of the historical adventures of David Balfour in *Kidnapped* and *Catriona* ensured that they would be illustrated time and again. William Hole, one of the most popular illustrators of the last century, and a particular favourite of Stevenson, was the first illustrator of both these stories.

Stevenson's *Strange Case of Dr Jekyll and Mr Hyde* presented a different kind of challenge to illustrators, with its short story shocker format, and this is reflected in the style of illustrations: initially, striking and colourful bookcovers, and later, the towering expressionist monochrome of S.G. Hulme-Beaman. Although laced with themes similar to *Dr Jekyll and Mr Hyde*, *The Master of Ballantrae* was at first illustrated by tried and tested artists such as William Hole and Walter Paget, with the latter working this time in colour. More recently, however, the striking colour illustrations by Lynd Ward present a more imaginative interpretation of the story.

The final chapter ranges far and wide, attempting to give a flavour of the illustrations that have accompanied Stevenson's less well known works. The famous frontispiece by Walter Crane from *Travels with a Donkey* is there alongside the images by A. Brunet-Debaines and R. Kent Thomas from the first edition of *Edinburgh: Picturesque Notes*. Wyeth, not surprisingly, appears again, but only briefly, because the majority of the illustrations are concerned with Stevenson's South Seas tales and the haunting interpretations of his *Fables*.

With such a wealth of illustrative material it is impossible to be exhaustive and, inevitably, favourites will have been left out. Above all, however, the aim is to offer some perspective on how successive generations of illustrators have interpreted the timeless stories and poems of Robert Louis Stevenson.

1. *The Works of Robert Louis Stevenson*, Tusitala Edition, 35 vols (London: Heinemann, 1924), XXIX, 149.
2. National Library of Scotland, Adv. MS. 26.8.2. fol.6 (Stevenson to Henley, [summer 1875?]).
3. *The Letters of Robert Louis Stevenson*, ed. Sir Sidney Colvin, 5 vols (London: Heinemann, 1924), II, 199 (RLS to R.A.M. Stevenson, [Davos-Platz, April 1882]). Hereafter *Letters*.
4. *Letters*, II, 177.
5. *Letters*, II, 255 (RLS to Alison Cunningham, [Summer 1883]).
6. *Letters*, III, 252 (RLS to W.H. Low, 20 May 1889).
7. *Letters*, IV and V, especially, IV, 85, 112, 229, 246; V, 4-5, 24, 34, 79.

A Child's Garden of Verses

The poems in *A Child's Garden of Verses* are bound up with Stevenson's own childhood experiences of illness, loneliness and play; a record, in a sense, of his childhood. That they are dedicated to Cummy, Stevenson's nurse and constant companion, further underlines their autobiographical nature. And yet these verses, with their simple rhymes and nostalgic content, appeal to children and adults alike. Children because they understand the frustration of poems like 'Bed in Summer' and adults because of the evocation of childhood memories:

> And does it not seem hard to you,
> When all the sky is clear and blue,
> And I should like so much to play,
> To have to go to bed by day?

And again the sentiment invoked in 'Good and Bad Children':

> Cruel children, crying babies,
> All grow up as geese and gabies,
> Hated, as their age increases,
> By their nephews and their nieces.

But there is more to this *Garden*, published in 1885, than meets the eye. It is the world as viewed by the child, yet without the sugary affectation normally associated with such verse. The innocence of the child is there though it has to confront a world that is real. The child is often alone, scared, confined to bed, at play, or dreaming of adventure. There is darkness and light, illness and play, dream and nightmare, spring and autumn, summer and winter. Often each experience has two sides. Sleep can bring 'frightening sights' as in 'The Land of Nod' or delightful dreams of 'armies and emperors and kings' as in 'Young Night Thought'.

It is a world where by day the child can climb a tree and see roads that 'lead onward into fairy land' ('Foreign Lands'), but where at night the child can feel in its hair 'the breath of the Bogie' whilst climbing the stairs to bed ('North-West Passage'). More than just pleasing rhyming couplets from the nursery, *A Child's Garden* is a vivid exploration of the child's world, at once deeply personal yet triggering the memories of us all.

A Child's Garden of Verses is distinctive amongst R.L.S.'s most popular works, and the artists who have illustrated it are from the world of children's books. Each artist, however, has stamped his or her illustrations with an intimate interpretation that places the child at the centre of the picture, as Stevenson had intended. Charles Robinson, the first illustrator of *A Child's Garden* chose, in some cases, to integrate the verse into his flowing and imaginative drawings. An important element in the American artist Jessie Willcox Smith's treatment is her use of both colour and black and white illustrations to convey the world of the child alone. Similarly, the Dutch artist H. Willebeek le Mair focuses on the single child. Interestingly, however, she creates scenes that evoke not Edinburgh but her own particular environment, which, rather than appearing incongruous, reveals a rich new dimension to this universal collection of poems.

FOR THE LONG NIGHTS YOU LAY AWAKE
AND WATCHED FOR MY UNWORTHY SAKE:
FOR YOUR MOST COMFORTABLE HAND
THAT LED ME THROUGH THE UNEVEN LAND:
FOR ALL THE STORY BOOKS YOU READ:
FOR ALL THE PAINS YOU COMFORTED:
FOR ALL YOU PITIED, ALL YOU BORE,
IN SAD AND HAPPY DAYS OF YORE:—
MY SECOND MOTHER, MY FIRST WIFE,
THE ANGEL OF MY INFANT LIFE—
FROM THE SICK CHILD, NOW WELL AND OLD,
TAKE, NURSE, THE LITTLE BOOK YOU HOLD!

AND GRANT IT, HEAVEN, THAT ALL WHO READ
MAY FIND AS DEAR A NURSE AT NEED,
AND EVERY CHILD WHO LISTS MY RHYME,
IN THE BRIGHT, FIRESIDE, NURSERY CLIME,
MAY HEAR IT IN AS KIND A VOICE
AS MADE MY CHILDISH DAYS REJOICE!

R. L. S.

Decorated dedication to Stevenson's beloved nurse 'Cummy',
from the first illustrated edition of *A Child's Garden of Verses*.
Charles Robinson
(London, 1896)

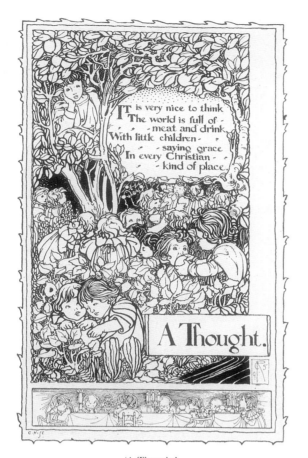

'A Thought'
Charles Robinson
(1896)

'At The Seaside'
Charles Robinson
(1896)

'Whole Duty of Children'
Charles Robinson
(1896)

'Happy Thought'
Charles Robinson
(1896)

A CHILD'S GARDEN OF VERSES
ROBERT LOVIS STEVENSON

WITH ILLVSTRATIONS BY
JESSIE WILLCOX SMITH

Front cover for one of the most popular illustrated editions.
Jessie Willcox Smith
(New York, 1905)

JESSIE WILLCOX SMITH.

In Winter I get up
at night
And dress by yellow
candle-light.'
From 'Bed In Summer'.
Jessie Willcox Smith
(1905)

*Up into the cherry-tree
Who should climb but
    little me?
I held the trunk with
    both my hands
And looked abroad on
    foreign lands.'*
From 'Foreign Lands'.

Jessie Willcox Smith
(1905)

Half-title for 'The Child Alone' sequence in
A Child's Garden of Verses.
Jessie Willcox Smith
(1905)

*'And many frightening sights abroad
Till morning in the land of Nod.'*
From 'The Land of Nod'.

Millicent Sowerby
(London, 1908)

*'Should a leaflet come to land
Drifting near to where I stand,
Straight I'll board that tiny boat
Round the rain-pool sea to float.'*
From 'The Little Land'.

Millicent Sowerby
(1908)

'Come up here, O dusty feet!
Here is fairy bread to eat.'
From 'Fairy Bread'.

Ruth Mary Hallock
(Chicago, 1919)

'I see the people marching by,
As plain as day, before my eye.
Armies and emperors and kings,
All carrying different kinds of things,
And marching in so grand a way,
You never saw the like by day.'
From 'Young Night Thought'.

Kate Elizabeth Olver
(London, [1927])

'There, in the night, where none can spy,
All in my hunter's camp I lie,
And play at books that I have read
Till it is time to go to bed.'
From 'The Land of Story-Books'.

Kate Elizabeth Olver
([1927])

'I saw you toss the kites on high
And blow the birds about the sky.'
From 'The Wind'.

Clara M. Burd
(Akron, Ohio, 1930)

I have to go to bed and see
The birds still hopping on the tree,
Or hear the grown-up people's feet
Still going past me in the street.'
From 'Bed in Summer'.

H. Willebeek le Mair
(London, 1931)

'*When I was sick and lay a-bed,*
I had two pillows at my head,
And all my toys beside me lay
To keep me happy all the day.'
From 'The Land of Counterpane', one of the most
autobiographical poems in the *Child's Garden* sequence.

H. Willebeek le Mair
(1931)

23

'They saw me at last, and they chased me with cries,
And they soon had me packed into bed;
But the glory kept shining and bright in my eyes,
And the stars going round in my head.'
From 'Escape at Bedtime'.

H. Willebeek le Mair
(1931)

'My tea is nearly ready and the sun has left the sky;
It's time to take the window to see Leerie going by;
For every night at tea-time and before you take your seat,
With lantern and with ladder he comes posting up the street.'
From 'The Lamplighter', the poem most associated with Edinburgh, and
with which most Edinburgh children are familiar.

H. Willebeek le Mair
(1931)

'Black are my steps on silver sod;
Thick blows my frosty breath abroad;
And tree and house, and hill and lake,
Are frosted like a wedding-cake.'
From 'Winter-Time'.

H. Willebeek le Mair
(1931)

'Now in the falling of the gloom
The red fire paints the empty room:
And warmly on the roof it looks,
And flickers on the backs of books.'
From 'Armies in the Fire'.

H. Willebeek le Mair
(1931)

TREASURE ISLAND

In a letter from Braemar, Scotland, to his friend W.E. Henley, in August 1881, Stevenson's enthusiasm for a new story he was writing, then called 'The Sea Cook, or Treasure Island: A Story for Boys', is evident:

> If this don't fetch the kids, why, they have gone rotten since my day. Will you be surprised to learn it is about Buccaneers, that it begins in the 'Admiral Benbow' public-house on the Devon coast, that it's all about a map, and a treasure, and a mutiny, and a derelict ship, and a current, and a fine old Squire Trelawney. . . and a doctor, and another doctor, and a sea cook with one leg, and a sea-song with the chorus 'Yo-ho-ho and a bottle of rum'. . . the trouble is to work it off without oaths. Buccaneers without oaths – bricks without straw. But youth and the fond parent have to be consulted.[1]

Youth and fond parents were indeed consulted and they liked what they read, for *Treasure Island* has gone through numerous editions, both English and foreign, since its first publication. It has become a classic, like *Alice in Wonderland* and *Gulliver's Travels*, and was a model for subsequent adventure stories such as H. Rider Haggard's *King Solomon's Mines*. It is today the most famous and most enduring of Stevenson's novels.

The story first appeared as a serialisation in the story paper for boys and girls, *Young Folks*, with Stevenson writing under the pseudonym, 'Captain George North', but it was not a great success. Despite this, Stevenson agreed to the story's publication in book form, and was overjoyed at the publisher's offer. As he related to his parents, 'there has been offered for *Treasure Island* – how much do you suppose?… A hundred pounds, all alive, O ! A hundred jingling, tingling, golden-minted quid. Is not this wonderful?'.[2]

Treasure Island is almost faultless as an adventure story. The narrative is descriptive, economical, and each sentence urges the reader on. It is one of the few books in the English language that a reader literally cannot put down. Perhaps its greatest quality is the way in which Stevenson, with the skill of a painter, sketches the most vivid of scenes in prose. We feel the tingling anticipation when the map is discovered; and we are relieved when there is not a moment's hestitation as Squire Trelawney resolves to go to Bristol 'to-morrow' to charter a ship for the island. Not next week, not next month, but 'to-morrow'. The tussle between Jim Hawkins and Israel Hands on board the *Hispaniola* is riveting and we are involved at a similar level when the pirates race across the island in pursuit of Flint's treasure. Finally, we are part of the infectious euphoria at the conclusion of the story, when the pirates are vanquished and the treasure is found.

Treasure Island has been illustrated more times than any of Stevenson's other books, and has presented a challenge to each generation of illustrators to interpret and reinterpret the main scenes and characters. Of all these artists, Walter Paget, John Cameron, N.C. Wyeth, Mervyn Peake and Ralph Steadman are the most notable. Stevenson himself was pleased with the efforts for the first illustrated English edition and happily conveyed the news to his father in a letter from Bournemouth, England, in October 1885:

> An illustrated *Treasure Island* will be out next month…so full of fire and spirit…it is my new toy, and I cannot divorce myself from this enjoyment.[3]

It was not until 1899 that *Treasure Island* found its first single illustrator, Walter Paget. He was a figure painter whose illustrations became synonymous with the story and were reproduced numerous times in later editions.

A decade later, two accomplished painters and illustrators, John Cameron and N.C. Wyeth, using the latest techniques, produced illustrations that added not only vibrant colours, but depth of composition together with personal interpretation. Wyeth's pirates, in particular, are more robust and expressive than anything previously attempted. They have movement, power, threat and clarity of composition.

Another two contrasting artists are Mervyn Peake and Ralph Steadman, who illustrated the book in 1949 and 1985 repectively. Whilst Peake's line drawings have an ethereal quality, Steadman's orgies of colour highlight the menace and violence in the story, and his harrowing interpretation of the pirates' attack on the stockade is far removed from the gentlemanly realism of Paget and Cameron.

1. *Letters*, II, 168 (RLS to W.E. Henley, [25 August 1881]).
2. *Letters*, II, 238 (RLS to Mr & Mrs Stevenson, 5 May [1883]).
3. *Letters*, III, 56 (RLS to Thomas Stevenson, 28 October 1885).

TREASURE ISLAND;
OR,
THE MUTINY OF THE HISPANIOLA.

By CAPTAIN GEORGE NORTH.

PROLOGUE.—THE ADMIRAL BENBOW.

CHAPTER I.
THE OLD SEA DOG AT THE ADMIRAL BENBOW.

SQUIRE TRELAWNEY, Dr. Livesey, and the rest of these gentlemen having asked me to write down the whole particulars about Treasure Island, from the beginning to the end, keeping nothing back but the bearings of the island, and that only because there is still treasure not yet lifted, I take up my pen in the year of grace 17—, and go back to the time when my father kept the Admiral Benbow Inn, and the brown old seaman, with the sabre cut, first took up his lodging under our roof.

I remember him as if it were yesterday, as he came plodding to the inn door, his sea-chest following behind him in a hand-barrow; a tall, strong, heavy, nut-brown man; his tarry pig-tail falling over the shoulders of his soiled blue coat; his hands ragged and scarred, with black, broken nails; and the sabre cut across one cheek, a dirty, livid white. I remember him looking round the cove and whistling to himself as he did so, and then breaking out in that old sea-song that he sang so often afterwards:—

"Fifteen men on the dead man's chest—
Yo-ho-ho, and a bottle of rum,"

in the high, old tottering voice that seemed to have been tuned and broken at the capstan bars. Then he rapped on the door with a bit of stick like a hand-spike that he carried, and when my father appeared, called roughly for a glass of rum. This, when it was brought to him, he drank slowly, like a connoisseur, lingering on the taste, and still looking about him at the cliffs and up at our signboard.

"This is a handy cove," says he, at length, "and a pleasant sittyated grog-shop. Much company, mate?"

My father told him no, very little company, the more was the pity.

"Well, then," said he, "this is the berth for me. Here, you, matey," he cried to the man who trundled the barrow, "bring up alongside and help up my

(column 2)

walking the plank, and storms at sea, and the Dry Tortugas, and wild deeds and places in the Spanish Main. By his own account he must have lived his life among the wickedest fiends of men that ever sailed upon the sea; and the language in which he told these stories shocked our plain country people almost as much as the crimes that he described. My father was always saying the inn would be ruined, for people would soon cease coming there to be tyrannized over and put down, and sent shivering to their beds; but I really believe his presence did us good. People were frightened at the time, but on looking back they rather liked it; it was a fine excitement in a quiet country life; and there was even a party of the younger men who pretended to admire him, calling him a "true sea-dog," and a "real old salt," and such like names, and saying there was the sort of man that made England terrible at sea.

In one way, indeed, he bid fair to ruin us; for he kept on staying week after week, and at last month after month, so that all the money had been long exhausted, and still my father never plucked up the heart to insist on having more. If ever he mentioned it, the captain blew through his nose so loudly that you might say he roared, and stared my poor father out of the room. I have seen him wringing his hands after such a rebuff, and I am sure the annoyance and the terror he lived in must have greatly hastened his early and unhappy death.

All the time he lived with us the captain made no change whatever in his dress but to buy some stock-

(column 3)

last broke out with a villanous, low oath: "Silence, there, between decks!"

"Were you addressing me, sir?" says the doctor; and when the ruffian had told him, with another oath, that this was so, "I have only one thing to say to you, sir," replies the doctor, "that if you keep on drinking rum, the world will soon be quit of a very dirty, low scoundrel!"

The old fellow's fury was awful. He sprang to his feet, drew and opened a sailor's clasp-knife, and, balancing it open on the palm of his hand, threatened to pin the doctor to the wall.

The doctor never so much as moved. He spoke to him, as before, over his shoulder, and in the same tone of voice; rather high, so that all the room might hear, but perfectly calm and steady:—

—"THE CAPTAIN AIMED AT THE FUGITIVE ONE LAST BLOW, WHICH, HOWEVER, WAS STOPPED BY THE SIGN BOARD."

"If you do not put that knife this instant in your pocket, I promise, upon my honour, you shall hang at next assizes."

Then followed a battle of looks between them; but the captain soon knuckled under, put up his weapon, and resumed his seat, grumbling like a beaten dog.

"And now, sir," continued the doctor, "since I now know there's such a fellow in my district, you may count I'll have an eye upon you day and night. I'm not a doctor only; I'm a magistrate; and if I catch a breath of complaint against you, if it's only for a piece of incivility like to-night's, I'll take effectual means to have you hunted down and routed out of this. Let that suffice."

Soon after Dr. Livesey rode away; but the captain

(column 4)

was for a person who stayed in our house, whom we called the captain.

"Well," said he, "my mate Bill would be called the captain, as like as not. He has a cut on one cheek, and a mighty pleasant way with him—particularly in drink—has my mate Bill. We'll put it, for argument like, that your captain has a cut on one cheek; and we'll put it, if you like, that that cheek's the right one. Ah, well! I told you. Now, is my mate Bill in this here house?"

I told him he was out walking.

"Which way, sonny? Which way is he gone?" And when I had pointed out the rock, and told him how the captain was likely to return, and how soon, and answered a few other questions, "Ah," said he, "this'll be as good as drink to my mate Bill."

The expression of his face as he said the words was not at all pleasant, and I had my own reasons for thinking that the stranger was mistaken, even supposing he meant what he said. But it was no affair of mine, I thought, and, besides, it was difficult to know what to do. The stranger kept hanging about just inside the inn door, peering round the corner like a cat waiting for a mouse. Once I stepped out myself into the road, but he immediately called me back, and as I did not obey quick enough for his fancy, a most horrible change came over his tallowy face, and he ordered me in, with an oath that made me jump.

As soon as I was back again, he returned to his former manner, half-fawning, half-sneering, patted me on the shoulder, told me I was a good boy, "and he had took quite a fancy to me. I have a son of my own," said he, "as like you as two blocks, and he's all the pride of my 'art. But the great thing for boys is discipline, sonny—discipline. Now, if you had sailed along of Bill, you wouldn't have stood there to be spoke to twice—not you. That was never Bill's way, nor the way of sich as sailed with him. And here, sure enough, is my mate Bill, with a spy-glass under his arm, bless his old 'art, to be sure. You and me 'll just go back into the parlour, sonny, and get behind the door, and we'll give Bill a little surprise,—bless his 'art, I say, again."

So saying, the stranger backed along with me into the parlour, and put me behind him in the corner, so that we were both hidden by the open door. I was very uneasy and alarmed, as you may fancy, and it rather added to my fears to observe that the stranger was certainly frightened himself. He cleared the hilt of his cutlass and loosened the blade in the sheath; and all the time we were waiting there he kept gulping as if he felt what we used to call a lump in his throat.

At last in strode the captain, slammed the door behind him, without looking to the right or left, and marched straight across the room to where his break-fast waited him.

"Bill," said the stranger, in a voice that I thought he had tried to make bold and big.

The captain spun round on his heel and fronted us; all the brown had gone out of his face, and even his nose was blue; he had the look of a man who sees a ghost, or something worse, if anything can be; and, upon my word, I felt sorry to see him, all in a moment, turn so old and sick.

"Come, Bill, you know me; you know an old ship-

'The Captain aimed at the fugitive one last blow, which would certainly have
split him to the chin had it not been intercepted by
our big sign-board of Admiral Benbow.'
Young Folks: A Boys' and Girls' Paper of Instructive
and Entertaining Literature (Michaelmas Double Number, 1881).

The famous map which has accompanied every
edition of *Treasure Island* since its first
appearance in book form in 1883.
(London, 1883)

The title-page for the first English illustrated edition (London, 1885).

'"One more step, Mr. Hands," said I, "and I'll blow your brains out!
Dead men don't bite, you know," I added, with a chuckle.'

J. L'Admiral
(1885)

'Down went Pew with a cry that rang high into the night.'

Walter Paget
(London, 1899)

'On our little walk along the quays, he made himself the most interesting
companion, telling me about the different ships that we passed by.'

Walter Paget
(1899)

'Gray, following close behind me, had cut down the big boatswain ere he had
time to recover from his lost blow.'

Walter Paget
(1899)

'Right in front of me, not half a mile away, I beheld
the Hispaniola under sail.'

Walter Paget
(1899)

One of the most exciting covers for an edition of *Treasure Island*.

John Cameron
(London, [1915])

*'I lay for some time, watching the bustle which
succeeded the attack. Men were demolishing
something with axes on the beach near the
stockade; the poor jolly-boat,
I afterwards discovered.'*
One of the twelve illustrations in a limited
edition of 250 copies bound in decorated vellum.

John Cameron
(London, 1911)

*'The doctor hailed them and told them of the
stores we had left, and where they were to find
them. But they continued to call us by name, and
appeal to us, for God's sake, to be merciful, and
not leave them to die in such a place.'*
John Cameron
(1911)

Endpapers from the Cassell Illustrated Classics *Treasure Island* by **N.C. Wyeth** (London, 1911)

'*All day he hung around the cove, or upon the cliffs, with a brass telescope.*'
Captain Bill Bones, scourge of the Admiral Benbow.

N.C. Wyeth
(1911)

The fight between Bill Bones and Black Dog. This image can be compared with the more passive illustration from *Young Folks*, above, p. 27.

N.C. Wyeth
(1911)

'. . . but there he remained behind, tapping up and down the road in a
frenzy, and groping and calling for his comrades.'
Blind Pew is abandoned by Johnny, Black Dog,
Dirk and his other 'mates'.

N.C. Wyeth
(1911)

'The boarders swarmed over the fence like monkeys.'
The pirates' first attack on the stockade.

N.C. Wyeth
(London, 1911)

'About half-way down the slope to the stockade, they were collected in a
group; one held the light; another was on his knees in their midst, and I saw
the blade of an open knife shine in his hands with varying colours, in the
moon and torchlight.'
The pirates prepare another black spot, this time for Long John Silver.

N.C. Wyeth
(1911)

'I had a line about my waist, and followed obediently after the sea-cook, who
held the loose end of the rope, now in his free hand, now between his
powerful teeth. For all the world, I was led like a dancing bear.'
The beginning of the treasure hunt.

N.C. Wyeth
(1911)

Opposite:
*'Well, there we stood, two on one side,
five on the other, the pit between us,
and nobody screwed up high
enough to offer the first blow.
Silver never moved; he watched them, very
upright on his crutch, and looked as
cool as ever I saw him.
He was brave and no mistake.'*
A classic illustration of Silver
from the 1930s by the Scottish artist
Monro S. Orr
(London, 1934)

Striking the 'Jolly Roger'. Jim Hawkins reclaims the *Hispaniola*.
Edmund Dulac
(London, 1927)

*'He . . . called roughly for a glass of rum. This, when it was brought to him,
he drank slowly, like a connoisseur, lingering on the taste.'*
Frontispiece.
Rowland Hilder
(London, 1929)

Long John Silver
Rowland Hilder
(1929)

MONRO S. ORR

Another illustration of Long John Silver,
this time by a Scots-born American.

Edward A. Wilson
(New York, 1941)

Captain Smollett
Edward A. Wilson
(1941)

Squire Trelawney
Edward A. Wilson
(1941)

*'He sprang to his feet, drew and opened a sailor's clasp-knife,
and, balancing it open on the palm of his hand,
threatened to pin the doctor to the wall.'*
The confrontation between Bill Bones and
Doctor Livesey at the Admiral Benbow.
Mervyn Peake
(London, 1949)

*'His left leg was cut off close by the hip, and under the left shoulder he
carried a crutch, which he managed with wonderful dexterity, hopping about
upon it like a bird. He was very tall and strong, with a face as big as a ham
– plain and pale, but intelligent and smiling.'*
Mervyn Peake
(1949)

*'Just before him Tom lay motionless upon the sward; but the murderer
minded him not a whit, cleansing his blood-stained knife the while upon a
whisp of grass.'*
Jim witnesses Silver's killing of loyal Tom.
Mervyn Peake
(1949)

Silver drags Hawkins along on a line during the treasure hunt. Here, Peake
opts to show only Silver with the line in his teeth, which can be compared
with N.C. Wyeth's version of the same scene, above, p. 35.
Mervyn Peake
(1949)

'In I got bodily into the apple barrel, and found there was scarce an apple left . . . a heavy man sat down with rather a clash close by . . . and I was just about to jump up when the man began to speak. It was Silver's voice, and, before I had heard a dozen words, I would not have shown myself for all the world.'

The most famous, and most frequently illustrated, incident in *Treasure Island*, given added power, menace and colour by

Ralph Steadman
(London, 1985)

41

'Squire and Gray fired again and yet again;
three men fell . . .'
A nightmare vision of the attack on the stockade.

Ralph Steadman
(1985)

KIDNAPPED AND CATRIONA

Kidnapped and *Catriona* are two halves of the one story, albeit separated by seven years and eight thousand miles. *Kidnapped* was completed in Bournemouth and published in 1886, and *Catriona* was written in Samoa and published in 1893, the year before the author's death. Stevenson had intended to write the two halves as one, but, when the narrative thread began to slip, he was persuaded by his friend and mentor, Sidney Colvin, to end the story with David Balfour arriving in Edinburgh to claim his inheritance. *Catriona* starts where *Kidnapped* ended, with Balfour exiting the British Linen bank in Edinburgh which he had been about to enter at the end of *Kidnapped*.

Published in July 1886, *Kidnapped* followed the appearance of *Strange Case of Dr Jekyll and Mr Hyde* in January of the same year. Although it was the success of *Jekyll and Hyde* that ensured a wider audience for *Kidnapped*, the latter was the story that broke new ground in Stevenson's development as a writer: the completion of a novel in which the author's imagination and his fascination with Scottish History came together. Since returning from America in 1880, Stevenson's interest in Scotland had gained a renewed impetus, a surge that came more easily after a period abroad. As he had done so often in his youth, he responded to Scottish history and landscape; he took a fresh look at the assassination of Colin Campbell of Glenure, the so called 'Appin Murder', and generally let his imagination journey through Scotland in the wake of the '45 Rebellion.

What he came up with was *Kidnapped*, a worthy successor to *Treasure Island*, but in many ways much more than a romantic quest for buried treasure. *Kidnapped* is Stevenson's first Scottish historical novel and it supersedes the romantic characters of Long John Silver and Jim Hawkins with Alan Breck Stewart and David Balfour of Shaws. The personification of divided Scotland, Breck represents the wild, romantic Highlands and the Jacobite Cause, and Balfour the respectable, Lowland Scotland, loyal to the Hanoverian succession. The relationship between these two conflicting spirits, combined with the evocation of Scottish landscape, makes *Kidnapped* much more than an adventure story.

On the surface, *Catriona* ties up the unresolved plot-threads of *Kidnapped* and brings David Balfour's adventures to a conclusion. But there is more to it than mere anecdote, since Stevenson himself conceded: 'I shall never do a better book than Catriona, that is my high water mark'.[1] Of course there are familiar elements such as David being abducted again, and the race to Inverary recalls some of the most exciting moments in *Kidnapped*. But the story differs in at least two important ways from its predecessor. First, a serious attempt is made to introduce female characters of some depth, in the form of Catriona Drummond, David's delicate Highland sweetheart, and the beautiful Miss Barbara Grant, Lord Advocate Prestongrange's meddlesome daughter. And second, the astonishing 'Tale of Tod Lapraik', told in Scots by Black Andie during David's imprisonment on the Bass Rock, stands as a monument, along with *Thrawn Janet*, to Stevenson's ability to write in Scots.

William Hole and N.C. Wyeth, two of the artists shown here, have illustrated both *Kidnapped* and *Catriona*, providing style and continuity over the two books. Indeed the black and white images of William Hole and the vibrant colours of Wyeth enhance the adventures of David Balfour in different ways. Unmatched, perhaps, is Wyeth's dynamic composition of Balfour and Breck, used for the cover of the 1913 Scribner's edition of *Kidnapped*.

1. *Letters*, V, 125 (Stevenson to Mrs Sitwell, April 1894).

YOUNG FOLKS PAPER.

FOR OLD AND YOUNG BOYS AND GIRLS.

VOL. XXVIII.—No. 805.] Printed and Published by the Proprietor, JAMES HENDERSON, at Red Lion House, Red Lion-court, Fleet-street, London.—MAY 1, 1886. [PRICE ONE PENNY; by Post, Three Halfpence.

"'THAT IS THE HOUSE OF SHAWS!' THE WOMAN CRIED. 'BLOOD BUILT IT; BLOOD STOPPED THE BUILDING OF IT; BLOOD SHALL BRING IT DOWN. SEE HERE!' SHE CRIED AGAIN. 'I SPIT UPON THE GROUND AND CRACK MY THUMB AT IT! BLACK BE ITS FALL!'"

KIDNAPPED;

OR,

THE LAD WITH THE SILVER BUTTON

By ROBERT LOUIS STEVENSON,

Author of "Treasure Island," "The Strange Case of Dr. Jekyll," &c.

CHAPTER I.

I SET OFF UPON MY JOURNEY TO THE HOUSE OF SHAWS.

I WILL begin the story of my adventures with a certain morning early in the month of June, the year of grace 1751, when I took the key for the last time out of the door of my father's house. The sun began to shine upon the summit of the hills as I went down the road; and by the time I had come as far as the manse, the blackbirds were whistling in the garden lilacs, and the mist that hung around the valley in the time of the dawn was beginning to arise and die away.

Mr. Campbell, the minister of Essendean, was waiting for me by the garden gate, good man! He asked me if I had breakfasted; and hearing that I lacked for nothing, he took my hand in both of his and clapped it kindly under his arm.

"Well, Davie lad," said he, "I will go with you as far as the ford, to set you on the way." And we began to walk forward in silence.

"Are ye sorry to leave Essendean?" said he, after a while.

"Why, sir," said I, "if I knew where I was going, or what was likely to become of me, I would tell you candidly. Essendean is a good place indeed, and I have been very happy there; but then I have never been anywhere else. My father and mother, since they are both dead, I shall be no nearer to in Essendean than in the Kingdom of Hungary; and to speak truth, if I thought I had a chance to better myself where I was going, I would go with a good will."

"Ay?" said Mr. Campbell. "Very well, Davie. Then it behoves me to tell your fortune; or so far as I may. When your mother was gone, and your father (the worthy, Christian man) began to sicken for his end, he gave me in charge a certain letter, which he said was your inheritance. 'So soon,' says he, 'as I am gone, and the house is redd up and the gear disposed of' (all which, Davie, hath been done), 'give my boy this letter into his hand, and start him off to the house of Shaws, not far from Cromond. That is the place I came from, he said, 'and it's where it befits that my boy should return. He is a steady lad,' your father said, 'and a canny goer; and I doubt not he will come safe and be well liked where he goes.'"

"The house of Shaws!" I cried. What had my poor father to do with the house of Shaws?"

"Nay," said Mr. Campbell, "who can tell that for a surety? But the name of that family, Davie boy, is the name you bear—Balfours of Shaws; an ancient, honest, reputable house, peradventure in these latter days decayed. Your father, too, was a man of learning as befitted his position; no man more plausibly conducted school; nor had he the manner or the speech of a common dominie; but (as ye will yourself remember) I took aye a pleasure to have him to the manse to meet the gentry; and those of my own house, Camp-

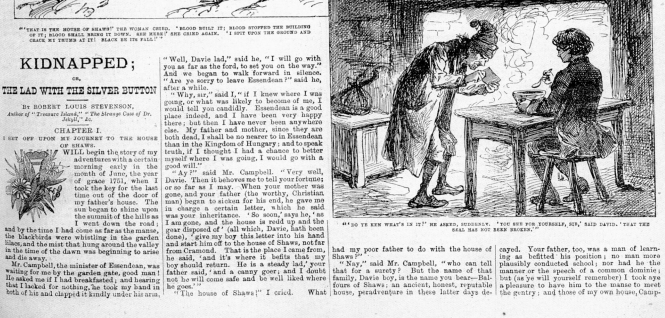

"'DO YE KEN WHAT'S IN IT?' HE ASKED, SUDDENLY. 'YOU SEE FOR YOURSELF, SIR,' SAID DAVID. 'THAT THE SEAL HAS NOT BEEN BROKEN.'"

Like *Treasure Island*, *Kidnapped* made its first appearance in this popular storypaper, though this time *Kidnapped* was the lead story in the *Young Folks Paper* (1 May 1886).

45

The fight in the roundhouse, from the *Young Folks Paper* (22 May 1886).

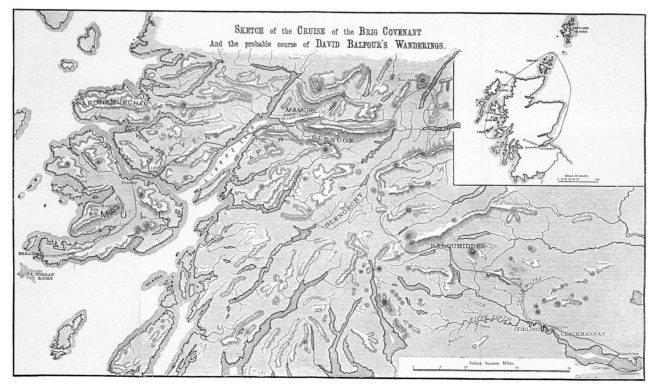

The map of David Balfour and Alan Breck's wanderings which, like the
Treasure Island map, has accompanied each successive edition of
Kidnapped. This map is from the first English edition (London, 1886).

'A main entrance, it was plainly meant to be, but never finished; instead of gates of wrought iron, a pair of hurdles were tied across with a straw rope.'
The first illustrated edition.

William Hole
(London, 1887)

'I took a pleasure in this game of blind-man's buff; but the catechist grew angrier and angrier, and at last began to swear in Gaelic and to strike for my legs with his staff.'
Balfour's encounter on the island of Mull
with the blind catechist, Duncan Mackiegh.

William Hole
(1887)

'I gave a piercing cry – "Help, help! Murder!" – so that both sides of the anchorage rang with it, and my uncle turned round where he was sitting, and showed me a face full of cruelty and terror.'

W.R.S. Stott
(London, 1913)

'"And how is yourself, Cluny?" said Alan. "I hope ye do brawly, sir."'

W.R.S. Stott
(1913)

'And the spirit of all that I beheld put me in thoughts of far off voyages and foreign places.' At Queensferry.

N.C. Wyeth
(1913)

'I had scarce time to measure the distance or to understand the peril before I had followed him, and he had caught and stopped me.'
The torrent in the valley of Glencoe.

N.C. Wyeth
(1913)

'But Alan and Cluny were most of the time at the cards.'
At the cards in Cluny's cage.

N.C. Wyeth
(1913)

'I, on my part, clambered up into the berth with an armful of pistols and something of a heavy heart, and set open the window where I was to watch.'
The siege of the Roundhouse, used as the frontispiece to this edition.

Louis Rhead
(London, 1921)

Another depiction of Balfour's encounter
with the blind catechist, this time by

Rowland Hilder
(London, 1930)

Two monochrome illustrations used as chapter headings.

Rowland Hilder
(1930)

Three Chapter headings:
'The flight in the heather: the moor',
'The flight in the heather: the quarrel',
and 'Good-bye'.

Hans Alexander Mueller
(New York, 1938)

CATRIONA

Catriona, front cover to the 1902 re-issue.
William Hole
(London, 1902)

*"What did they suffer for?" I asked. "Ou, just for the guid cause," said she.
"Aften I spaed to them the way that it would end. Twa shillin' Scots: no
pickle mair; and there are twa bonny callants hingin' for 't! They took it frae
a wean belanged to Brouchton."'*
Notice the initials 'RLS' and 'WH' carved at the bottom of the gibbet!
First illustrated edition.

William Hole
(London, 1898)

*"Tod was a wabster to his trade; his loom stood in the but. There he sat, a
muckle fat, white hash of a man like creish, wi' a kind of a holy smile that
gart me scunner."'*
'The Tale of Tod Lapraik', as told by Black Andie.

William Hole
(1898)

*"Keep back, Davie! Are ye daft? Damn ye, keep back!"
roared Alan.'*

William Hole
(1898)

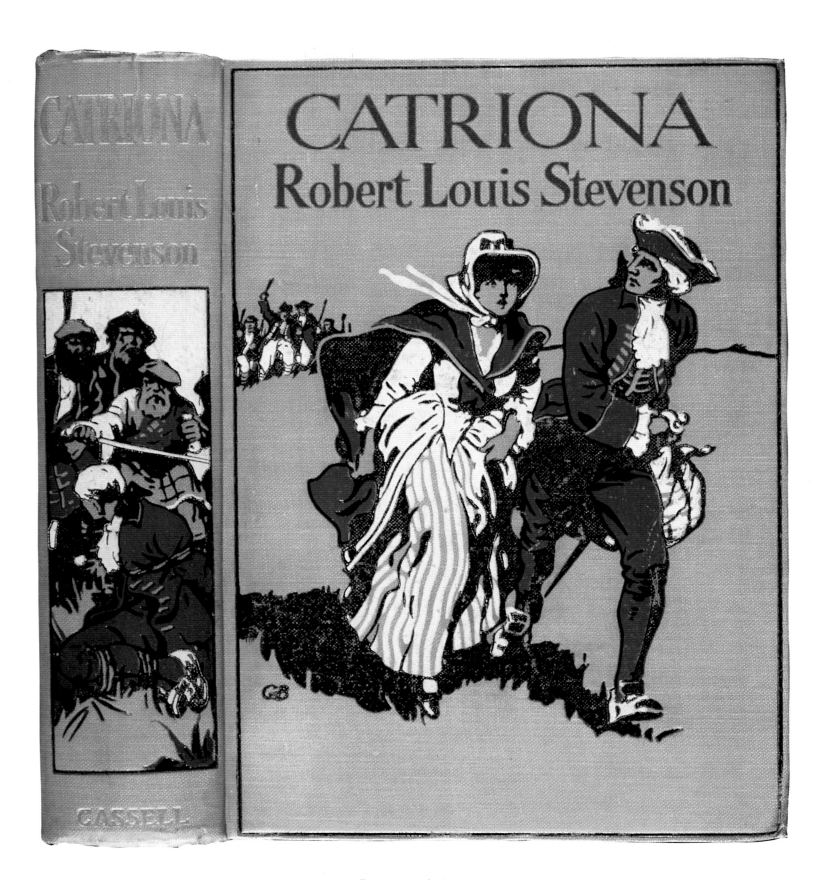

Front cover and spine
G.B.
(London, [1915])

4.22 *'I followed, accordingly, and took off my new hat to her*
the best I was able.'
David and Catriona meet for the first time.

A.C. Michael
(London, [1915])

'At that word, they came all in upon me like a flight of birds upon a carrion,
seized me, took my sword, and all the money from my pockets, bound me
hand and foot with some strong line,
and cast me on a tussock of bent.'
The second kidnapping of David Balfour.

A.C. Michael
([1915])

58

DAVID BALFOUR

© C. S. S.

by

ROBERT LOUIS STEVENSON

With Pictures by N.C.WYETH

NEW YORK
CHARLES SCRIBNER'S SONS
MCMXXXV

Illustrated title-page
N.C. Wyeth
(New York, 1935)

'At this he rose from his chair, lit a second candle, and for a while gazed upon me steadily. I was surprised to see a great
change of gravity fallen upon his face, and I could have almost thought he was a little pale.'
David's first meeting with Lord Advocate Prestongrange, at which he informs him that he witnessed the murder in Appin of Colin Campbell of Glenure.

N.C. Wyeth
(1935)

The fight between Catriona's father, James More, and Alan Breck.
N.C. Wyeth
(1935)

Strange Case of Dr Jekyll and Mr Hyde
·
The Master of Ballantrae

Strange Case of Dr Jekyll and Mr Hyde is one of the most popular stories ever written. It was composed in Bournemouth at breakneck speed, in the last few months of 1885, in a desperate attempt to make money. Intended as a 'shilling shocker', a popular Victorian literary form, the inspiration came from 'a fine bogey tale' that Stevenson had dreamt one night. The first version was thrown in the fire after his wife, Fanny, complained that the content was too shallow and should include an allegorical element. In ten days Stevenson had rewritten it, retaining the shocking details of human transformation and the separation of good and evil, but adding deeper observations on their significance.

It is the tale of a young doctor who concocts an elixir which brings the evil side of his personality to the fore and turns him into the diminutive Mr Hyde. The key theme is the duality of the human psyche, the degree to which good and evil is contained in everyone. Not only was this a strong theme in the Calvinist religion in which Stevenson had been reared, but it was an idea explored by writers such as Fyodor Dostoevsky (*Crime and Punishment,* 1866). Stevenson had already alluded to the duality theme in his drama *Deacon Brodie* and, arguably, in the character of Long John Silver in *Treasure Island*.

Yet the main aim in *Dr Jekyll and Mr Hyde* was to write a good yarn, a money-spinner, a story that was gripping and easily understood. And on its publication in January 1886 the story exceeded all expectation, becoming an instant success both in Britain and America. It was just as quickly absorbed into popular culture, and the term 'Jekyll and Hyde' passed into the language as being synonymous with a personality exhibiting qualities of good and evil – 'nice and nasty'. It was *Dr Jekyll and Mr Hyde* that made Stevenson's name, not *Treasure Island*.

The theme of good and evil is one that is also at the heart of *The Master of Ballantrae: A Winter's Tale* though it is part of a curious mixture that goes stale half way through. This time it is expressed in the form of two brothers, Henry and James Durie. Henry is the weak, younger brother while James, the eponymous Master, is, according to Stevenson, 'all I know of the devil'.[1] Set in the now familiar period of the 1745 Rebellion and beyond, the story ranges from Scotland to India and is finally brought to a sub-zero conclusion in the American wilderness. Despite borrowing the same historical period as *Kidnapped* and employing pirates, it is an uneasy, though fascinating, tale that ends with the two brothers buried in the same grave.

One might have expected illustrators to have been queuing up to work on *Dr Jekyll and Mr Hyde*, but unfortunately this has not been the case. Instead, publishers, following the shilling shocker format, issued the story in decorated paper wrappers with a striking front cover. However, the publication in 1930 of S.G. Hulme-Beaman's illustrations interpreted the whole of the story, and all the artists who have followed him stand on his shoulders. When we turn to *The Master of Ballantrae* we find the familiar monochromes of William Hole alongside Walter Paget's successful foray into colour. Yet Lynd Ward's sparing use of colour and inventive composition perhaps create a more memorable effect.

1. *Letters*, III, 171 (RLS to Sidney Colvin, 24 December 1887).

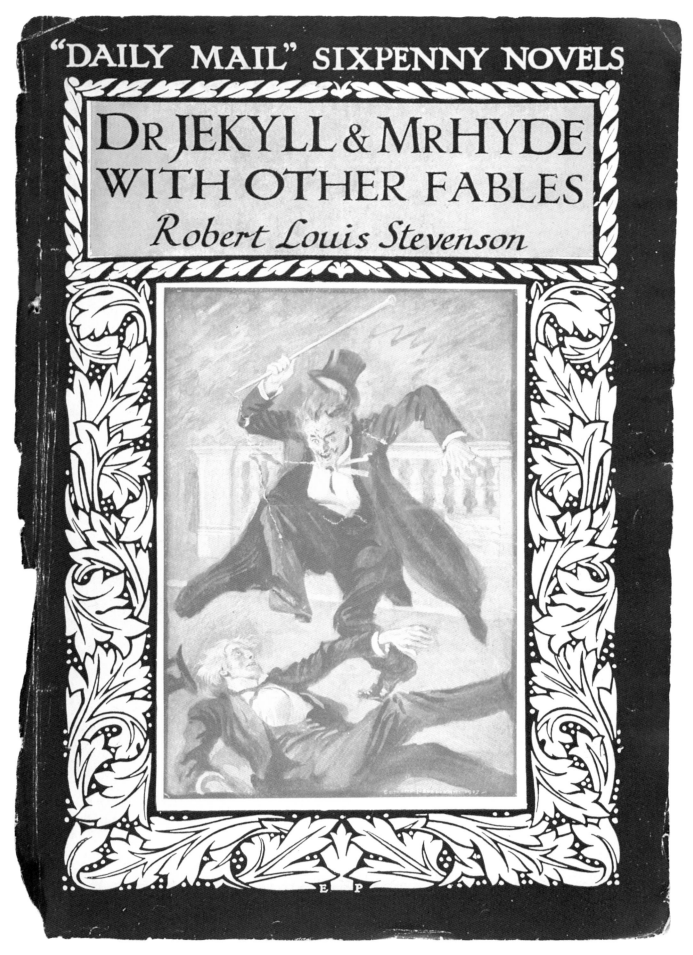

A popular paper-cover edition.
Edmund J. Sullivan
(London, [1897?])

Paper cover
H. Flygare
(Stockholm, 1921)

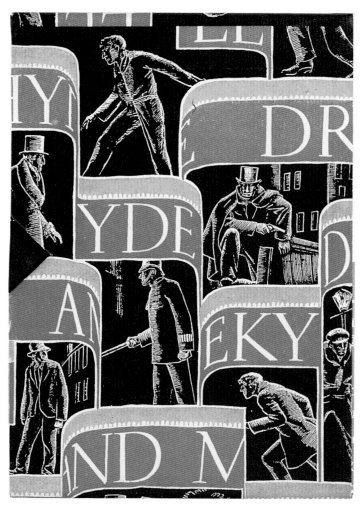

Illustrated slipcase
W.A. Dwiggins
(New York, 1929)

'I saw for the first time the appearance of Edward Hyde.'
W.A. Dwiggins
(1929)

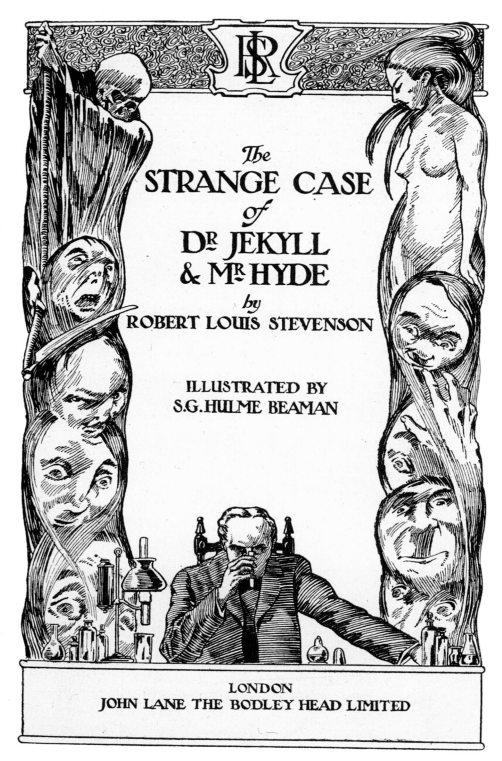

The
STRANGE CASE
of
Dr JEKYLL
& Mr HYDE
by
ROBERT LOUIS STEVENSON

ILLUSTRATED BY
S.G. HULME BEAMAN

LONDON
JOHN LANE THE BODLEY HEAD LIMITED

Illustrated title-page
S.G. Hulme-Beaman
(London, 1930)

'And still the figure had no face by which he might know it; even in his dreams, it had no face, or one that baffled him and melted before his eyes.'
Mr Utterson's troubled thoughts on Mr Hyde.

S.G. Hulme-Beaman
(1930)

'... and as I looked there came, I thought, a change – he seemed to swell his face became suddenly black, and the features seemed to melt and alter.'

S.G. Hulme-Beaman
(1930)

'I became, in my own person, a creature eaten up and emptied by fever, languidly weak both in body and mind, and solely occupied by one thought: the horror of my other self.'

S.G. Hulme-Beaman
(1930)

'The murderer was gone long ago; but there lay his victim in the middle of
the lane, incredibly mangled.'
The murder of Sir Danvers Carew.

Helen A. Martin
(Edinburgh, 1946)

Mr Hyde in Dr Jekyll's ill-fitting clothes.

Mervyn Peake
(London, 1948)

Mr Utterson 'set forth in the direction of Cavendish Square'.

Mervyn Peake
(1948)

'. . . his face was so ghastly to see that I grew alarmed
both for his life and reason.'

Harry Horse
(Edinburgh, 1986)

An exaggerated illustration of Mr Hyde by the Danish illustrator
Paul Høirup
([Copenhagen, 1970?])

Jekyll's hand and Hyde's hand
Barry Moser
(Lincoln, Nebraska, 1990)

'. . . they agreed to steer a middle course, one son going forth to strike a
blow for King James, my lord and the other staying at home to keep in
favour with King George.'
The toss of a coin decides that the Master shall join the Rebellion of 1745
and that Henry, his younger brother, shall stay at home.
First illustrated edition, *The Master of Ballantrae*.

William Hole
(New York, 1889)

'Some night birds arose from the boughs upon our coming, and then settled
back; but Secundra, absorbed in his toil, heard or heeded not at all.'

William Hole
(1889)

Cover and spine for the Cassell edition of *The Master of Ballantrae*,
which used only four of the twelve colour illustrations by

Walter Paget
(London, [1916?])

'"*It is cut on the inside,*" *said I.*'
The evidence that the Master tried a foul stroke in the duel with his
brother. Frontispiece to the Cassell edition of
The Master of Ballantrae with twelve illustrations by

Walter Paget
(London, 1911)

'Close in the chimney sat two men. The one that was wrapped in a cloak and wore boots, I knew at once: it was the bird of ill omen back again.'

Walter Paget
(1911)

'The frost was not yet very deep, and presently the Indian threw aside his tool, and began to scoop the dirt by handfuls.'
Just before the final, disturbing, scene in which the Durie brothers die.

Walter Paget
(1911)

'Day in, day out, he would work upon her, sitting by the chimney-side with his finger in his Latin book, and his eyes set upon her face with a kind of pleasant intentness that became the old gentleman very well.'
The old Lord tries to persuade Miss Alison Graeme to marry Lord Henry Durie in place of the Master, whom they believe to have fallen at Culloden.

Lynd Ward
(New York, 1965)

'Presently he comes on deck, a perfect figure of fun, his face blacked, his hair and whiskers curled, his belt full of pistols; chewing bits of glass so that the blood ran down his chin, and brandishing a dirk.'
Teach the pirate, in satanic mood.

Lynd Ward
(1965)

A FINAL MEDLEY

As the title of this chapter suggests, a group of images are presented here which have not been covered in the preceding sections but which may prove to be essential in creating a deeper impression of the range of illustrations that Stevenson's writing has inspired while, at the same time, showing parallels in style and technique to what has been before. Indeed, the ubiquitous N.C. Wyeth's interpretation of *The Black Arrow* provides at least one measure of continuity. The wood engravings by Walter Crane for the frontispiece of Stevenson's first two books, *An Inland Voyage* and *Travels with a Donkey*, take us back to the beginning of Stevenson's career when he was struggling to establish himself as a writer. Moving to the end of his short life *The Beach of Falesá* encapsulates the Western impact on the South Seas and is notable too for its native female heroine, Uma, who, in one of the illustrations here, helpfully translates a word for her new husband, Wiltshire.

The most interesting of the early illustrations from the first edition of *Edinburgh: Picturesque Notes* have been included too: an etching by A. Brunet-Debaines and two wood engravings by R. Kent Thomas. On the opposite page, the dreamlike illustration by Norman Wilkinson shows Stevenson's beloved 'lamplighter' on an Edinburgh street. The rough woodcut by Fanny's son-in-law, Joseph Strong, captures the primitive interior of the miner's cabin, perched high in the Californian mountains, where the newly-wed Fanny and Louis stayed in the summer of 1880. Much more controversial was Morgan's illustration for 'The Body Snatcher' which caused quite a commotion when it appeared at Christmas 1884, because it featured a corpse.

Less violent, though perhaps more disturbing, is the illustration which was used as the frontispiece to *The Wrecker* (1892), showing Wicks about to drive a knife through his open hand. Coming as it did after Stevenson's perceptive observations in his travel essays, *In the South Seas*, *The Wrecker*, in its final stages, alludes to the more mature South Seas fiction that was to emerge in *The Beach of Falesá* and, arguably, *The Ebb-Tide* (1894).

Stevenson's *Fables*, originally published with *Jekyll and Hyde*, broke free at the end of the nineteenth century to stand on their own with accompanying illustrations. The three examples shown here from editions of the *Fables*, etchings by E.K. Martin, a drawing by E.R. Herman, and woodcuts by Rachel Russell, present contrasting visual experiences and their existence highlights another part of the Stevenson publishing explosion that occurred in the decades after his death.

To conclude our journey through some of the illustrations that have become such an important part of the works of this much travelled Scot, it is perhaps appropriate to return again to Stevenson's *Edinburgh: Picturesque Notes*:

> There is no Edinburgh emigrant, far or near, from China to Peru, but he or she carries some lively pictures of the mind, some sunset behind the Castle cliffs, some snow scene, some maze of city lamps, indelible in the memory and delightful to study in the intervals of toil.[1]

1. *Edinburgh: Picturesque Notes* (London, 1879), p.39.

Right: Marquesan warrior in fighting dress. 'The South Seas: A Record of Three Cruises', in *Black and White*.
N.P.D.
(London, 1891)

Frontispiece from Stevenson's first book, an account of a canoeing trip in
Belgium and France with his friend, Walter Simpson.
An Inland Voyage
Walter Crane
(London, 1878)

Frontispiece from Stevenson's famous account of his tour in France with
Modestine, his temperamental, four-legged companion.
Travels with a Donkey in the Cévennes
Walter Crane
(London, 1879)

Detail from front cover,
Travels with a Donkey in the Cévennes
(Boston, 1879).

The old city from Salisbury Crags.
Edinburgh: Picturesque Notes, first edition.
R. Kent Thomas
(London, 1879)

' . . . while, above all, the brute mass of the Castle and the summit of
Arthur's Seat look down . . .'
R. Kent Thomas
(1879)

Greyfriars Kirkyard
A. Brunet-Debaines
(1879)

The Castle from Princes Street.
T.H. Crawford
(London, 1896)

The Old Town from the Calton Hill.
T.H. Crawford
(1896)

'God bless the lamplighter!' from 'A Plea For Gas Lamps'. *Virginibus Puerisque and Other Papers*
Norman Wilkinson
(London, 1921)

Stevenson and Fanny honeymooning in a disused silver miner's cabin. *The Silverado Squatters*, frontispiece.
Joe Strong
(London, 1883)

PALL MALL CHRISTMAS "EXTRA"

R. Louis Stevenson's
THE BODY SNATCHER

Morgan

Twenty Guinea Prizes.

FOR PARTICULARS SEE CONTENTS.

OFFICE, 2, NORTHUMBERLAND STREET, STRAND, LONDON, W.C.

1884.

Illustration by **Morgan** to accompany Stevenson's
Christmas ghost story, 'The Bodysnatcher'.
Pall Mall Christmas 'Extra' (London, 1884).

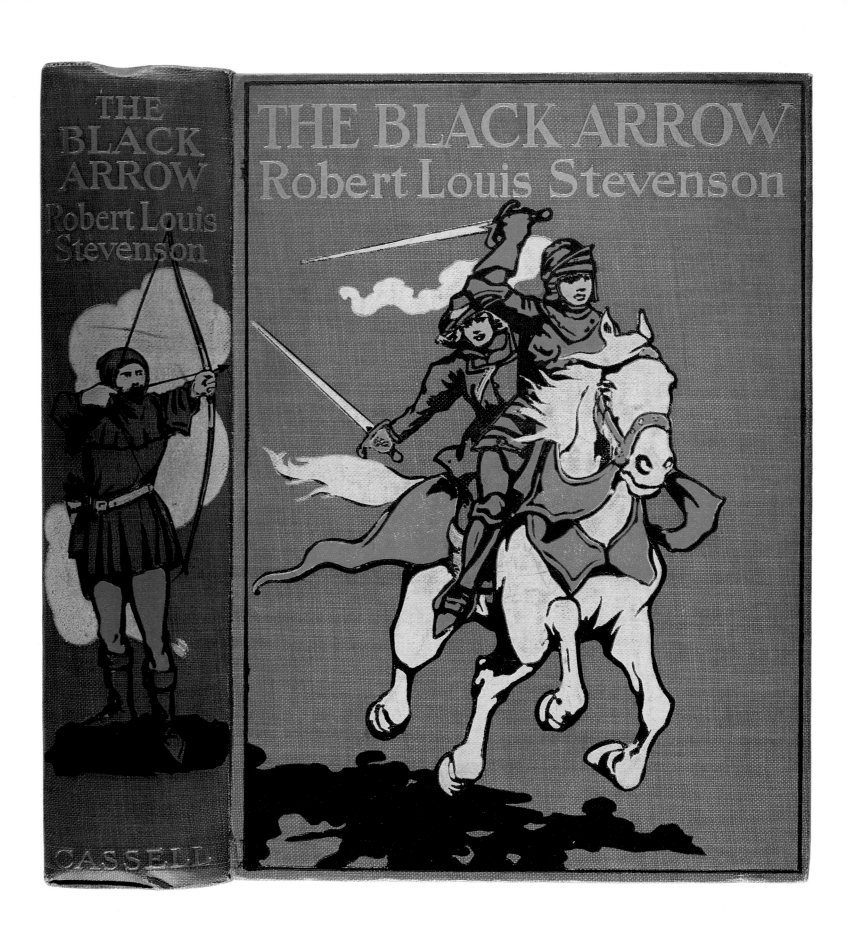

Cover and spine, *The Black Arrow.*

Cyrus Cuneo
(London, [1915])

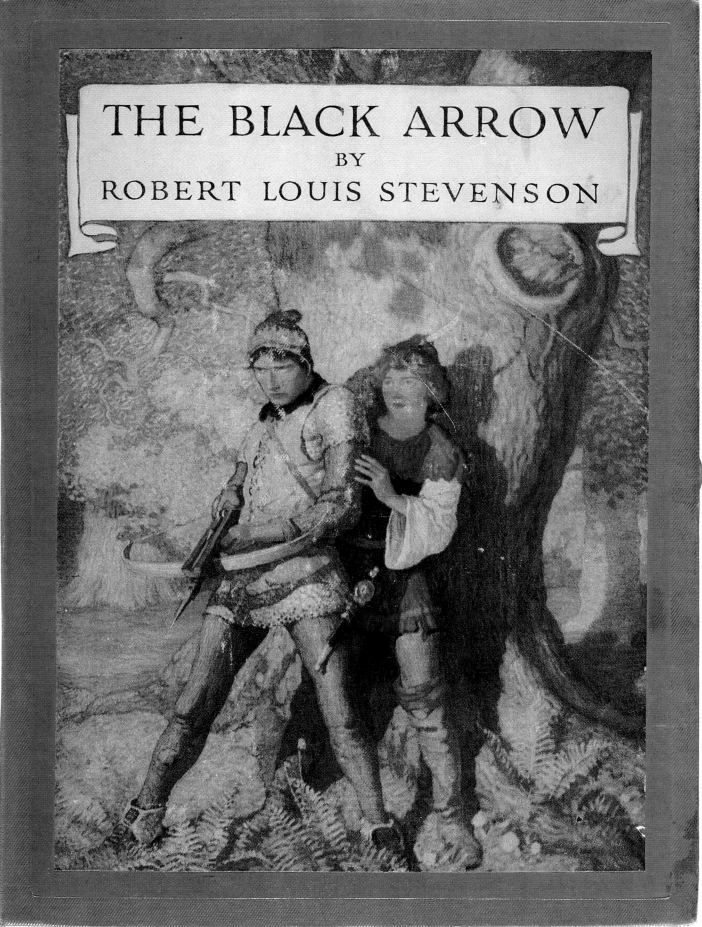

Cover, *The Black Arrow.*
N.C. Wyeth
(London, 1916)

Endpapers, *The Black Arrow.*
N.C. Wyeth
(1916)

'. . . and Lawless, keeping half a step in front of his companion and holding
his head forward like a hunting-dog upon the scent . . . studied out
their path . . .'
The Black Arrow

N.C. Wyeth
(1916)

'Wicks spread his hand face-up on the table, and drove a
knife through his palm. "That kind of an accident," said he.'
The Wrecker, with Lloyd Osbourne.

W.L. Metcalf
(London, 1892)

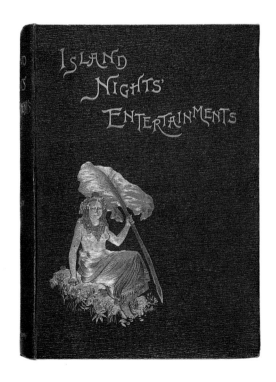

Cover of *Island Nights' Entertainments*, first edition.

Gordon Browne and W. Hatherell
(London, 1893)

'"What does fussy-ocky mean?" I asked of Uma, for that was as near as I
could come to it. "Make dead," said she.'
'The Beach of Falesà', in *Island Nights' Entertainments*.

Gordon Browne
(1893)

'So he went on after the bloodless thing.'
'The House of Eld', in *Fables*.

E.K. Martyn
(London, 1902)

*'And she was aware of the thing as it were a babe unmothered, and she took
it to her arms, and it melted in her arms like air.'*
'The Poor Thing', in *Fables*.

E.K. Martyn
(1902)

*'Then they sat together; and the sea beat on the terrace, and the gulls cried
about the towers, and the wind crooned in the chimneys of the house.'*
'The Song of the Morrow', in *Fables*.

E.K. Martyn
(1902)

'The Persons of the Tale', *Fables*, frontispiece.
The puppets in the foreground are
Long John Silver and Captain Smollett.

E.R. Herman
(London, 1914)

Two illustrations from:
'The Penitent', in *Fables*.

Rachel Russell
(London, 1928)

'"Drink" sang the daughter of Miru.'
'Something In It', in *Fables*.

Rachel Russell
(1928)

Cover of *Memories.*
Jessie M. King
(London, [1912])

BIBLIOGRAPHY

R.L.S. ILLUSTRATED WORKS
AND SELECTED ILLUSTRATORS

Where possible, the original form from which the illustrations were taken is provided, normally before the illustrator's name. The names of the illustrators are given in bold type.

The Black Arrow
London: Cassell & Co., [1915]. **Cyrus Cuneo** (*1879-1916*)
London: Cassell & Co., 1916. From original paintings. **N.C. Wyeth** (*1882-1945*)

The Bodysnatcher
in *Pall Mall Christmas 'Extra'* (1884), London: [s.n.], 1884. Engraving. **Morgan**

Catriona (published in U.S.A. as *David Balfour*)
London: Cassell & Co., 1898. From original paintings. **William Hole** (*1846-1917*)
London: Cassell & Co., 1902. **William Hole** (*1846-1917*)
London: Cassell & Co., [1915]. From original paintings. **G.B. & A.C. Michael** (*fl. 1903-1928*)
New York: Charles Scribner's Sons, 1935. From original paintings. **N.C. Wyeth** (*1882-1945*)

A Child's Garden of Verses
London: Bodley Head, 1896. From pen and ink drawings. **Charles Robinson** (*1870-1937*)
New York: Charles Scribner's Sons, 1905. From original paintings, and monochrome pen and ink drawings. **Jessie Willcox Smith** (*1863-1935*)
London: Chatto & Windus, 1908. From original paintings. **Millicent Sowerby** (*1878-1967*)
Chicago: Rand McNally & Co., 1919. From original paintings. **Ruth Mary Hallock** (*1876-1945*)
London: Collins, [1927]. From original paintings. **Kate Elizabeth Olver** (*d. 1960*)
Akron, Ohio: Saalfield Publishing Co., 1930. From original paintings. **Clara M. Burd**
London: Harrap & Co., 1931. From original paintings. **H. Willebeek le Mair** (*1889-1966*)

Edinburgh: Picturesque Notes
London: Seeley, Jackson, & Halliday, 1879. Etchings and engravings. **A. Brunet-Debaines** (*b. 1845*) & **R. Kent Thomas** (*b. 1816*)
London: Seeley & Co., 1896. From original paintings, and etchings. **T.H. Crawford** (*b. 1860*)

Fables
London: Longmans Green & Co., 1902. Etchings. **E.K. Martyn** (*1859-1923*)
London: Longmans Green & Co., 1914. From original pen and ink drawings. **E.R. Herman**
London: The Swan Press, 1928. Wood engravings. **Rachel Russell**

The History of Moses
Daylesford, PA: Privately printed, 1919. From coloured drawing. **Robert Louis Stevenson**

An Inland Voyage
London: C. Kegan Paul & Co., 1878. Engraving. **Walter Crane** (*1845-1915*)

Island Nights' Entertainments
London: Cassell & Co., 1893. From original paintings. **Gordon Browne** (*1858-1932*) & **W. Hatherell** (*1855-1928*)

Kidnapped
in *Young Folks Paper. For Old and Young Boys and Girls* (vol. XXVIII, 805, 1 May 1886 & 808, 22 May 1886), London: James Henderson, 1885 [-1891] vols 26-38. Engravings.
London: Cassell & Co., 1886. Engraving.
London: Cassell & Co., 1887. Engravings. **William Hole** (*1846-1917*)
London: Cassell & Co., 1913. From original paintings. **W.R.S. Stott** (*fl. 1905-1934*)
New York: Charles Scribner's Sons, 1913. From original paintings. **N.C. Wyeth** (*1882-1945*)
London: Harper & Brothers, 1921. From original paintings. **Louis Rhead** (*1857-1926*)
London: Oxford University Press, 1930. From original drawings. **Rowland Hilder** (*b. 1905*)
New York: Limited Editions Club, 1938. Wood engravings. **Hans Alexander Mueller** (*b. 1888*)

The Master of Ballantrae: A Winter's Tale
New York: Charles Scribner's Sons, 1889. From original paintings. **William Hole** (*1846-1917*)
London: Cassell & Co., 1911. From original paintings. **Walter Paget** (*1863-1935*)
London: Cassell & Co., [1916?]. **Walter Paget** (*1863-1935*)
New York: Heritage Press, 1965. Lithographs. **Lynd Ward** (*b. 1905*)

Moral Emblems & Moral Tales - see *A Stevenson Medley*

'A Mountain Town in France'
Article containing reproductions of drawings by **Robert Louis Stevenson** in *The Studio* (Winter number 1896-7), London: [s.n.], 1893[-1964]

R.L. Stevenson Memories
London: T.N. Foulis, [1912]. From original painting. **Jessie M. King** (*1875-1949*)

The Silverado Squatters
London: Chatto & Windus, 1883. Engraving. **Joe Strong** (*1852-1900*)

'The South Seas: A Record of Three Cruises' (published in book form as *In the South Seas*)
Illustrated article in *Black & White. A Weekly Illustrated Record and Review*, 32 vols (London: Black & White Publishing Co., 1891[-1906]), I, 23-24, 46-48, 78-80, 114-15, 144-45, 177-78, 208-09, 305-06, 334-35, 365-67, 443-44, 544-45, 606-07, 638-39, 672-74; II, 32-33, 52-53, 102-03, 174, 374, 440, 470-72, 572, 663, 696-97, 780-81. Engravings. **O. Lacour** (*fl. 1886-1891*) & from original drawings by **Fairfax Muckley, N.P.D.** and others.

A Stevenson Medley
London: Chatto & Windus, 1899.
(Containing reproductions of woodcuts by **Robert Louis Stevenson** which first appeared in *Moral Emblems. A Collection of Cuts and Verses*, Davos-Platz: S.L. Osbourne & Co., [1882], and in *Moral Tales*, Davos-Platz: S.L. Osbourne & Co., [1882])

Strange Case of Dr. Jekyll and Mr. Hyde
London: Amalgamated Press, [1897?]. **Edmund J. Sullivan** (*1869-1933*)
Stockholm: Björck & Börjesson, 1921. **H. Flygare**
New York: Random House, 1929. Engravings. **W.A. Dwiggins** (*1880-1956*)
London: Bodley Head, 1930. Photogravures, and silhouettes from original pen and ink drawings. **S.G. Hulme-Beaman** (*1887-1932*)
Edinburgh: Robert Grant & Son, 1946. Lithographs. **Helen A. Martin**
London: Folio Society, 1948. From original drawings. **Mervyn Peake** (*1911-1968*)
New York: Limited Editions Club, 1952. Lithographs. **Edward A. Wilson** (*1886-1970*)
[Copenhagen: Selskabet Bogvennerne, 1970?]. From original drawings. **Paul Høirup**

Edinburgh: Canongate, 1986. From original drawings. **Harry Horse**
Lincoln, NEB: University of Nebraska Press, 1990. Wood engravings.
  Barry Moser (*b. 1940*)

The Sunbeam Magazine
Edited and illustrated in pen and wash by **Robert Louis Stevenson**.
  (Cover reproduced in *Autograph Letters, Original Manuscripts, Books,
  Portraits, and Curios from the Library of the late Robert Louis
  Stevenson*, sale catalogue of Stevenson's library, part II, lot 298.
  New York: Anderson Auction Co., 1914[-1916]. 3 parts.)

Travels with a Donkey in the Cévennes
London: C. Kegan Paul & Co., 1879. Engraving. **Walter Crane** (*1845-1915*)
Boston: Roberts Brothers, 1879.

Treasure Island
in *Young Folks: A Boys' and Girls' Paper of Instructive and Entertaining
  Literature* (vol. XIX, 565, Michaelmas Double Number, 1881),
  London: James Henderson, 1879[-1884]. 25 vols. Engravings.
London: Cassell & Co., 1883.
London: Cassell & Co., 1885. Engravings. **J. L'Admiral**
London: Cassell & Co., 1899. Engravings. **Walter Paget** (*1863-1935*)
London: Cassell & Co., 1911. From original paintings. **John Cameron** (*fl.
  1917-1925*)
London: Cassell & Co., 1911. From original paintings. **N.C. Wyeth**
  (*1882-1945*)
London: Cassell & Co., [1915]. From original paintings. **John Cameron**
  (*fl. 1917-1925*)
London: Ernest Benn, 1927. From original paintings. **Edmund Dulac**
  (*1882-1953*)
London: Oxford University Press, 1929. From original paintings, and pen
  and ink drawings. **Rowland Hilder** (*b. 1905*)
London: Frederick Muller, 1934. From original paintings. **Monro S. Orr**
  (*b. 1874*)
New York: Limited Editions Club, 1941. Lithographs. **Edward A. Wilson**
  (*1886-1970*)
London: Eyre & Spottiswoode, 1949. From original pen and ink drawings.
  Mervyn Peake (*1911-1968*)
London: Harrap, 1985. From original paintings. **Ralph Steadman** (*b. 1936*)

Virginibus Puerisque and other Papers
London: Chatto & Windus, 1921. From original paintings. **Norman
  Wilkinson** (*1882-1934*)

The Wrecker (with Lloyd Osbourne)
London: Cassell & Co., 1892. From original paintings. **W.L. Metcalf**
  (*1858-1925*)

FURTHER READING ON STEVENSON

Balfour, Graham, *The Life of Robert Louis Stevenson*, 5th edn
  (London: Methuen, 1910)
Bell, Ian, *Dreams of Exile: Robert Louis Stevenson: A Biography*
  (Edinburgh: Mainstream, 1992)
Calder, Jenni, *RLS: A Life Study* (Glasgow: Richard Drew, 1990)
—— ed., *Stevenson and Victorian Scotland* (Edinburgh: Edinburgh
  University Press, 1981)
Colvin, Sidney, ed., *The Letters of Robert Louis Stevenson*, Tusitala
  Edition, 2nd edn, 5 vols (London: William Heinemann, 1926)
—— *Vailima Letters: Being Letters Addressed by Robert Louis Stevenson to
  Sidney Colvin*, 2 vols (Chicago: Stone & Kimball, 1895)
Daiches, David, *Robert Louis Stevenson* (Norfolk, CONN: New Directions,
  1947)
Furnas, J.C., *Voyage to Windward: The Life of Robert Louis Stevenson*
  (London: Faber & Faber, 1952)
Hennessy, James Pope, *Robert Louis Stevenson* (London: Jonathan Cape,
  1974)
Hirsch, Gordon, see **Veeder, William**
James, Henry, 'The Art of Fiction' in *Longman's Magazine*, 46 vols
  (London: Longmans Green & Co., 1883[-1905]), IV, 502-21

—— 'The Letters of Robert Louis Stevenson', in *The North American
  Review*, 173 vols (New York: North American Review Publishing Co.,
  1815[-1901]), CLXX, 61-77
—— 'Robert Louis Stevenson' in *Century Illustrated Monthly Magazine
  (Scribner's Magazine)*, 100 vols (New York: Charles Scribner's Sons,
  1887[-1936]), XXXV, 869-879
Knight, Alanna, *The Robert Louis Stevenson Treasury* (London:
  Shepheard Walwyn, 1985)
Noble, Andrew, ed., *Robert Louis Stevenson* (London: Vision Press, 1983)
—— ed., *From the Clyde to California: Robert Louis Stevenson's Emigrant
  Journey* (Aberdeen: Aberdeen University Press, 1985)
Stevenson, Robert Louis, 'Books which have influenced me', in *Works*,
  Pentland Edition, 20 vols (London: Cassell & Co., 1906[-1907]), XV, 302-09
—— 'Byways of Book Illustration', in *Works*, Vailima Edition, 26 vols
  (London: William Heinemann, 1922[1923]), XXIV, 134-49. Article
  originally published in *The Magazine of Art* (February, 1882)
—— 'A Chapter on Dreams', in *Works*, Pentland Edition, XV, 197-211
—— 'The Genesis of 'The Master of Ballantrae', in *Works*, Pentland Edition,
  XV, 378-81
—— 'A Humble Remonstrance', in *Longman's Magazine*, 46 vols (London:
  Longmans Green and Co., 1883[-1905]), V, 139-47.
—— 'Memoirs of Himself', in *Works*, Tusitala Edition, 35 vols (London:
  William Heinemann, 1924), XXIX, 145-68
—— 'The Morality of the Profession of Letters', in *Works*, Vailima Edition,
  IV, 410-13
—— 'My First Book "Treasure Island" ', in *Works*, Skerryvore Edition, 30
  vols (London: William Heinemann, 1924[-1926]), II, xxvii-xxxvii
—— 'A Note on Realism', in *Works*, Pentland Edition, XV, 262-68
Veeder, William, and **Hirsch, Gordon**, eds, *Dr Jekyll and Mr Hyde After
  One Hundred Years* (Chicago: University of Chicago Press, 1988)

SELECTED READING ON BOOK ILLUSTRATION

Anderson, Patricia, *The Printed Image and the Transformation of Popular
  Culture 1790-1860* (Oxford: Clarendon Press, 1991)
Chester, Tessa Rose, see **Whalley, Joyce Irene**
Feaver, William, *When We Were Young: Two Centuries of Children's Book
  Illustration* (London: Thames & Hudson, 1977)
Felmingham, Michael, *The Illustrated Gift Book 1880-1930* (Aldershot,
  Hampshire: Wildwood House, 1989)
Gascoigne, Bamber, *How to Identify Prints* ([London]: Thames & Hudson,
  1986)
Greutzner, A., see **Johnson, J.**
Heller, Steven, and **Pomeroy, Karen**, *Designing with Illustration*
  (New York: Van Nostrand Reinhold, 1990)
Houfe, Simon, *The Dictionary of British Book Illustrators and Caricaturists
  1800-1914*, Revised edn (Woodbridge, Suffolk: Antique Collectors'
  Club, 1981)
Johnson, J., and **Greutzner, A.**, *The Dictionary of British Artists 1880-1940*
  (Woodbridge, Suffolk: Antique Collectors' Club, 1976)
McLean, Ruari, *Victorian Book Design & Colour Printing* (London: Faber
  & Faber, 1963)
Micklethwait, Lucy, see **Peppin, Brigid**
Peppin, Brigid, and **Micklethwait, Lucy**, *Dictionary of British Book
  Illustrators: The Twentieth Century* (London: John Murray, 1983)
Pomeroy, Karen, see **Heller, Steven**
Wakeman, Geoffrey, *Victorian Book Illustration: The Technical Revolution*
  (Newton Abbot: David and Charles, 1973)
Whalley, Joyce Irene, and **Chester, Tessa Rose**, *A History of Children's
  Book Illustration* (London: John Murray, 1988)
Wood, Christopher, *The Dictionary of Victorian Painters*, 2nd edn
  (Woodbridge, Suffolk: Antique Collectors' Club, 1978)
Wyeth, Betsy James, ed., see under **Wyeth, N.C.**
Wyeth, N.C., *The Wyeths: The Letters of N.C. Wyeth, 1901-1945*, edited by
  Betsy James Wyeth (Boston: Gambit, 1971)